Ivor Bertie Gurney, composer and poet, was born in 1890 in Gloucester. He won a permanent place in the Gloucester Cathedral choir when he was only ten years old, then became an articled pupil to the Cathedral's organist and, in 1911, won a scholarship to the Royal College of Music.

Four days after Britain declared war on Germany, Gurney volunteered but was refused by the army on medical grounds. However, he volunteered again in 1915, was drafted into the 2nd 5th Gloucesters and saw front-line action the following year. On Good Friday, 1916, he was wounded and, six months later, gassed at Passchendaele.

Gurney was still in hospital in Edinburgh when his first collection of poems, *Severn and Somme*, was published. He had made new friends – and fallen in love with Nurse Annie Drummond – but a physical and emotional crisis culminated in his attempted suicide in 1918.

He was discharged from hospital a month before the Armistice. A period of hectic and impressive creativity – during which his second collection of poems, *War's Embers*, was published – came to an end when he suffered a more complete collapse. In 1922, Gurney was sent to the City of London mental hospital, where he was to stay until his death in 1937.

R. K. R. Thornton was born in Huddersfield in 1938 and educated at Manchester University. He has written numerous articles and his eight books include *Poetry of the 'Nineties, Gerard Manley Hopkins: The Poems* and John Clare's *The Rural Muse*. His most recent work, *The Decadent Dilemma*, was published in 1983.

Dr Thornton is Senior Lecturer and head of the English Literature Department at the University of Newcastle upon Tyne.

IVOR GURNEY

War Letters

A selection edited by
R. K. R. Thornton

THE HOGARTH PRESS
LONDON

Published in 1984 by
The Hogarth Press
40 William IV Street, London WC2N 4DF

First published in Great Britain by Mid Northumberland Arts Group and
Carcanet New Press 1983
Hogarth edition offset from first British edition with corrections
Text copyright © J. R. Haines, the Trustee of the Ivor Gurney Estate 1983
Introduction, selection and other editorial matter
copyright © R. K. R. Thornton 1983

British Library Cataloguing in Publication Data
Gurney, Ivor
1. Gurney, Ivor – Biography
2. Poets, English Twentieth Century – Biography
3. Composers, English – Biography
I. Title   II. Thornton, R. K. R.
780′.92′4   PR6013.U693Z
ISBN 0 7012 0567 9

Printed in Great Britain by
Redwood Burn Limited
Trowbridge, Wiltshire

ACKNOWLEDGEMENTS

The editor and publishers would like to thank: J. R. Haines, Gurney's literary executor, not only for his permission to print the material from the Gurney archive, but also for his encouragement and help; Gloucestershire County Library Service and the staff of the City of Gloucester Public Library, especially Jill Voyce and Neville Chapman, and G. R. Hiatt, the Divisional Librarian; Kathleen O'Rawe and Doris Palgrave for their typing; Professor Denis Matthews for help with the music; and Ben Thornton.

The Mid Northumberland Arts Group (MidNAG) is the area arts association for central Northumberland. It is sponsored by Wansbeck District Council in association with Northumberland Technical College, administered by the Leisure and Publicity Department of Wansbeck District Council, and grant aided by Northern Arts.

CONTENTS

WAR BOOKS

What did they expect of our toil and extreme
Hunger — the perfect drawing of a heart's dream?
Did they look for a book of wrought art's perfection,
Who promised no reading, nor praise, nor publication?
Out of the heart's sickness the spirit wrote
For delight, or to escape hunger, or of war's worst anger,
When the guns died to silence and men would gather sense
Somehow together, and find this was life indeed,
And praise another's nobleness, or to Cotswold get hence.
There we wrote — Corbie Ridge — or in Gonnehem at rest —
Or Fauquissart — our world's death songs, ever the best.
One made sorrows' praise passing the church where silence
Opened for the long quivering strokes of the bell —
Another wrote all soldiers' praise, and of France and night's stars,
Served his guns, got immortality, and died well.
But Ypres played another trick with its danger on me,
Kept still the needing and loving of action body;
Gave no candles, and nearly killed me twice as well,
And no souvenirs though I risked my life in the stuck tanks,
Yet there was praise of Ypres, love came sweet in hospital
And old Flanders went under to long ages of plays thought in my
   pages.

INTRODUCTION

Ivor Gurney is one of the finest composers of song in the English tradition, and is becoming increasingly recognised as a poet whose literary work is as significant and interesting as his music. P. J. Kavanagh's Oxford edition of Gurney's poems attests to that deserved growth of interest in his poetry. Some of his distinctiveness must lie in his conjunction of music and verse, but much of the fascination stems from the life of this extraordinary man. Michael Hurd's *The Ordeal of Ivor Gurney* (1978) satisfied biographical interest to some extent, but the letters which Hurd used to such effect and the description of the extensive Gurney archive in the City of Gloucester Public Library from which they came, inevitably created a demand for the publication of further material from that archive to help understand the life and times of Gurney, that odd and impressive figure whom Herbert Howells (in *Music and Letters*, xxxv, 1954) called a "strange, erratic, lovable, brilliant, exasperating, unteachable but wholly compelling youth."

Ivor Gurney was a writer of awkward genius. There is no doubting the beauty, power and interest of much of his work; there is equally no doubting that the distinctiveness of character which made his work so individual could also express itself in exasperating wilfulness, in difficulties in conforming to conventional society, in self-doubt, self-disgust, and perhaps even the destruction of the very self which created. The problems, rooted in his family and himself, began to show themselves during his years just before the First World War at the Royal College of Music. With the War and Gurney's enlistment it seemed for a while that the imposed rigidities of army life might save him, though Gurney never was to satisfy the army's love of smartness – when told to look more like a soldier he asserted "I'm not a soldier. I'm a *dirty civilian*" (letter of 5 July 1916). His letters, particularly those to Marion Scott, helped him to keep in contact with the literary and musical world and he kept on writing them when he was invalided home after over a year on the battlefields of France. At first he seemed to find himself; in the Edinburgh War Hospital he met new comrades to admire, fell in love with a nurse, and his book *Severn and Somme* (1917) was published. But he was separated from his friends; Annie Drummond, according to Marion Scott, "played fast and loose with Ivor till she drove him to desperation in 1917 and 1918" (Gurney archive 61.140); and his earlier problems, compounded by the physical and emotional effects of his war service, drove him to the breakdown which finds expression in his suicide note of 19 June 1918. He was sent from hospital to hospital dealing with those suffering from shell shock and neurasthenia, and finally went home to Gloucester at the end of the War. The publication of *War's Embers* (1919) and a period of hectic and impressive creativity, with attempted resumption of studies at the R.C.M. and a variety of casual musical and manual jobs, were the prelude to a more complete breakdown. In 1922 he was sent to Barnwood House, Gloucester, and then to the City of London Mental Hospital at Dartford, Kent, where he lived until his death in 1937, occasionally writing music but more often letters, appeals, poems (or amalgams of all three) in alarming and wonderful profusion and with a degenerating coherence quite dreadful to observe.

Gurney wrote hundreds of letters, particularly during his time in the army and in the City of London Mental Hospital, and the problem of publishing them is one of selection, since common sense and economics agree that it is not time for the complete letters which may one day be possible. I have decided to confine this selection to the War letters, covering his career from enlistment in February 1915, through his training in the 2nd 5th Gloucesters and his service at the front from May 1916 to September 1917, to his stay in various hospitals in Scotland and England and his return home towards the end of the War. This provides a coherent and whole narrative, from his letter written at home in Barton Street declaring "Well, here I am, and a soldier" (letter of February 1915) to his return to Barton Street and the wish for the dishing out of "Peace Bread" at the War's end (letter of 2 November 1918). It provides a variety of interests to balance the intense personal concentration of their author; where the asylum letters seek to express a world known only to Ivor Gurney, the army letters deal with a great public event and its wider impact and the lively world of music and literature which fascinated both Gurney and his correspondents. The War letters also help to chart Gurney's modulation into poetry from music; with no piano on which to practise and precious little musical companionship, his interest in poetry – always there as a companion to music in his love of song – grew and was fostered by the caring and stimulating correspondence of Marion Scott in whose interest and sympathy he was remarkably fortunate. By concentrating on this limited period of Gurney's life, it is possible to give fuller representation of his ideas and experiences in that period. It is a vital period for him, and the letters have a double relevance, the immediate and the delayed. They are the context for many of the poems of nostalgia, of looking away from the battlefield to his beloved Gloucestershire which the title of *Severn and Somme* (and even more the proposed titles of *Songs from Exile* or

Remembered Beauty – see letter of March 5 1917) aptly expresses; but they describe those events which themselves form the memories of the later poems. "First Time In" for example relates closely to those experiences described in the letters of June 1916:

> And then one took us courteously
> Where a sheet lifted, and gold light cautiously
> Streamed from an oilsheet slitted vertical into
> Half light of May. We entered, took stranger-view
> Of life as lived in the Line, the Line of war and Daily
> Papers, dispatches, brave-soldier talks, the really, really
> Truly Line; and these the heroes of story.
>
> Never were quieter folk in teaparty history.
> Never in "Cranford", Trollope, even. And as it were, home
> Closed round us. They told us lore, how and when did come
> Minnewerfers and grenades from over there east;
> The pleasant and unpleasant habits of the beast
> That crafted and tore Europe. What line mending was
> When guns centred and dugouts rocked in a haze
> And hearing was difficult – (wires cut) – All necessary
> Common sense workmanlike cautions of salutary
> Wisdom – the mechanic day-lore of modern war-making,
> Calm thought discovered in mind and body shaking.
> The whole craft and business of bad occasion.
> Talk turned personal, and to borders of two nations.
> Gone out; Cotswold's Black Mountain edges against august
> August after-suns glow, and air a lit dust
> With motes and streams of gold. Wales her soul visible
> Against all power West Heaven ever could flood full.
> And of songs – the Slumber Song, and the soft Chant
> So beautiful to which Rabelaisian songs were meant;
> Of South and North Wales; and David of the White Rock:
> What an evening! What a first time, what a shock
> So rare of home-pleasure beyond measure
> And always to Time's ending surely a treasure.

(Poems of Ivor Gurney, p. 65)

Sometimes the War experience finds its way directly into the poems, as in "Firelight" in the letter of 3 February 1917, although the treatment is much more raw; as Gurney writes in the letter of 3 August 1915, "Great poets, great creators are not much influenced by immediate events; those must sink in to the very foundations and be absorbed."

I am conscious that concentration on the War period leaves out the early enthusiasms of the pre-War Royal College of Music days, ignores the excitements and creative bursts of that immensely productive post-War period when some of Gurney's best work was produced, and avoids the strange fascinations, incoherences and difficulties of the asylum years. But a book aiming not to price itself beyond the reach of the general reader cannot include everything, and it seemed best to present one period reasonably fully. Even so, as much has had to be rejected as included, most of it with some insight into Gurney's personality, the situation of the soldier, or the state of music and literature in the 1914–1918 period.

Gurney was in some ways conscious of the interest in his letters. He wrote to Marion Scott in August 1916:

> I guess that you are out of danger, and will soon be able to resume that correspondance which is inevitably fated some day to be the joy and wonder of my biographers. That is, if my biography is not fated to be one line in the casualty list, with the wrong number and a J. instead of an I – as is set forth on my identification disc.

His own sense of his potential to write something worthy of his county and his country was a driving force and a weight, a burden of guilt and responsibility. He developed a sense of having earned in the war, through both suffering and creative work, the respect and consideration of his country; and his country's apparent refusal to grant him a full pension and its vocal thanks was a source of indignation and another weight. It had been clear before the War that he was not well, with his dyspepsia and neurasthenia, but after the War his illness became more unmanageable. It can no longer be claimed that Gurney's madness was caused by the War; it is plain from the letters that he himself recognised the possibility of the War experience clearing both body and mind, which for a time it seemed to be doing. Equally, it is impossible to claim that the War had no effect on him. Not only in his sense of deserving reward (he was planning a third collection to be called *Rewards of Wonder*), but also in the powerful consciousness of the shattering experiences and shattered responses, one can see the way in which the War seized his mind and occupied it as much as Gloucestershire had done while he was at the front. The War was, with Gloucestershire, the shaping experience of his life, resonating in his poems right up to his death, occupying his mind when his mind had no longer a context worthy to occupy it.

For a time, from 1915 to 1917, he seemed to lose some of his doubts and his worst problems in his involvement with the War. He was given exercise, regular food, a purpose, comrades and corres-pondence. All held him together, in spite of the atrocious surroundings which the War, the weather and the enemy contrived for the forces at the front. Out of these conditions came music – song settings of "By a Bierside" for example – and, more frequently because of the lack of a piano, poetry, to which he increasingly turned to express his creative drive.

Gurney's accounts of his experience and feelings bear out what has become familiar in other poets in the First World War: like Wilfred Owen, he wished to write poems with his comrades in mind: "Old ladies wont like them, but soldiers may, and these things are written either for soldiers or civilians as well informed as the French what 'a young fresh war' means" (14 February 1917), or "Things like the 'Signallers Vision' are meant to appeal to such people as are in this room with me – not to the experimenters in Greek metres" (29 March 1917). He is equally conscious of the need for spontaneity and the impossibility of refinement: "It would need quiet and continued thought – whereas the things are finished as quickly as possible: often finished at one go" (29 March 1917). He has the same lack of hatred for his enemy: "In the mind of all the English soldiers I have met there is absolutely no hate for the Germans, but a kind of brotherly though slightly contemptuous kindness – as to men who are going through a bad time as well as themselves" (17 February 1917). And he has the same love for his fellow soldiers, their humanity and strength, that other soldier poets had. Whether one calls it homoerotic or covertly homosexual is less important than to recognise it as a strong innocent admiration, love and respect for the calm, strength, wholeness and nobility of his comrades.

What helps to make Gurney distinctive and important, however, is that he is a private soldier and has, like his fellow-private Isaac Rosenberg, a distinct ability in two arts. His sense of his distinctness from the officers can be seen in his sonnets of "counterblast" against Rupert Brooke's which were "by an officer (or one who would have been an officer)", as he writes in the letter of 14 February 1917. The only thing which could make him (the "wangler" as he saw himself) think of officer training was that it might delay his return to the front. So we have in the letters and poems an important record of a conflict which is notably poorly provided in accounts from the viewpoint of the private soldier.

It might be thought that the poems which Gurney was sending back to Marion Scott and which eventually made up *Severn and Somme* and *War's Embers* should not be printed here in space which might well be occupied by letters. I indeed began with the same opinion, considering that the poems had been published elsewhere; but more and more it became apparent that there was an exciting relationship between letter and poem which would be lost by such a separation. The letters are the context from which the poems spring and indeed the poems are as much part of the letters as the more conversational and mundane material. Part of the directness of Gurney's approach in his verse and the narrative vitality of style perhaps stem from the easy modulation between the forms which circumstance forced on him in the trenches.

For similar reasons, I have printed only complete letters, feeling that the whole balance is important, even if one does have the repeated trivia of enquiries after health and the weather.

The letters are presented without annotation. It would have been possible to find reasons for a great deal, and many letters could be annotated to a length equalling the letter itself, with page references to newspaper articles, biographical details, identification of literary and musical quotations, historical and geographical information, details of printings and variants of poems and settings; but it seemed more valuable to give all the space to Gurney's letters, which are the main interest and purpose of the book, trusting that all can be made clear by using the index, standard reference books and, of course, Michael Hurd's *The Ordeal of Ivor Gurney*, which provides the best context and commentary.

The dates of the letters are important and I have ordered them chronologically. I have provided as full information about dating as possible, although Gurney is fairly casual about dating his letters. I have given a full and standardised style of dating, wherever the information came from. When Gurney did date the letter, I have signified this with (G) after the date; where there is an envelope with a legible date of posting, I have used that and signified it with (P), though I recognise the possibility that letters could have changed envelopes, as in one case has obviously happened; if there is an annotation by a recipient or earlier editor, I have accepted it if handwriting, style, paper and content fitted in with dated letters, and acknowledged it with the symbol (E); lacking all these, I have assigned a date from all evidence available and signified this conjectural date with a question mark (?).

It would have been pedantic and largely pointless to reproduce information from the envelopes in which the letters were posted, but it is worth pointing out that letters from France would typically have the Field Post Office number franking, the stamp of the censor saying "Passed Field Censor" with his number and signature, and Gurney's note in the top left hand corner "On Active Service" instead of a stamp. This information becomes quite telling when one sees the envelope of his suicide note (letter of 19 June 1918), where he has written "Wounded Soldiers Letter" in place of the stamp which he otherwise always put on his letters sent in the British Isles. It is a small but expressive sign of his sense of being owed something for his service.

The marks of the Censor are very slight: the deletion of the address on the letter of 7 June 1916, and four lines of gloomy prognostication in the letter of 5 July 1916. But the effect of the Censor is perhaps still strong in what is *not* said: Gurney is reticent in reporting his own acts of courage or fighting, of which one gathers fragments indirectly, but he also consciously refrains from full information and particular types of information because of the Censor. In the letter of 7 August 1916, he remarks that it is "difficult in these letters to interest you, and yet avoid trouble with the Censor", and on 29 September 1916 he explains that "My letters in future will not be so long; by special request of the Censor". It is presumably this last request which makes him begin the next letter (8 October 1916) with the declaration "Pas de contraband/Lectures pour tous/De la musique De la litterature etc etc etc". Some of his letters from hospital contain information which one imagines would not have passed the Censor, and his later poems, lacking that constraint, fill in some of the activities which he is in correspondence so reluctant to mention.

The addresses given on Gurney's letters are in a variety of styles and with a variety of punctuations. Since he had a little system in the matter and did not seem particularly to care, I have saved space by standardising the presentation of addresses to a continuous line which I have punctuated.

I have indented the beginning of paragraphs whether Gurney did or not, and have tried to represent his paragraphing as far as possible, though on his small sheets of paper and with his erratic practice it is not always clear what he intends. I have closed brackets where he allowed the edge of the paper to represent that closure for him; and I have kept his spelling and punctuation.

I have transcribed Gurney's music as carefully as possible, and Professor Denis Matthews has helped to get rid of some of my mistakes; but it must be remembered that these fragments are hurriedly-noted sketches and reminiscences which the neatness somewhat misrepresents. Gurney's omissions and casualnesses seem more startling when carefully transcribed, but it should not be assumed that they are his final thoughts.

All the letters printed here are from the Gurney Archive in the City of Gloucester Public Library. The number printed at the head of each letter opposite the date is the reference number of the letter in that collection, the box number followed by the place in the box. The numbering is not chronological and there is an occasional duplication, but researchers should have no difficulty in locating any of the letters used.

When one has finished the task of bringing some order to a part of this wild mass of creativity, one must say of the whole collection of letters what Herbert Howells wrote to Joy Finzi about the letters Gurney wrote to him:

> They are – as you will see – of a strangely mixed order and quality. But they are astonishingly vivid as a reflection of the man we knew in the wasted days of 1914–18, and in the wretched aftermath. To me, as I re-read them now, they are sometimes more moving than I can express (Letter 3.34 in the Gloucester Collection).

CORRESPONDENTS

Frederick William HARVEY (1888–1957). Early friend and poetic example for Gurney, he was born at Murrell's End, Hartpury, and grew up in Minsterworth. He went to school at Rossall, trained as a solicitor, and enlisted in 1914 in the 5th Gloucesters. *A Gloucestershire Lad at home and abroad* (1916) was written in the trenches. He won the D.C.M. after an encounter with the enemy in No Man's Land, was commissioned, captured, and attempted to escape. *Gloucestershire Friends: poems from a German prison camp* (1917) reaffirmed the commitment to his native county which marks his life and work. His most famous poem is probably the title poem of *Ducks, and other verses* (1919). Other collections of verse include *Farewell* (1921), September (1925), a selection of 31 poems in the Augustan Books series (1926) and a selection *Gloucestershire* (1947). *Comrades in Captivity; a record of Life in seven German prison camps* (1920) is in prose.

Herbert HOWELLS (1892–1983). Articled pupil to A. H. Brewer of Gloucester Cathedral, he won a scholarship to the Royal College of Music, where his teachers were Stanford and Charles Wood. His Mass was performed in 1912 in Westminster Cathedral, and his first Piano Concerto in 1913 at Queen's Hall. His first appointment as sub-organist at Salisbury Cathedral was cut short by serious ill health, but he survived to teach composition at the R.C.M. from 1920 until well into the '70s. He succeeded Holst as director of Music at St. Paul's Girls' School (1936–62), and was King Edward VII Professor of Music at London University. A distinguished composer who has not yet received due recognition, his *Hymnus Paradisi* is considered his masterpiece. (See C. Palmer's *Herbert Howells: a Study*, 1978.)

Marion Margaret SCOTT (1877–1953). Attended Royal College of Music 1896–1904, being taught violin by Arbos. She remained closely associated with the College, helping to found the R.C.M. Union in 1906, editing the *R.C.M. Magazine* 1936–44, and being awarded an honorary A.R.C.M. shortly before her death. She was a founder of the Society of Women Musicians in 1911 and its president from 1915–1916. She published a book of poems in 1905, wrote music criticism, led her own string quartet, organised concerts, and was for a time leader of Morley College Orchestra under Gustav Holst's direction. She wrote a book on Beethoven and many articles on Haydn, though she never completed her projected book on the latter. (See Herbert Howells's "Marion Margaret Scott", in *Music and Letters*, XXXV, 1954, p. 134 and Kathleen Dale's "Memories of Marion Scott", *ibid*, p. 236.)

Ethel Lillian VOYNICH (née BOOLE, 1864–1960). A friend from Gurney's time at the R.C.M. before the war, Mrs. Voynich was composer, translator, and novelist. Her music includes songs, and a Cantata in memory of Roger Casement. Her translations include *Chopin's Letters* (1931), *The Humour of Russia* (1895), and Stepniak's pamphlets. Her novels, of which the most often reprinted and translated is *The Gadfly* (1897), also include *Jack Raymond* (1900), *Olive Latham* (1904), *An Interrupted Friendship* (1910), and *Put Off thy Shoes* (1945).

ABBREVIATIONS

AB   Arthur Benjamin
AND   Annie Nelson Drummond
ASC   Army Service Corps
BEF   British Expeditionary Force
CB   Confined to Barracks
CCS   Casualty Clearing Station
CHHP Sir Charles Hubert Hastings Parry
CVS   Sir Charles Villiers Stanford
DCM   Distinguished Conduct Medal
ET   Edward Thomas
FPC   Field Post Card
FWH   Frederick William Harvey
GKC   Gilbert Keith Chesteron
GLA   Grand Literary Agent
HE   High Explosive
HNH   Herbert Norman Howells
MGC   Machine Gun Corps
MH   Margaret Hunt
MMS   Marion Margaret Scott
RAMC Royal Army Medical Corps
RB   Robert Bridges
RCM   Royal College of Music
RCO   Royal College of Organists
RLS   Robert Louis Stevenson
RSM   Regimental Sergeant Major
RT   Radio Telephone
RVW   Ralph Vaughan Williams
S and J Sidgwick and Jackson
SKen   South Kensington
TLS   Times Literary Supplement
TMS   Trench Mortar Strafe

A BRIEF CHRONOLOGY

1890   Ivor Bertie Gurney born 28 August at 3 Queen Street, Gloucester, his father a tailor. Alfred Cheesman stood as godfather.

1890s   Move to 19 Barton Street. Attends National School and All Saints' Sunday school.

1896   Purchase of family piano.

1899   Graduates to full membership of Choir of All Saints.

1900   Wins place in Cathedral Choir, and goes to King's School; begins to learn the organ; meets F. W. Harvey.

1905*ff*   Years of intimacy with Cheesman, and Margaret and Emily Hunt, who encouraged his artistic talents.

1906   Articled pupil to Dr. Herbert Brewer, organist of Gloucester Cathedral. Herbert Howells a fellow pupil from 1907.

1911   Wins scholarship of £40 per annum to Royal College of Music; takes it up in the Autumn.

1912   Friendship with Herbert Howells and Arthur Benjamin. Meets Mrs. Voynich. Composition of the "Elizas". Early signs of physical and mental illness.

1914   Britain declares war on Germany, August 4th. Gurney volunteers August 8th and is refused.

1915   Volunteers again. Drafted into army February 9th and joins 2nd 5th Gloucesters as Private no. 3895.
Battalion leaves for Northampton in early February; to Chelmsford in April; to camp at Epping on 17th June; back to Chelmsford in August. In band in September.

1916   To Tidworth on Salisbury Plain in February and thence to Park House Camp for Active Service Training. 25th May, departure for France. 15th June, first Front Line fighting (in the Fauquissart–Laventie sector). August, in hospital for teeth and glasses. Plans book of poems. December to February, has job in Sanitary Section.

1917   April, wounded on Good Friday. Sent to hospital at Rouen for 6 weeks. Given new number 241281 and transferred to Machine Gun Corps. Battalion moves to Ypres front in August. September 10th (?) gassed at St. Julien (Passchendaele). Shipped to hospital in Edinburgh. Publication of *Severn and Somme*. Falls in love with Nurse Annie Nelson Drummond. Transferred to Command Depot at Seaton Delaval.

1918	February, in Newcastle General Hospital for "stomach trouble caused by gas". March, at Brancepeth Castle. June, in Lord Derby's War Hospital at Warrington. July, transferred to Napsbury War Hospital, St Albans. Discharged in October. Armistice declared, November 11th. Return to R.C.M.
1919	Publication of *War's Embers*.
1922	Sent first to Barnwood House, Gloucester, then to City of London Mental Hospital at Dartford in Kent.
1937	Dies at Dartford on 26th December. Buried at Twigworth.

I
IN TRAINING

To F. W. HARVEY   41.1
February 1915 (?)   19 Barton St, Gloucester.

Dear Willy: Well, here I am, and a soldier, in your own regiment's
2nd reserve — to go to Northampton on Monday for the first
Reserve.

   I am glad you are pretty well now, a week should put you·right,
and make you happy. Tonight I have been reading the Georgian
Poetry Book, and it is this that has made me write to you. Our young
poets think very much as we, or rather as we shall when body and
mind are tranquil. Masefields feeling of beauty and its meaning
strike chords very responsive in ourselves. I found myself remembering old things, old times together as I read "Biography", and it
brought you very near. May 1925 see us both happy and revered by
the few who count and know the good when they see it.

   Meanwhile there is a most bloody and damnable war to go
through. Let's hope it'll do the trick for both of us, and make us so
strong, so happy, so sure of ourselves, so crowded with fruitful
memories of joy that we may be able to live in towns or earn our
living at some drudgery and yet create whole and pure joy for
others. It is a far cry for me, but who knows what a year may do?
And I mean to touch music no more till I must.

   The Sea, the Sea will be my home for a while, and the hard
friendly life of that wrestle with that most untameable, unknowable
element of God. Could we only do it together! Do you read much
now, are you (most wisely maybe) letting yourself float on the
stream of common consciousness; just living and taking the nearest
thing as your present fulfilment? Do you look forward, or do you
wear blinkers and cultivate short sight and a narrow perception?

   This is all rather blithering, but that book made me think of you
and our common aims.

   And I would give much for a couple of hours teadrinking and
smoking with a piano and book-talk; but that's not yet, indeed it
may be very far away, worse luck.

   Good bye: Yours ever   IBG

To F. W. HARVEY   61.392
*February 1915 (?)   Pte. I. B. Gurney, B Company, 2nd 5th
Gloucesters, Northampton.*

Dear Willy: Well, here I am; hard worked and, apparently able
to stand about 7 hours a day drill, praise be to God. I think it will be

all right. If so, May should see me considerably better and much happier.

Today was a sailing day, and I thought of the day when I should first sight the Plate or Spain or even Ireland from the bow of a three master.

And of that further day, when, all difficulties being removed, health and technique and inspiration restored, I should get an appointment on shore. And last, when I should be acknowledged great in Art by those whose judgement I value. Let em all come!

The Army biscuits suit me. Of course they are too hard for my poor teeth, but hot tea and patience helps one past all.

It was an experience worth the writing about, when we recruits stood at ease in the dusk while the 5th Gloucesters crowded around us with cries of welcome and recognition and peered into our faces to make sure of friends. It gave me a thrill such as I have had not for long enough.

I have already changed billet, and the chaps here are very nice indeed. Good men, which is a great point. But in this new democracy almost everyone is jolly, or tries to be.

Kiplings little 6^d book on the new Armies is very good. Hast seen it? Good bye and best luck and health and willing endurance of all: Yours ever   I.B.G.

To Mrs Voynich   41.2

April 1915 (E)   Pte Gurney, 6 Platoon, B Company, 2nd 5th Glosters, Chelmsford, Essex.

Dear Mrs Voynich: Well, here I am; a soldier of the King, and the best thing for me — at present. I feel that nowhere could I be happier than where I am, (except perhaps at sea) so the experiment may be called a success. What the future holds has to be kept out of sight, and indeed that is easily to be done here where noone talked of the war until the last few days, and only now because the regiment of which we are the reserve has already been in the trenches and perhaps in action.

They are good sorts, most of these boys; and will surely fight as well as those who have already gone — though there is no word of war; nothing but a gentle grumbling about the rations or the sergeant major.

It is indeed a better way to die; with these men, in such a cause; than the end which seemed near me and was so desirable only just over two years ago. And if I escape; well, there will be memories for old age; not all pleasant, but none so unpleasant as those which would have come had I refused the call.

Now I am tired; but tired with many others, Hungry, but honestly so. And if I *must* grumble there is always a good reason somewhere. The army meat would make Falstaff misanthropic (and reduced his bulk.)

I hope your health is good now. Europe is not now a fit subject for sick people to read about, and if you are not well this must very much depress you. But heres the spring — and Framilode, Minsterworth, Maisemore and the Severn villages must be full of flowers and peace.

Your little garden must look well under these skies of the last week or so.

Did you go to this three Bs festival? They did some great stuff.

I was glad to see that Verbruggen had taken liberties with the scoring of the Choral Symphony.

Have you read "The Undying Past" by Sudermann. It struck me very much indeed, and I doubt whether any of our young men could touch it. It is German — very much so — everything so intense and volcanic and half-mad, except Hertha.

(This letter has been left more than a week and shall go now for fear it should be left for ever.)

Good bye and best wishes yours very sincerely   Ivor Gurney

To HERBERT HOWELLS   3.3

8 April 1915 (P)   Pte I B Gurney, 6 Platoon, B Company, 2nd 5th Glosters, Chelmsford.

Dear Howells: Well, if you and Miss Higgs could make out "I praise the tender flower" to C H H Ps satisfaction, you are very deserving of praise — I did not mean that to be sung; there were corners to be rounded off too. But still, if "Edward" went well, I am content.

What had you done for the exam? Anything besides your suite? And are you quite well now, and able to let fly with the nimble pen?

And how is Benjamin?

As to whether I like soldiering. I am convinced that had I stuck to music, complete health would have been a very long job. This life will greatly help.

Secondly, supposing I had not joined, and never attained my high aim in music — I could not have forgiven myself.

Thirdly, that if I get shot, it wont matter to me what my possibilities (with health) might or might not be.

4thly. That the life, though hard, and the food scant and coarse, makes me as happy as I can be made without a yacht and money. It is hard, and always I am tired, but struggle through in a very much happier frame of mind than that I have had for some time — probably 4 years.

There's your answer, and longer than you wanted I daresay.

As to chances of fighting — our first battallion is already in France. We fill up gaps, and generally stop up holes in it. So that May or June may see us, and myself, in the fighting line.

The chaps are rough, but as a general thing good inside. And never a word do they say about wanting to fight, or being in the trenches. Their attitude is — We dont want to fight, but someone must do it — the best attitude of all.

Will Harvey is already in France with the 1st 5th Glosters. Now I suppose you are in Glostershire; and soon will see apple blossom and the pear trees "praising God with sweetest looks". Sometimes my heart aches for Framilode, and my little leaky boat; my gun and the ever changing Severn, now so full in Flood.

And through my thoughts when indigestion has lessened and left my brain clearer, there runs the symphonic greatness of the "Wedge" Prelude and Fugue! Curious, is it not?

Work lately has been
6.45 – 7.30
8.45 – 12.45
2.0 – 4.30
and occasionally night operations. One of which was 11 – 2.15 pm – am There was language! 18 carat, full blooded, above proof, purple verbiage, in broad Glostershire.

If you can get hold of Masefields "Philip the King" read it. Besides "Philip" there is a poem named "August"— the best of the war poems. Well, Good bye, and the very best wishes for all happiness: Yours   I.B.G.

To MARION SCOTT   41.4

9 May 1915 (P)   Pte Gurney, 6 Platoon, B Company, 2nd 5th Gloucesters, Chelmsford, Essex.

Dear Miss Scott: Thank you for your kind letter, and the reminder of College life. It is a happy friendly life there — at S. Ken — and if it were not for my unworthy body, I should have nothing but pleasurable memories of London. As for me — I am well; in the sense that I am able to hang on in everything they have done as yet, but in the sense of feeling well there is improvement but nothing else. But fatigue from the body brings rest to the soul — not so mental fatigue.

Do you know that the Glosters have the second best roll of battle honours in the British Army? So it is. And though we are a rough lot in some ways, (and the Bosches will discover some of them,) we have no end of a good domestic reputation, so to speak.

The less that is said of our musical taste the better; but in full chestedness and knowledge of ragtime etc we excel. Our Colonel is Bathurst ("Benny") an M.P. Our Captain is Sewell of some note as a cricketer; S. African and Gloucestershire. And our talk is rough, a dialect telling of days in the open air and no books. We do not talk about the war, although we have taken to looking at the casualty lists now our 1st regiment is in the trenches, and our friends are astonishing the fields of Flanders with strange talk.

And so Rupert Brooke is dead; still he has left us a legacy of two sonnets which outshine by far any thing yet written on this up-heaval. They are as beautiful as music. They are so beautiful that at last one forgets that the words are there and is taken up into ecstasy just as in music.

> "These had seen movement, and heard music; known
> Slumber and waking; loved; gone proudly friended;
> Felt the quick stir of wonder; sat alone;
> Touched flowers and furs and cheeks. All this is ended.

But the Times Literary Supplement for March 11 quotes two in full; there you must find them. Galsworthy calls Beethoven's 7th Symphony the most wonderful piece of music in the world; (in the "Patrician", I think;) and that is not so bad a guess. It holds at any rate the spirit of our armies.

Beethoven, Bach, Mozart, Schubert seem to be left high above war-mark, with folksong and Palestrina and our madrigals. I should think that Brahms chamber music is often insufferable now.

But oh, to hear the "Sea Symphony" again! How is Vaughan Williams? If he goes, and with Rupert Brooke dead, we shall have suffered severely enough on the side of Art.

It is possible that I may get leave this week end, and if so I shall probably come up to College on Monday morning (I must be on first parade (6.30) on Tuesday.)

There and then I shall find out what Howells is doing and all the other little etceteras that I want to know.

Poor Concerto — so fine, so strong, so beautiful; when will you be done again?

I will let you know about my visit. It may be from 1 oclock till four
on Monday (tomorrow week.):
Yours very sincerely   Ivor Gurney.

To MARION SCOTT   41.6

*16 June 1915 (P)   Pte Gurney, B Company, 2nd 5th Glosters,
Chelmsford, Essex.*

Dear Miss Scott: Thank you for your letter, and the kind things;
not to say flattery.

The Library here possesses but one copy of Shakespeare's
Historical Plays, and that is out. But I should guess it to be either
from King John, Henry V, or Henry IV. Certainly it is Shakespeare.

What date is the College at Home? I feel that I should like to
come to it, and could probably do so. Tomorrow we march to camp,
somewhere near Epping; but your letter would be forwarded at
once.

Stanford wrote to me a short time ago — very kindly but hiero-
glyphically. (?)

My health is still slowly improving; and as my mind clears, and as
the need for self-expression grows less weak; the thought of leaving
all I have to say unsaid, makes me cold. Could I only hand on my
gift! Anyway, I have been rejected for second-reinforcements, and
Territorial 3rd reinforcements will be late in going. The war
however seems like lasting a year, and there is none of the
exhilaration of battle in hot weather training.

Still, I chose this path, and do not regret it; do not see what else I
could have done under the circumstances; and if the Lord God
should have the bad taste to delete me
"Deil anither word tae God from a gentleman like me".

Anyway there's the Elizabethan songs, Edward, the Twa
Corbies, the Sea, and Kennst du das Land — two of which seem to
be lost and one a sketch.

Masefield is with the Red Cross in France.

John Drinkwater's new book seems to be good. Have you read
any of Neil Munro's books? John Silence, The New Road, Doom
Castle? They are very good, and exciting in the R.L.S. style. What a
fine speech was Churchill's, at Dundee. The man has pluck enough.

"Land and Water", Belloc's affair is optimistic but John Buchan
thinks it highly probable that there will be another winter campaign
— farther east though.

One of the best signs of healthy taste at present, is the significant fact that though Rabinadrath Tagore has been knighted, the critics I read did not pretend to be transported by his work — Not so much, indeed, as before the war: Yours very sincerely   Ivor Gurney.

To MARION SCOTT   41.5

28 June 1915 (P)   *Pte Gurney, 2nd 5th Glosters, Wintry Farm Camp, Epping, Essex.*

Dear Miss Scott: Very sorry, miss, but it couldn't be helped. They left me uncertain up to the last moment, and the leave was not granted, so I heard, simply through the carelessness of an orderly corporal.

I hope that everything went off well in spite of the unfortunate hiatus.

Edward Thomas reviewed Brooke's poems in the Chronicle, and I got another sonnet out of that —

Now God be thanked that has matched us with this Hour
                          another very good one.

It *is* curious how little great youthful-seeming poetry has been written; and sonnets seem especially fated to be the work of "solemn whiskered men, pillars of the state".

Well, here we are in camp, and a nice old mix up it is! Whatever is wanted out of the ordinary is at the extreme wrong end of the kitbag. Everything has to come out, and at last in exasperation one stuffs things of hourly necessity in first, and language flows not wisely but too well. This lengthens the act of cleaning up at least 250%. But this is good for me.

The unmentionable by-products who manage this brigade (there are the Bucks, the Oxford and Bucks and the Glosters here) give us reveillé at 5. Breakfast at 6 Parade at 7. Dinner at 2. Tea somewhere about 4.30 — 5.30. May their iniquity be remembered at the last!

And such tea!

At present I am "on sick" with lumbago, a horrid name. But this came just in time to prevent C.B. for a dirty rifle, which is thus put off — may it be forgotten!

"Land and Water" is still very optimistic. My thoughts go onward to the dim time after the war, and the politics in ten years time. Here is Belloc gaining a great following; who is a very strong opponent of the Party System, a Strong Anti-Socialist, and though once a Liberal M.P. with a strong contempt for it. He is certain to show large in public opinion, and there will be many and curious rows and large and generous bewilderments.

A 100 reinforcement went off on Friday to the front, and there was some excitement — "some" in the American sense.

The cheering was immense, overwhelming, cataractic. The only things that can give you an idea of that sound are either elemental sounds like the war of winds and waves or the greatest moment in music — the end of the development in the 1st movement of the Choral Symphony. Like the creative word of God.

I have discovered an original essay on Spring! In a book called "Southward Ho" by Holbrook Jackson in Dent's Wayfarers Library — a good book.

There is nowhere to put books here — nowhere! Only in that comic-tragic kit bag, Gott strafe it. A slot machine is what I want, or a valet.

Do you know anything about our people in the Army? What has happened to Benjamin? Warren? And that person Brown whom I disliked so much. What are they doing at rehearsal now? Will there be an Opera?

Please excuse writing and the pencility thereof, but nothing else is possible in camp: with best wishes:

Yours very sincerly   Ivor Gurney

To Herbert Howells   3.2

June 1915 (?)   Pte Gurney, B Company, 2nd 5th Glosters, Wintry Farm, Epping, Essex.

Dear Howells: It couldn't be managed. One has to make such applications 5 or 6 days before, and so the chance was missed. I hope the estimable A.B is all right, and not so sick of the Army as we are here; but poor privates may only guess at the riot of extravagance and debauchery which make up the lives of lieutenants and such folk.

At the moment of writing, I am lying precariously on the edge of a pool, watching for signs of khaki over a hedge half a mile away and cursing the army strongly and long. The aim of training troops is to make them as tired as possible without teaching them anything. Take em for a route march, stand em on their heads, muck about with em in any fashion so long as they get tired and sick of soldiering. It is an unintelligent affair for the infantry nowadays. If you do what you are told and have no objection to sudden death, that means a good soldier.

What are you writing now? Let's have another, simpler string quartett or V and P sonata. I would like to hear that bloated monstrosity of a Concerto of yours again though. Glad to see you were publicly recognised as the most deserving pupil. I hope the medal is not too large to roll or bowl to the pawn shop.

My health still improves very slowly, though if it had not been for 5 easy days (for inoculation etc) last week I should have come a cropper. They are mad as hatters here. Reveille at 5. Roll call and rifle inspection at 6. Breakfast at 6.30. Parade at 8.15 March or summat. Dinner 1.30–2.30. Bayonet Practice 3.30. Tea 4.30. So the meals come at 6.30, 1.30 about, and 4.30. O Generation of vipers! And I joined to cure my belly!! May the Lord play dirty tricks in great abundance on such malapert cock-knaves. Please remember me to C.V.S. C.H.H.P. Mr Waddington Dr Alcock and Dr Davies; who I suppose will still be splitting hairs while I am splitting cocoanuts. How do the composition-cubs get on? Write me a newsy letter or at least P.C.:   Yours etc   I B G

To MARION SCOTT   41.7

3 August 1915 (P)   Pte Gurney, B company, 2nd 5th Glosters, (tomorrow to be) Chelmsford, Essex.

Dear Miss Scott: I am so sorry about the bloodvessel; sufficiently exciting for one who had a mind in favour of peace and whole organisms. But now it is more or less over (as I hope) now you may reap some benefit. As how saith the sage — A headache may seem a poor investment while in full blast, but when it is slackening is worth a dollar a minute.

J. E. Patterson has written a book around Minehead, perhaps "Fishers of the Sea", or no — "Love like the Sea"; which I liked. Perhaps you might. He has power, but an amateurish trick of underlining his points which is irritating.

Belloc has a passage in one of his Essays; the one called the Views of England I believe; in which he speaks of the strange and secret enchantment and the haunted tides of all that Sou Western coast.

You did not at all bore me by your description of the West; if it had been dull, probably I should have skipped it, but every word was read and enjoyed; behind it all, the continual aching current — "Shall I ever sing it all"? Indeed England has been poorly off for musicians, or at least (I believe) for musical output. Schubert so full of happy memories of orchards, and Mozart so clear in spirit and expression like a Spring sky, cannot we produce these? The country that produced the man who could write such a speech as

"Ye elves of hills, brooks, standing lakes and groves"

could produce anything. Our young men must write on a diet largely composed of Folk Song and Shakespeare.

The Sonnet of R.B. you sent me, I do not like. It seems to me that Rupert Brooke would not have improved with age, would not have broadened; his manner has become a mannerism, both in rhythm and diction. I do not like it. This is the kind of work which his older lesser inspiration would have produced. Great poets, great creators are not much influenced by immediate events; those must sink in to the very foundations and be absorbed. Rupert Brooke soaked it in quickly and gave it out with as great ease. For all that we have very much to be grateful for; but what of 1920? What of the counterpart to "The Dynasts" which may still lie within another Hardy's brain a hundred years today?

Thank God we leave camp tomorrow! In it we have suffered all the horrors of slum life. They have driven us to distraction with parades and unexpected unnecessary swoops on our (supposedly) free time. Rainy weather was our only respite, and that on clayey soil how appalling! Shackles and over and underdone roast. Execrable tea, margarine crying to Heaven and the Sanitary inspector for deracination. Bread often fit for museums. Bacon virginal — unspoiled pig. The Canteen was a bright spot, but a bright spot cherished and administered by swindlers and rogues of nameless birth.

From this we go to billets — not to grumble; not to grumble, but to make sacrifices before the altar of the Godess of Home, that estimable female who, like all her sex, is not allowed in camp.

What we are to do, what destiny confronts us the Gods themselves may well be to confused to know in all the rumours excursions and alarms which surround those condemned for their sins to dwell in camp.

(This is a queer letter. Once more it is taken up and perhaps may be completed this time.)

What do you say, for an ending, to an original

To the Poet before Battle

Sonnet

Now, Youth, the hour of thy dread passion comes;
Thy lovely things must all be laid away,
And thou, as others, must face the riven day
Unstirred by the tattle and rattle of rolling drums
Or bugles strident cry. When mere noise numbs
The sense of being, the fearsick soul doth sway,
Remember thy great crafts honour, that they may say

Nothing in shame of Poets. Then the crumbs
Of praise the little versemen joyed to take
Shall be forgotten: then they must know we are,
For all our skill in words, equal in might
And strong of mettle, as those we honoured. Make
The name of Poet terrible in just War;
And like a crown of honour upon the fight.

Please criticise this very frankly, and with no eye on Wordworth's "September 1802" "London 1802" "It is not to be thought of", "October 1803" "November 1806", or any such. It is not meant to compete.

Kitchener reviews us on Thursday.

I am in the band — a new one — playing the baryton, a bass cornet arrangement. It is a fine instrument, and three days practice — even to me — are inadequate to do it justice.

Good bye and good-luck

Yours very sincerely

Ivor Gurney

Oh, what do you think of the Ballade to Beelzebub? Barring one line, it is worthy of anyone. It was written by my best friend for the 5th Gloster Magazine, a trench paper. Have I not right to be proud of him? Is it not gorgeously *meaty*?

To MARION SCOTT   41.10

September 1915 (E)   *Pte Gurney, B Company, 2/5th Glosters,*
Chelmsford, Essex.

Dear Miss Scott: Thank you very much for your letter which pleased me very much.

It is easier to take a letter bit by bit as you did.

The Glosters have no prospect of camping in Windsor Park; neither do they wish it — Billetts are in every way better. Thanking you kindly; but it is curious that some Essex troops have just gone there from Chelmsford.

I was glad to hear of Shimmin, and have wiped off a long standing debt of a letter, and hope to hear from him soon, though that is undeserved. Tell him I write many more letters now than once I did. He will get little enough sleep in camp I am afraid. He must rest between tea and bedtime, if they let him alone then.

But I had written before you sent your letter and it went to Marlborough Road way.

Belloc's Essay on the Views of England is in either "First and Last", "On Everything" or "On Anything".

As to the "Dynasts" all you say is true; and what you say establishes it high enough. You did not mention the songs though, some of which are magnificent. His bad verse inevitably recalls Browning, to me. His good, is splendidly direct. Milton could never have imagined the Dynasts; and at least Hardy spares us that vile Latin-English, and Latin constructions. The puzzle is that Hardy's sense of Humour in some things so strong has not restrained him oftener.

As to Faith.

There is an excellent article in this week "Saturday Westminster", a paper of which I am very fond. It is a review by Walter de la Mare, and is that poet's confession of Faith. (There is also a charming poem on Bach, called "during Music".) I repose myself on a blind faith that all evil is somehow unavoidable, and therefore necessary, and that in the End a complete explanation of and compensation for the least scrap of evil is to come.

I hate all formal ceremonies and Churches, and my master in all these things is Wordsworth, and my place of worship his. (The article is not de la Mare's, but one called Religion and the War. I wish you would get that number.) The important thing to remember now is that there are no problems now that were not equally urgent two years or 2000 years ago. A Faith which needs reconstruction now will need it often again maybe.

Let us play — the 48.

People who find their Faith shocked by this war, do not need a stronger faith only, but a different one, without blinkers. The whole question is summed up in the last line of the A♭ Prelude. 2nd Book. There you will find a complete and compendious summary of all necessary belief.

I count myself lucky to be in the band. Fancy getting an interesting job in the noble profession of Arms! There's something wrong within the state of Denmark. We made our debut at this (Sunday) morning's Church-parade with that first of all march tunes, "Marching through Georgia" — bugles and brass. O, but it was hard work! The band is a soft job usually, but not on the march. Our chaps marched splendidly, as they can when they choose.

At present I am writing a ballad of the Cotswolds, after Belloc's "South Country". And there are two sonnets which may come with this. I find ballad writing very grateful and comforting to the mind, and to praise one's own county makes it not the less joyous. Someday maybe I'll write music with not less facility.

I call this hefty good verse. Yet it flows (as R.L.S. said) like buttermilk from a jug.

When I am old and cannot bide
The grimy townships more,
When dreams and images will not
Assuage my longing sore,
I'll shake their (the towns') mire from my quick feet
And shut an alien door,

And get me home to my dear West
Where men drive ploughing teams, —
And smell the earth, sing earthy songs,
Drink careless, dance, swim streams
Of Crystal, Jest with God; I'll have
Dreams Substances not dreams.

There in the creeper clad old houses
Of beautiful grey stone,
I'll have my friends, and make amends
For bleak years spent alone
Deep-snug in a black old chimney seat
   Close to the hearth-stone.

I repeat, Madam, that strikes me as being a damgood piece of
verse, and yet when I feel like it, it means the simple trouble of
sitting down and opening my poetical pores and exuding as fast as
pen will write — almost. But not so this.

Satan above the Battle

Think you that he who made the skies was ever
Able before to make a scene accurst
As this one? Nay; now God hath done his worst,
His keenest spite hath poured on Man's endeavour
To live and dream — like Him! Nor would he sever
His countenancing help from Man, nor burst
That bubble of Love; till those, his creatures, had first
Near equalled Him in might. O clever! Clever!
But, Son of God, and Man, what think you of this?
What is your Passion worth? Three days in Hell
Under protection. Poverty. Judas' kiss?
(O Sentiment!) Or can it be you came
Too soon? These daunting triumphs of Science . . . ! Well,
That's all; but were I you I'd burn with shame.

Afterwards

Those dreadful evidences of Man's illdoing
The kindly Mother of all shall soon hide deep,
Covering with tender fingers her children asleep,

Till Time's slow cycle turns them to renewing
In other forms their beauty — No grief, no rueing
Irrevocable woe. They'll lie, they'll steep
Their hearts in peace unfathomed, till they leap
Quick to the light of the sun, as flowers strewing,
Maybe, their own friends paths. And thats not all,
When men who knew them walk old ways alone,
The paths they loved together at even-fall,
Then the sad heart shall know a presence near,
Friendly, familiar, and the old grief gone,
The new keen joy shall make all darkness clear.

In this band of ours I have discovered a delightful creature. A Great broadchested heavy chap who has been a morris dancer and whose fathers and grandfathers uncles and other relations know all the folk song imaginable. High Germanie High Barbary. O No John. I'm Seventeen Come Sunday — whole piles of 'em. He is a very good player too and a kind of uncle to the band. Chock full of an immense tolerance and good humour and easy to get on with. "I loved him for his great simplicity", and hope to be like him some day. So strong in himself, set fast on strong foundations. Not likely to be troubled with neurasthenia. He whistled "Constant Billy" which I had never before heard.

My leave starts on Thursday most likely — 5 whole days. O Cranham, Minsterworth, Framilode, Maisemore. All of you love me and I return the compliment. It is you that have poured into my as yet defective mould that fluid of beauty which shall one day take form in me and make others aware of your graces and sweet looks. Let but the Germans leave me alone, and in 5 years time the Lord Almight may relax that critical brow with which he yet regards me and decide not to delete me as yet. Gloster in September! Gloster's fairy tower against the hills. September mists. Fruitpicking in the orchard, even that orchard from which my dearest friend has gone and is now on other work overseas. I send you a song which you have not yet seen. When you have finished, please send it and the letter to Sir Hubert, for whom it is meant. Meanwhile I am occupied on a march for the Glosters those inheritors of fame and a long roll of honour.

Do you not like Laurence Binyon's verses in the Times Supplement? Those and Hardy's and Kipling's are the best of the bunch. Though I like Watson Grenfell and Noyes. Hardys grows on one. Did you ever read his last book of short stories — the Changed Man. Have you read any of D F Lawrence? I have just finished an extraordinary book called "The White Peacock", full of arresting studies of character and most essentially breathing of earth and clouds and flowers — though not a pleasant book:

    Goodbye yours very sincerely   Ivor Gurney.

P.S. There are two important items of news. One is that I have just had a birthday — my 25th. The other that we had Zeps here about a fortnight ago. Two bombs were dropped on Chelmsford itself, both on or near the Glosters billetting area. The damage was perhaps 5£ worth. It cured an old lady of muscular rheumatism, indeed it made an athlete, a sprinter of her — she went down the street in her nightgown like a comet or some gravity-defying ghost. One of the bombs was terrifying and must severely have shocked the elm tree which it mostly affected. Our supply guard did a roaring trade in old iron, and if it ever occurs to some wealthy enthusiast to buy up the two bombs in bits for purposes of reconstruction, he will probably get prostrated either by worry or rage; some of the guard may also suffer prostration.

[*encloses copy of F. W. Harvey's "In Flanders"*]

To MRS VOYNICH   41.11

Late September 1915 (E)   *Pte Gurney, B Company, 2nd 5th Glosters, Chelmsford, Essex.*

Dear Mrs Voynich: Thank you very much for your letter. I enjoyed it all, but have no comment to make on the earlier parts.

You say that Bach and Milton are first cousins. Maybe, but if heredity were a calculable affair, and supposing their fathers really to have been brothers, I should say that Bach's father must have considerably annoyed Milton's dad and vice versa. Oh the dogmatics — the blank stares at fun and humour — the self-absorption and the wide outlook — the difference in ideas on God and the Universe! The tolerant admiration on the one side and the slightly contemptuous fatheadedness on the other!

Milton is one of the great men not worth crossing the streets to speak to. Bach was worth a hungry pilgrimage to see.

Do you remember Shakespeare's "native woodnotes wild?"

I have not yet read "Samson", though this is one of the things I firmly intend to tackle soon. In the extract you sent (It begins "Among them he a spirit of mischief sent") one thing jars me a good deal — "desire" and "destroyer" for consecutive line endings is very bad.

A tiny P.S. says that Meredith is not Hardy. Which is only slightly truer than that Hardy is not Meredith. Shakespeare never drew such women! Hardy's sins are chiefly the result of a narrow spiritual outlook, or a dryness of soul. Meredith's are mostly technical, and probably come from the striving of an original mind to be more original. (I don't wonder . . . he lived in the age of Tennyson and George Eliot.) But his boys, his girl-women and his best men are superb.

He never could have so spoilt a book as Hardy has spoilt "The Return of the Native", with sins against Art and Probability and all those feelings that make one lump the world's experiences, and use laughter born of Tragedy, and that half cynical nobility and clearness of eye that forbid men to complain much. The book is perverse. Besides, most of Hardy's chief characters are essentially uninteresting in themselves. Stuck up against Egdon Heath they do well, but they leave Egdon Heath the pride of place. However we cannot mould our great men; we must take Hardy's peasant-characters as being what they are and be grateful. Why some people have the cheek to compare Shakespeare's country characters to Hardy's I cannot guess. They (S's) are sometimes good — even brilliant sketches, but no more. And if Meredith's prose is tortured, Hardy's is often that of the leading article, or the magazine writer — dessicated and non-committal.

Walt Whitman is my latest rediscovery, and he has taken me like a flood. One of the greatest of teachers. And as a poet, he among others has this enormous virtue — that when he has nothing to say, you may divine it a mile off. A marked copy may be read in half an hour; but oh, what gorgeous stuff it is!

One line (and fit for us today)
"And how the same inexorable price must still be paid for the same great purchase".
"In the name of these States shall I scorn the antique?
Why these are the children of the antique to justify it." (By the way, this reminds me that my mind-picture of triumph and restrained gloriously-trembling exultation is this chord on trumpets.

And that last quotation has it — that tingle of expectancy and jubilation.)

On Death he says the supreme word.
On the Making of men also.
On the Open Air and its revelations.
And he is Democracy's own poet and prophet. This line on the

sea — "Where the fierce old mother endlessly cries for her castaways."

The titles of his poems will be a complete inspiration to a sensitive musician in tune with his spirit

"Ethiopia saluting the Colours"
"To the leavened soil they trod."
"Darest thou now O Soul"
"Thou Mother with thy equal Brood".
"Out of the Cradle Endlessly rocking"
"Song for all Seas, All Ships."
"Year that trembled and reeled beneath me."

And the end of "This Compost." (This poem is all about the chemistry of Earth.)

One line runs
        "Yet behold . . . .
The summer growth is innocent and disdainful above all those strata of sons dead."

And the End
"Now I am terrified at the Earth . . . . . .
. . . .
It renews with such unwitting looks its prodigal annual sumptuous crops. It gives such divine materials to men and accepts such leavings from them at last."

Well, we're here still. If I hear definitely or almost definitely that we are to go to France or the Mediterranean, straightway shall I go in for a commission. It is best to get paid for taking risks. Meanwhile my instrument is not any other than the baryton, a kind of bass cornet, for we have not long formed a brass band, and I, moi-même am a performer therein. Great fun, it is, and my co-Orpheuses are all goodnatured and bottomlessly tolerant. My bridge playing has improved quite perceptibly since I left the company . . . . . .

One word our company will give to the next Oxford Dictionary — and I love it. This word signifies (let me be lexicographical) "One of small intellectual powers"
                Twallet
Doesnt it sound like it?
This noun is, as you may guess, not infrequently qualified . . . . . .

My best friend has just got the D.C.M. Also he has written this
                Flanders.

I'm homesick for my hills again!
    My hills again!
To see above the Severn plain
Unscabbarded against the sky
The blue high blade of Cotswold lie,

> And giant clouds go royally
> By jagged Malvern with a train
> Of shadows. Where the land is low,
> *Like a huge imprisoning O;*
> I hear a heart that's sound and high,
> I hear the heart within me cry
> "I'm homesick for my hills again,
>   My hills again!
> Cotswold or Malvern, sun or rain,
>   My hills again!"

That will be in anthologies hundreds of years hence, surely.

Well, my 5 days leave is past and over, and Gloster's delicate colours, long views and sea breezes are the whole breadth of England away. That soil bore me and must ever draw my dreams and for ever be home to me. It is to [be] torn up by the roots for me to live flatly in a flat marsh like Essex, where the air is stagnant and unalive. But if we stay here the eastern winds will give us sea airs — sharper than the serpents tooth. May it come soon.

I hope you enjoyed your holiday with the Taylors. If I had been able to come along, we might have formed fours and squad and columns of platoons like the Guards, after a period of probation. But that was not to be. Your remarks about the refugees pleased me very much.

(An inversion has just occurred to me "If I were God, how I would pity the hearts of men" — to (an angel-being's soliloquy) (cynical) If I were a man how I would pity the heart of God.) That was caused by your sheet on Poland. One has seen the dummy at bridge keep silence for some time while his partner seems bent on destruction, but near the end at some apparently-lunatic play he glances up with a countenance in which distrust has almost swallowed up belief. One can imagine the heavenly beings watching Poland, and secretly scanning God's inscrutable face. . . . "Can it be smugness or may there be a purpose"? "Certainly he has rounded some nasty corners, and his technique is perfect of course, but. . . ." "Can he have left things to a bureaucracy to manage?" "The office boy's forgot. . . ." "He's wound it up and lost the key . . .'

The Budget seems to be a very good one, don't you think?

If I get any idea when we are to go to the front; or any idea we are not going to India, immediately I shall try for a commission. One may as well get paid for taking risks.

My health gradually improves, but it is hard to control the mind. I only hope it will be as quick in the right direction one day. Have you read any D. F. Lawrence? "The White Peacock" is an early work I believe; but, though it is black in outlook and is obviously carrying the world on his shoulders, he is very good at characterisation, and his feeling for Nature is superb.

Someone has lent me two of Tchekof's plays — the "The Seagull" and "The Cherry Orchard". The first I have read twice and am very struck with it — for its truth and its well drawn characters. I must read the other again before I decide, but it will probably not please me so much. (There is a lovely phrase in a review this morning, about our young men, who are continually pulling up their emotions by the roots to see how they are getting on.)

Hauptmann's Sunken Bell is good, but not very good, I think.

Well, that is all I find to say in this queer letter.

We are expecting Zeps tonight as there is a rumour of four somewhere about. But Chelmsford is a straggly place and probably not easy to spot.

They discovered a spy at Epping, and made one or two very interesting discoveries. One was that his garden shone phosphorescent at night with an arrow pointing to London.

I rail against Lady Fortune inasmuch as baccy the solace and reconciler to destiny is to be 2d on the ounce dearer. Nectar and ambrosia are untouched. Here I remain with best wishes:

Yours very sincerely   Ivor Gurney

To MARION SCOTT   41.13

Late September 1915 (?)   *Pte Gurney, Band – D Company.,*
2/5 Glosters, Chelmsford, Essex.

Dear Miss Scott: Thank you very much for the jam, which looks very nice, but my uneasy conscience will not let me be — on the grounds that if I am unable to afford jam on 8/- a week, I can hardly deserve it to be sent. It would be best to send some money home for some Gloster jam, which, it is an article of creed with me, can hardly be equalled.

There was no train, as I expected, that Sunday night; and after a 3d doss which I very much enjoyed, arrived at Chelmsford at 6 a.m., but wangled the sergeant into saying nothing. In this sort of thing, as the Immortal Bard observes, "there's nothing so becomes a man as modest stillness and humility", with which I dosed the sergeant, to the desired end. In a recollection of our conversation, I remember the subject ran from my being able to do railway work, to the discussion, or rather assertion that I could not imagine a one sided brain of any greatness. I hope that you did not suppose me so humourless as to refer even distantly to myself then, but my memory makes it seem very like it. We happened on one of the few things I think about on route marches, and which is an article of salvation with me. Carlyle has not put it too strongly in "Heroes". It is chiefly a matter of environment with the really great men what shape they take in their power; but with the smaller men, such as Wordsworth, I am not quite sure. Whether I could do railway work or not, which of course I *can*, referred not at all to this. What made me more sensitive to this is that I have just bought Wordsworth's life in Jack's 6d Home Series, and his colossal complacency makes one anxious. What a crowd they must have been — Wordsworth, Dorothy and Coleridge!

But how a poor wandering mind like mine must envy Wordsworth's strong self-sufficiency! How must his mind have been filled with those pictures that are the all-in-all to any artist! Here in Essex there are no sunsets, and no colour; no mystery in woods, no sense of other-worldliness. Nothing but common life in the light of common day. When my mind can escape from its imprisoning body, it reaches out desperately to the memory of Malverns purple and, later, black against afterglow, or Cranham trees transfigured to shapes of colour and form and seeming without substance, merely imagined, stuff of dreams. (Cotswold man beside me)

> "Here's luck to the world as sound as a wheel
> Death is a thing we all must feel.
> If Life were a thing that money could buy,
> The Rich would live, and the poor would die.

It is Fred Bennett — the morris dancer of old time, who is alternately telling stories or answering questions in broad Glostershire, and playing cadenzas and hymn tunes on his trombone — so things must be as they may as regards mistakes.

"Redgauntlet" is amazingly good where it is good, and the dull parts can be detected from a mile away.

I hope you'll like the Chesterton book I am sending. Some of the things are as good as could be — as the Grocer. Old Noah. The Song on Cocoa; all jolly and rollicking in good hefty English.

Have I ever quoted a phrase from a "Morning Post" review on a book by some young "naturalist"? It is — that "our young men are continually pulling their emotions up by the roots to see how they are getting on."

I hope you are not doing so much work as you were, and are now pretty well. To have weak nerves is rather like the sensation a strong man must have, struggling in treacle. You had better read the "Prelude" for a sedative. Or "The Excursion" as a soporific. Or the "Daily Mail" as a galvanic.

Have you noticed the Eastern (or N.E.) sky about 10 oclock at night lately? What there is about the stars to make them more impressive than any other object I do not know. But the sight of Orion and the three stars nearby moves me as much as Beethoven. How garish, how vulgar, how Raphael-Tuckish the moon is to such, save only when it is a thin curve and seems a sort of star, or crescent out of which stars will be cut, or delicate scimitar for the making thereof.

In winter when the trees are naked, and frost binds all moist things with iron, and breath goes strangely up in vapour – then who goes out from the warm neighbourly comforting firelight and stands in mere starlight and earthy gloom, what a continual surprise, what a revelation of unknown purposes is his who turns his eyes upwards and sees that majestical roof fretted with golden fire! It is a strong assurance to man that his mind, confronted with the sight of all those worlds, some of them thought to be dead, many dying, as even this our own; that his mind, I say, though humble before these unintelligible mysteries is exalted with an uprushing of fierce and tender joy, and strangely, of a pride in God's Handiwork, as if a private should view his Chief Commanders handiwork or a molecule take pleasure in the soft fantastic imagery on English Autumn trees. (Copyright in U.S.A.) (Forget the Clamour.):

Yours very sincerely   Ivor Gurney

TO HERBERT HOWELLS   3.8

September/October 1915 (?)   Pte Gurney, Band – D Company, 2/5 Glosters, Chelmsford, Essex.

My Dear Howler: I am sorry not to have seen you for so long, but what time I have had in London has been either irregular or entirely unexpected, and so have made no appointment.

I hope you are forging ahead with epoch-makers, with a teeming brain and a full and happy mind: (the two are inseparable, I believe.)

As for me, behold a poor dyspeptic Tommy more sick than can be shadowed in words of the army; but with a kind of delirious joy at the back of his mind, because there is a chance of his getting a job in the Railway Transport at the front — opportunities to rise and 3/4 a day to start. I do not think, old chap, my health will improve much more in the army. I *must* have something to think about. That is, I am so far well as to try to shun the danger of introspection and self analysis. Two years of brain work and out door exercise would probably put me right. I cannot remember a time since schooldays when my health was better — anyway. You can imagine, too, what the hope of being able to praise England and make things to honour her is in me, as in yourself. You can imagine too what a conflict there is between that idea and warfare. . . . If only I could be convinced that there was nothing unique, nothing that was not easily paralleled in me, I would not care. But to be neurasthenic — to wonder what my capabilities are — to have patience only because, someday, there may come something to give joy to men and especially Englishmen . . . to suffer all this in the thought-vacuum in which the Army lives, moves and has its being, is a hard thing. The hardest thought of all is that I am deceiving myself, that nothing especially worthy is in me; and that I should take a commission at once. The Railway job would allow me to remain in the army; to get some money; to rise if it were at all interesting; and not to run into any great danger. But anything — anything to take my all too subtle observation off myself. Well, well; excuse the clamour — "Forget the clamour", I mean.

I say, old chap, I wish you would do myself and a lonely girl a favour. Harvey's cousin, Edith Harvey, is in London at some girl's club, earning her own living. Could you, would you send her some Concert tickets? She is an interesting plucky girl, and you would get on well with her, I think. Please do this. Her address is

Miss E. Harvey
11 St George's Square
S.W.

Which is a girl's club of a new sort, where they are allowed to do exactly as they please without let or hindrance. Coming in at 2 a.m. with a latchkey is nothing uncommon.

I often think of your Concerto and its strength and beauty. It is a work which must one day force itself on the attention of a world whose mind, alas, must for sometime be fixed on other things. Have you ever read Wordsworth's Prelude? There is nothing better for evoking those pictures in the mind which are the soil and seed of all art worthy the knowing. It is dull enough and egotistical enough at times but still is full of stimulation and packed memory.

How is Benjamin? Is *he* sick of the Army too? And your brother — still sick? Is he abroad yet? Well, I will leave this in hopes to see you again before long, some fine or otherways evening: but at present to the "Prelude" and to envy you, but, should this Railway business come off perhaps there will not be such cause. But say nowt about it! Please try to send those tickets. When are you going to write some Cotswold music? Oh, for a Symphony on "Henry IV"! You just look at it!

With best wishes

I subscribe and profess myself to be, Gracious Sir, your most obliged and humble servant.   I.B.G.

To MARION SCOTT   41.9

19 November 1915 (P)   *Pte Gurney, etc.*

Dear Miss Scott: I am so sorry about Sidney. He sent me a cheery P.C. which made me think he was well over the worst. Poor chap, he has not had the best of times.

As for the sonnets I shall be delighted to see them in the next number. In which, it may be safely prophesied that the verse alone will be worth the money.

I hope that by now you are much better than you were, and out of Cold's clutches, and more your own. If you are hard up for new things to read remember the "Century of Essays". (in "Everyman") There is much solace and delight therein, and a ripping little essay by Dekker on Winter; which ends, "When Thames is covered with ice, and men's hearts are covered over and crusted with cruelty, then mayst thou or any man be bold to swear, that it is Winter."

To end this note I send you a

Carol

Winter now has bared the trees,
Killed with tiny swords the jolly
Leafage that mid-summer sees
But left the ivy and the holly.
    Hold them high
    And make delight
For Christës joy that 's born tonight.

All green things but these have hid
Their heads, or died in melancholy,
Winter's spite them all has rid
Save only ivy and brave holly.
    Give them place
    In all men's sight
For Christës grace that's born tonight.

Baby eyes are pleased to see
Bright red berries and children jolly,
So shout and dance and sing with glee,

And honour ivy and prickly holly,
  Honour courage
  And make delight
For Christës sake that's born tonight.

Christus natus hodie!
Drink deep of joy on Christmas day.
Join hands and sing a roundelay.
For this is Christ's and children's day.
Christus natus hodie!
Hodie!

And now I have forgotten the corrections.
Very well, let it be "Unstirred by rattle of the rolling drums". I do
not understand the objection to it though.

$$\frac{4}{4}$$ *(musical notation)*

Just as
If England to herself do rest but true

$$\frac{4}{4}$$ *(musical notation)*

I'll guarantee to find a line of 13 actual syllables in "Paradise Lost".
The other objection I cannot meet. "Maybe" means maybe there. It
is not padding. For instance Jones has a friend, acquaintance, or
companion named Brown. Brown is stirred up by his young lady to
enlist. Jones is engaged on War Work, tying up parcels at the
Admiralty with odd bits of string which it is his business to untie and
use to purpose. (as per instructions on Economy.) Brown, who
becomes sick of the Army, lacks nevertheless the courage to desert.
Is shipped over to France in a cattle boat, and contracts a severe fit
of sea sickness which is only terminated, in an especially violent
paroxysm, by a 29.6 shell. Jones rises in the World, gets a string
contract from Government, acquires fame from his superb
collection of Knots (now in the Bruem, otherwise the Mittish
Bruseum), obtains through influence a free pass, and goes, after the
war, on a tour in Flanders. Is it not possible that he, maybe,
"maybe", mayhap to exterminate the solitary dandelion which has
sprung out of the former friend and companion of his youth —
Brown? I wot so: Yours very sincerely   Ivor Gurney

To Mrs Voynich   41.15

November 1915 (E)   *Pte Gurney, D. Company, 2/5 Glosters,*
Chelmsford, Essex.

Dear Mrs Voynich: Don't think I mind being slanged. A good
healthy quarrel, on literary matters especially was and is always
pleasing to my still unquiet mind. I take the truth about Milton to be
— that he was the greatest of all our word-craftsmen. That, he was
not nearly national enough. That, though he was self-critical
enough as to rythm and form, he wrote the most detestable half-
English; sounding more like a Bohn translation than anything else.
(But see Belloc's essay on his chief merit — "picturing".) That,
though his mind was huge in some ways, it was surprisingly limited
in others. And that to the universal charity and often careless
exercise of great powers that Shakespeare has, he can oppose only
those characteristics which have nothing to do with good-
fellowship. What has he to do with the Renaissance, or any rebirth
of spirit? In spite of his political ideals. Beethoven became deaf, and
wrote the C#minor Quartett and the Ninth Symphony. Milton
became blind, and wrote "Paradise Lost" and "Samson
Agonistes". His spirit was huge, but not generous, because he
lacked humour, and its attendant qualities.

We are to go abroad before long I think; somewhere about
January. As my health is improving, this does not please me. I am so
far well as to wish to get back to music $+$ (a big plus) football and
long walks. This is a far cry from last Feb: is it not? I hope you have a
similar, or rather, a better tale to tell of health: that you are indeed
quite well. These cold bright days of winter are salutary and good
for all sorts and conditions of men. Poor Sidney has had a hard time
of it, but from his postcard to me he is well out of the worst. He shall
have another letter in a day or two. Miss Scott too, is one of the
unhappy band, but she writes cheery letters — if that has anything
to do with health in *her*.

There was a chance, there is still a chance, of my getting a post in
the Railway Transport Office in France, but oh, it has dwindled
down to such a small one. So I suppose that I must take my chance
and trust to the "luck of the Gloucesters", a proverb in the Army.
The 28th Foot fought the rearguard action at Corunna as the most
trusted troops, so "Q" says in a book called "Shakespeare's
Christmas"; and they are the 1st Gloucesters and famous as any,
and as good.

My D.C.M. friend is in England — in Glostershire – training as an
officer, and no doubt invoking the Muse.

It is a fact that makes me think, that though I have had more

training in music than verse, yet a sonnet comes far easier to me
than a prelude or any other small form in music. Perhaps it is
because I am compelled to think of and have more to do with books
than music, but it is certainly true that arrangement of words comes
with less effort than the other. But it is probable work would alter
that.

Tonight there is a debate on "Spooks". Please goodness there
will be something [worth] hearing about them. At present, all I
know of them is very dull and hardly worth remembering.

How the A major Prelude (Book II) of Bach seems to be born of
the spirit that makes Christmas Carols! The UnMiltonic candour,
sweetness and childlike natural grace recalls the (Gloster) carol of
"A Virgin Unspotted"

Well, I'll away to the spooks, and end with best wishes
    Yours very sincerely   Ivor Gurney.

To Mrs Voynich   46.32.2

December 1915 (?)

Dear Mrs Voynich: It was kind of you to send such a jolly nice
parcel — a perfect sweet parcel. We are now altogether out of
civilisation — and were so then; and the advent of such chocolates is
decidedly an event.

The letter was very acceptable also — a link with the things I long
to return to, and which it is better save at such moments to forget.

I hope your health continues to improve, and you are becoming
more able, if not quite able, to do all you wish to do.

It is strange to turn from the gray monotony of doing continually
things I hate doing, to talk of things that draw the best of me, and
talk me out of myself.

I had a long talk with an RAMC man who knew Tolstoi, and runs
well in his pleasures with me, — It was like a glimpse of Heaven; so
sorely needed for a dyspeptic fish out of water. We talked of Tolstoi
and Bach and Rupert Brooke, and the end of the war. I saw Heaven
opening before my eyes and the lovely angels of Books and Music,
Music and Books, sending all kinds of pleasant greetings and
welcome.

I have come to the state where I know how good a Shakespeare
Sonnet is, but cannot wrap myself in it, and cannot dwell on the lines
to taste their sweetness; no not even in that beginning "That time of
year thou mayst in me behold", which has always shown me an

exquisite quiet sunset sky of winter, peaceful and serenely grave. Do you remember what happened to Peter in the Retreat? (War and Peace) I try to put myself in his place, and so fit myself for the task I wish to accomplish. Very well, but how much longer?

My letters now are all soliloquies; I can offer nothing better: a cuckoo, cuckoo with a very minor third, from sodden woodlands hopeless of the spring.

One is ashamed to complain for so many men take things smilingly almost till the moment that they drop. Indeed it is a great thing to be in company with such men, and to imitate them as far as my wavering will will allow. How much better than four years ago anyway!

What a fatheaded sort of letter this is to send to a friend! Please excuse it, this being the best I can manage. We live in a gray waste of time, in a gray wasteful business and in gray discouraged days without sunshine. Duty is a gray thing also, and cheers very little if it upholds.

At present I am on some duty connected with water carts, out of the Batt: which makes a change.

Well the best of possible Christmases to you, will Xmas day be a meatless day I wonder? May the kind Gods forbid! Let our home-friends celebrate it with great hunks of roast and steaming pudding. The spirit of Joy may the better descend upon us here:

Yours very sincerely   Ivor Gurney

To Mrs Voynich   41.16

Late December/early January 1916 (?)   Pte Gurney, D Company, 2/5 Glosters, Chelmsford, Essex.

Dear Mrs Voynich: What a jolly letter!

Thank you very much, and I hope you had an enjoyable Christmas in bed.

You must have had some exciting times in your war work, and some day I shall be glad to hear more; though female furies are not much in my line, as I prefer the more downright male in tantrums. But what a Xmas present for our enemies! May they receive many such.

We may quarrel about Milton, though my admiration for him is enormous, — as a master of words; and God knows I envy even more the mastery of his mind — but never about Bach. But the attitude towards Bach can hardly be called by so cold a word as admiration, it is an enormous and partly incredulous love; a wonder at such a wealth of wonderfulness and such a control. A Bach hand

grenade is worth a whole battery of howitzers of other names.
Shakespeare also
                    Do you know this — of Masefield?
Here is a marvellous city, built of marvellous earth,
Life was lived nobly here to give such beauty birth,

Death is so blind and dumb Death does not understand —
Death drifts the brain with dust, and soils the young limbs glory,
Makes empires idle tales, and Fame a travellers story
Death sends the naked soul to wander under the sky,
Death opens unknown doors. It is most grand to die.

I have sadly marred it, and omitted one line, but even then it must
strike you.

I shall be glad to be out of the army. The best thing for me is
brainwork again of some kind. I need something to fix my wandering thought in the morning. My health is very different to what it
was, but even now a true description of my mind at its best would
be, not unhappy. Would two years put me right now? I could walk
20 miles a day for weeks, and take pleasure in music or verse after
that. But *must* have work and movement not to be badly depressed.
At auction Bridge I am a cunning fiend, at least to such opponents as
one finds here. In the evenings I look with favour on the divine art of
Music; but in the afternoon I am a clod. Two years, think you?

As for going abroad, there are rumours only.

I pass with my comrades as one who is willing to be friendly with
almost anybody; looks depressed, but makes more jokes than
anyone around here. One who can play the piano above archangels,
who can read anything at sight, and makes (O wonder) classical
music interesting; but has an itch, a positive mania for arguing, and
discursing on weird and altogether unimportant subjects. A good
card-player, a good goal-keeper, a first-rate liar, (on occasions
needful) and a friend of the 1/5 D.C.M.

Please use my Christian name when you write to me. I feel
embarrassed. Private Gurney I know, and Ivor, but who is Mr
Gurney?

Martin Chuzzlewit entrances me just now, and I have just come
across a most delightful R.A.M.C. man who met Tolstoi in Russia.
You would like him. He showed signs of drifting into a confirmed
idealist at one time, but I think that will not happen now. You should
have heard our folk song concert. And a priest (R.C.) who has
heard the peasants sing all the Irish folk songs, nearly, I know. And
the reader at Cardinal Newmans old place. And O, lots more —
people you will never know. Lovable in themselves, and meaty stuff
for the full artist there may be in me; If only once I can get to the

stage of being able to think high and sustainedly for only two pages, as Prelude I Book II (the 48)! Then all the world shall have grace to know of the beauty of my County, of stars, and moving water, of friendship and the companionable solace of tobacco; all in little black dots of notes, and fiddle sounds and the harsher touch of the piano; but not in words, for towards Literature I feel slightly contemptuous. "All art strives constantly to the precondition of music."

Goodbye with best wishes: Yours sincerely   Ivor Gurney

To MARION SCOTT   41.20

1 January 1916 (P)   *Pte Gurney, 2/5 Glosters.*

Dear Miss Scott: Thank you very much for your presents – the first of which was perfect; the second I am only regretful to have because most of the extracts are taken from the "Path to Rome", a book I — have read. But very much "Thank you"!

I hear Sidney is with you now. Please remember me to him, and say that I hope he has received my last letter which was sent to Aylesbury. I hope he is getting better properly now. You shall have the songs right enough; but I hope to get leave in a little while, and to rummage them out, and perhaps retouch them. Would a fortnight be too long? If so, you shall have them before. "Twa Corbies" "Edward" and the Elizas; but not touched up.

Please let me have the Poetry Book when you have done with it. The markings were, almost, random guesses, or things I knew to be good. I hope to know it better before opinionising. How good our younger writers are. It is arguable that we have no great writers, but how good a foundation for another Colossus is this fashion of writing in clear direct and coloured English verses containing, as a general thing, no moralising, no recommendations save to love life, and to seize on its sweet moments when possible, and to make as many as possible; and still more to make existence a many coloured thing of joy.

I hope you are getting strong now, and able to feel things more as you wish. Our poets should help an invalid who can feel. They have a divine dissatisfaction with blindness and spiritual inactivity that is tonic and stimulation.

(O by the way, I am leader of the Opposition against a Socialist Government, next Monday and have ordered Belloc's book on the Servile State to make things hot for it.)

And I really feel, begin to feel, competent at last to feel and express dissatisfaction with Shakespeare. A great step. W.S. is not perfect often, but how much of the greatest things is perfect. Let us leave perfection to Tennyson and William Morris — in lengthy things, I mean.

The College Executive have held over my Schol: till the end of the war, which is very nice of them.

But here go I walking common ways;
Drab-souled things on every hand;
A sulky mist is all its haze . . . .
It's very dead desert this land.

Here I will wish you a happy new Year, full of keen experiences, and quietly joyful times of fallowness.

May the War end soon, and let us dream again, but nobly and to active ends. May England grow dearer, sweeter in herself (for we deserve better weather and more amiable smiles) and in our memories. And may the President of the Women Musicians be preserved to sanity. With best wishes:

Yours very sincerely   Ivor Gurney

To Ivor Gurney   61.144

17 February 1916   [*Printed circular from the Royal College of Music Union*]

Dear Mr Gurney: It has been brought to the notice of the R.C.M. Union General Committee that some of the Members who are on Active Service may have experienced difficulties in arranging for the maintenance of their professional musical interests during their enforced absence, and may be glad to know where to apply in the event of their wanting a temporary teacher for their pupils, a reliable deputy to take over a position, or a responsible representative to gather any royalties from publishers which may accrue.

It has therefore been suggested that it might be desirable to form a Sub-Committee of the R.C.M. Union for this purpose, but before any definite steps are taken the General Committee has requested us to enquire into the matter, and to ascertain the views of Members on Active Service. It will be of the greatest help to us if you will kindly let us know at your earliest convenience what your views are, and whether such a scheme would be of any service to you personally. Replies should be sent to the Hon. Secretary (MISS MARION SCOTT) at the above address: Yours faithfully,

Marion M. Scott   Harold Samuel
Mabel Saumarez Smith   Harold E. Darke.

To The R.C.M. Union Committee

[*Gurney's reply on the reverse of above circular.*]

Dear Committee: I have experienced no great difficulty in arranging for the maintenance of my professional musical interests, for at the best they were only slightly more than nil. As for requiring a temporary teacher, you could serve me little in this, but for any temporary pupils — at half a guinea a lesson of 20 minutes — I should feel most grateful. Your remark about collecting royalties happens merely to be ironic; and so does not give me anything like the pleasure the other offer does — that offer to provide a responsible deputy for my position. My position is at present that of a private in the 2/5 battallion of the Gloucesters, who are about to move to huts on Salisbury plain. Any deputy, trustworthy or otherwise, would be most gratefully welcomed, and fulsomely flattered, receive all my military decorations, and a valuable insight into the best methods of mud-cleaning with vocal accompaniment:

    Yours truly   Ivor Gurney

To Mrs Voynich   41.19

Late February 1916 (?)   *Pte Gurney, D.co 2/5 Glosters, Park House Camp, Salisbury.*

Dear Mrs Voynich: Thank you for your present, which gave me great pleasure — that brand being as I think the very best, and, worse luck, is not obtainable here. We are about 3 miles from Tidworth, in the middle of downs, a charming spot; far past our best hopes; and huts at worst are far better than tents, in winter at any rate; and who may deny that Winter is here now?

More and more, though still not very actively, I feel the need for brain work — Chess does all for me that is done as yet. I am very grateful for Chess; a noble and fascinating game.

The two camp pianos are distressing. One suffers badly from a disease, the opposite of aphasia. Its nervous system is so weak that some time must elapse before a note can be repeated. And may I pause here to repeat my firm faith that the slow movement of the C major Rasoumoffsky Quartett is one of the loveliest things in music?

How are your aliens? Some times I think that it would be nice to share your duties occasionally. We are firing and marking for a fortnight, which is an interesting and cushy job. It would tax

Shakespeare's mind to conceive the monotony of eternal bayonet fighting, squad drill, and fatigue.

Isn't "Vittoria Corombona" fine? ("The White Devil") "The Alchemist" "Catiline" and "All for Love" are very good too. But the later Jonson comedies are impregnably dull.

Snatch of Shakespearian wit, from Pte Tim Godding. A Sergeant was going round collecting birthdays, (not for generous purposes.) and one man hesitated to answer. Said T. G. 'He dont know his birthday. He dont know his name. The sun hatched it." Our men are far too fond of swearing, and quarrel, though not badly, on too small provocation; but they are a good lot, and are to be honoured. I believe we are not less in mettle than the 7th. Time will prove, and perhaps before long. Did you care for Henry James. If so, what books?:

With best wishes I remain, Yours very sincerely   Ivor Gurney

To HERBERT HOWELLS   3.33

February 1916 (?)   *Pte Gurney, D Co 2/5 Glosters, Park House Camp, Salisbury.*

My dear Howler: Here am I, not so very long ago an invalid, cohabiting with 30 others in a small hut; to feed on the first thing that comes along — so be the canteen is shut – to sleep on bare boards, now paliasses; in damp blankets; rising at midnight to stoke fires, or fulfill the needs of nature; going forth into snowdrifts 8 inches deep, as they are now; reading Shakespeare and composing in a continual and profane noise; meekly obeying my spiritual and temporal pastors and masters; not at all unhappy, and remembering always my dear Cranham, Framilode, Minsterworth. I am sure either to be killed or cured by this, hein? Well, about those songs, my benefactor. All's well with the Elizabethans save "Spring" of which there is another score, as the parts testify. There is very little difference between the two; but one difference is important — the line or so where there is a change to 3/4 time for a bar or so — or indeed one bar only. I have just rewritten "I praise the tender flower" also, in which you may make alteration as I am away from pianos. My brain is pretty clear now, however, at best, and I dont think there is much wrong.

Tidworth country, where we are, is supposed to be the nicest spot on the plain, and this is probably true as the lookout from D Co parade ground is not unlike Cranham, from which I suppose it is only about 50 miles direct. Here it is chalk, there limestone, but both look much alike at a distance, and woods are woods all England over. There is one horrid change however. Today the snow is 8 inches deep in places, and consequently there was no Times, no Daily News, my usual matutinal mental pabulum, as a really educated person would say.

I think we are quite near the front — the fighting line, but at least I have control enough of my mind to think very little of this. The only thought that disturbs me ever, is that all my continual striving and endeavour to become a fit and full man, ("full man" is Shakespeare) may be ended by a German bullet or bayonet. But then my belief in our destiny rises clear and strong and in spite of my sick mind, and by the help of the last volume or so of "War and Peace" I am calm again. Read it, boy, read it.

War and Peace & Shakespeare & Whitman & St Matthew & Wordsworth & Plutarch is a pretty complete diet — mental pabulum.

These men are rough as a rule who swear frightfully, but are good men inside, and full of things for such as I to imitate. Floreat Gloucestriencis 2/5 7 and 9th. French inspected us last Wed; a short kind faced gentleman. Good bye: Yours   I.B.G.

To MARION SCOTT   41.21

22 March 1916 (P)   Pte Gurney, D.Co 2/5 Glosters, Park House Camp, Salisbury.

Dear Miss Scott: The beginning of this letter is to commemorate Tim Godding — one of the most original people in all this regiment, a big word.

Here am I, sitting on my bed, against my kit bag, half-reading Carlyle, little soaking through to my dull mind, when I become aware that a boxing match is being arranged. Tim Godding will be obviously somewhere near the top of this. And presently. "No, mate, I cant say as I can box, but Ive had ——— good hidings from one bloke and another . . . . .'

Today also, when we were lying on our bellies, trying to load and reload and rereload with the quickness of those who get extra pay for it — though not likely to get the pay for those who have extra quickness — A skylark arose. Now Tim Godding has little bits of jargon, some of which I strongly suspect to be Hindustani. One of these is "Ipshi pris", a sign of high spirits, of salutation to a passing battallion, or the crown of a joke; anything joyful. So Tim Godding half turned over, looked up to the first blue of spring —

"Ipshi pris, skylark; ipshi pris"!

One night also, after lights out, he, as is the usual course of things gave voice to the feelings of the hut — this time on the universal distaste for army life.

"Ah, let me once get out of this bastard lot, and they wont see Tim again. The —— Germans can come and fight on our doorstep, and all as I'll say is."Fight on, lads, fight on". They can come and drag our old man out the front door, and Ill be up in the attic — washing me feet." It was also he who made answer to the doctor, when asked how he felt. —

"Bad all over doctor. Worse in some places than in others."

Our address is Salisbury, but in reality we are 14 miles or so away. Tidworth is our habitation more or less, and on a sunny day, the view from our camp is charming. Army life is for me full of long blanks of tedium. Would that I were sound in mind and body, and able to take all in that is to be taken! Hard for an artist to go self-condemned to partial blindness and deafness through that which might be so fruitful to him! But on the whole I take it as a price to be paid for my education, and dodder on as contented as maybe. But it is hard to long for beauty, and beauty obtained to remain unsatisfied — chronically discontent. But given time I think that my revenge on myself and my circumstances shall be long and sweet.

Last Sunday Crudlan and I lay out on a down so like our own; but the first violet had not yet arrived, whereas the woods must be happy-eyed with them at home — in Glostershire where Spring sends greetings before other less happy counties have forgotten Winter and the snow. Where the talk is men's talk, and eyes of folk are as kind as the soft airs. The best roads in England, the finest cider, the richest blossom in the most magical orchards, beauty content in security, strength quiet in confidence controlled, blood mixed of plain and hill, Welsh and English; are not these only of my county, my home? And yet were I there the canker in my soul would taint all these. But at least I have reached the position of longing for work, and of blaming myself for part of my misfortunes at any rate.

Now we are allowed to wear our honour, the back-badge: and great is the joy thereat. Today is the anniversary of that great day in Egypt when the rear rank of the double line faced about and the Old Braggs — 28th Foot — repelled two attacks in blood and glory.

Of course you may quote from my song, and accept my best wishes for a successful address.

Yes, that A minor 6/8 movement is the one I meant.

You ask me whether I will look at certain poems with a view to setting — after the war. The reason I do not write now, is not because there is a war on, but because I do not feel bound to write;

when my mind compels me, then I will write; then and not before.

I am not altogether in agreement with the Russian attitude to Suffering. It is too passive.

In a review of Rupert Brooke's "Letters from America", I found that Henry James had written to this effect, in the preface.

"I admire the British soldier. His mind seems to contain a moral hospitality to all the vagaries of fortune", etc. So it does. He grins nearly all the time that one might expect him to have little reason for doing so.

We are 14 miles from Salisbury, near Tidworth. If we stay any time I meant to visit Stonehenge.

Arthur Bliss a Captain!

A Captain!

!

There is no chance of coming to London; none at all. We shall see France, I guess, first.

I still read the "Times" Supplement with great pleasure. It is a good review. But dont read the leaders as a rule — dont heed Clutton's Brockings or Brock's Cluttonings. But I did read Andrieffs article, and that on Shelley, — both very good.

The Band is a washout.

And I am at present a Wesleyan, for the Wesleyan contingent is so small "that it 'scapes the thunderbolt" of particular Sunday inspections: With best wishes Yours very sincerely   Ivor Gurney.

To Mrs Voynich   41.8

April 1916 (?)   *Pte Gurney, B Co 2/5 Glosters, Park-house Camp, Salisbury.*

Dear Mrs Voynich: Thank you again for your parcel, which made a redletter day for me — partly on account of the unexpectedness of sweets of such a quality in such conditions. Chocolate and chocolate-cream is all that we can get here.

Mrs Taylor's parcel made much the same sensation, and lasted longer; we get pretty well fed, though not quite on those lines. But O! when is the war going to end? My legs and head might change places most days, and I not know the difference. As to going to France, that is a matter of indifference to me. Let me go, get not too painful or undignified a wound, and return to quietness and a space for digestion, which space is now occupied by evolutions in marching order. Yet out of all this mirk and gloom there shines the gleam of 5 days leave on Monday! And the doubt whether I shall be able to enjoy it or not . . . But Cranham, Framilode, Minsterworth, Crickley, May Hill, and the sight of Malverns . . . The soft air and kind faces that go in my mind with the name Gloucester.

I wonder how you are getting on with your alien work. Have you had any more difficulties with female desperadoes? And how the garden is getting on, and the little pool.

How are Geoffrey and Julian? Salonika has been a rest cure for him, by all accounts. I wonder whether we might be sent there. But France is the ever present word with us. And yet — there is the youth of us of the 3rd line recruits lately drafted in; and even more on account of the Home service men of other regiments attached to us, which make a mixed lot. These draft men signed on only a short time ago, and are really no more than conscripts. Why have they drafted other regiment's Home Service men on to us? Why not our own?

Tim Godding made a remark the other day, which might amuse you. Someone was poking fun at him, and Tim, patient for a time, got all his own back with "Ah, mate, I was born too near a wood to be frightened with owls."

But he is a Shakespearian character, and I am sorry to have left him in D Company, though I am happy and more at home in B.

But O, O, O to get back to my music, and time for books and walks. All manifestations of energy are hard for me, but I'd manage more work now than ever before in my nerve-ridden existence. Have you no observations by a Distinguished Neutral Observer to comfort me withal — that Peace is near to view? How long shall the tyranny of Officers and Non-coms endure? When shall the advent of the orderly sergeant inspire no fear?

But Floreat the 2/5. They are a clean minded comradely lot, whose cheerfulness and cork-like buoyancy fill me ever with admiration and love. Can there be mettle enough in the Germanies to meet this spirit if it be wide-spread? Will you please send me Sidney's address when you write? Or before, on a P.C. to

19 Barton St
Gloucester

Bless his heart! I believe he hates it more than I.

Do you know, Madam, that hut orderly — the lighter of fires and washer up of dishes etc for the day — is an enviable job, and sought after by myself not least? And Wash house fatigue? And firing and marking from 7 till 2 a dream of bliss? 3 hours trench digging after! Excuse these moans, But I am as a bottle in the smoke, a mouldy pelican in a howling wilderness of monkeys.

A miserable self analysis of a despised carcass-haunted spirit, or vice-versa. A being cut off from Civilisation by the fixed gulfs of Militarism and an extreme distaste for doing anything not forced on me. Hamlet in Khaki. A Macbeth without courage to Murder or fly.

Ah, well. They who funk Life have to pay! Perhaps I am lucky in paying hardly but more quickly than most in my position have to.

Anyway there is Tim Godding and many more, masters of life, and my unconscious kindly instructors.

My best wishes to the spring flowers:

Yours very sincerely   Ivor Gurney

To HERBERT HOWELLS   3.21

2 May 1916 (P)   Pte Gurney, B Company, 2/5 Bat., Glosters, Park House, Salisbury.

Dear Howler: I was delighted to see your name down as one of the composers of new works for Westminster. How I should like to hear them! Have they spoilt the Cathedral with frescoes? There has been some correspondence about it, and I should like to know what you think.

Today is a perfect Spring day, and so I must think of Glostershire and Shakespeare, and envy those who may look on our county's radiant green and joyful blossoming. O the richness in the ride from Gloster to Newnham! Someday, someday . . . .

What have you been writing this term? Something clear and English I hope. Does the war still obsess you? If so, you are, perhaps, less fortunate than your comrades in the Army, whose mind is full of pack and rifle, buttons and boots.

When you get back to London, ask Miss Scott for the two books of poems I lent her; you will probably find something to suit you. How I envy you the chance of seeing Shakespeare, a desire that is very strong in me. O to see "Antony" and to be thrilled once again by Antony's passion and the proud defiances of the great queen. If I must die think only this of me, that I sincerely wish that what rag of a mantle I possess should descend on you, and inspire you someday to turn your thoughts to an Antony symphony.

Do you know Miss Scott has been very ill, a near squeak this time apparently.

How is Benjamin? Tell him, as a friend I send a blessing; as a lootenant nothing but kicks. Floreat Armae Brittannicae, et exerciti whose motto is Fed Up. Fed Up: Yours ever   I.B.G. Miss Voynich has whooping cough.

To MARION SCOTT   41.22

17 May 1916 (P)   [*to Miss Scott but with no address or perhaps
even first page. Postmarked from Park House Camp*]

Your letter reads as though written by a radiantly healthy person,
but you say Yorkshire is too far to travel. You *must* have some go in
you. I meant to ask you in this where Hindhead is; but today reading
Cobbetts "Rural Rides" (in Nelsons 6d Library) I came across it.
Did you know that both Arun and Wey make their start near there?
I love Arun, not for the sight of it, of which I know nothing, but for
its name and for Belloc's continual affectionate references.
Especially that in an essay on either Death or Rest. Methuen now
publish a selection from him at 1/-. I forget the name unless it is "A
Goodly Company".

We are certainly to be off soon. Next Monday or Tuesday will be
the exact date most likely. All this leaves me merely indifferent, as I
set the extra danger against the not having to clean buttons; and not
being inspected every morning.

I mean to send with this a book on Keats by Edward Thomas. I
hope you will like it.

On Saturday the gods gave me a brief respite from servitude, and
I snatched a space at High Wycombe, after great gulfs of wasted
time at Andover, Basingstoke and Maidenhead and Reading. From
Basingstoke to Reading I travelled with a corporal of the Cold-
streams, who had been out since Mons. He was the kind of man who
would make an efficient and self-effacing member of a Church
Council. Quiet voiced and quiet-eyed he exhorted us never to spare
any Germans, never to take prisoners; and backed it up with some
effective evidence. It would have been the queerest thing, before
the war, to have seen this quiet man uttering the most bloodthirsty
wisdom. He did not hate, bore no malice apparently, but merely
was determined to kill every German he might lay hands on. One
thing he told us was that the Prussian Guard at Loos was a very
mixed lot and very inferior to the original. But dammy, I wish they
would let me transfer to the Navy or the Air service. This marching
and futile stunting-about bores me. And if I am to die, who would
not rather be dropped from an aeroplane than blasted up to
aeroplane height from a hole?

Sir C H H.P wrote me a cheery letter a few days ago, in which he
expressed his surprise that the love of music had survived in his
young men. It surely would persist in any whose love of music was
not merely a varnish, or a justification for long hair. (And O, how
they've clipped us!)

I must leave off now; there is a "buzzer" parade. (They have made me a signaller now), and must be off.

Need I say how delighted I am to be able soon to afford my amiable female correspondents the delight of saying that they have recently received "A Letter from the Trenches"?

Good bye. Your letters interest me very much. You say mine interest you, but Ill be scalped with a jack-knife if they do me.

With best wishes for new energy and spirits:

Yours very sincerely   Ivor Gurney.

To HERBERT HOWELLS   3.14

24 May 1916 (P)

Dear Howler: Finis est, or rather, Inceptus est (?) We go tomorrow. Little Howler, continue in thy path of life, blessing others and being blest, creating music and joy, never ceasing from the attempt to make English music what it should be, and calmly scornful — heedless of the critics.

Go on and prosper: and Au revoir.   I B G

II

AT THE FRONT

To Marion Scott   41.25

7 June 1916 (P)   *France.*

Dear Miss Scott: Your letter has just reached me, here, dans les tranchées. Where and how of course I may not say; bang in the front seats we are; so that when you read of a slight disturbance near Donawhere you may picture me standing gallantly to attention as near to the cookers as possible.

But O what luck! Here am I in a signal dugout with some of the nicest, and most handsome young men I ever met. And would you believe it? — my luck I mean; they talk their native language and sing their own folksongs with sweet natural voices. I did not sleep at all for the first day in the dugout — there was too much to be said, asked, and experienced: and pleasure in watching their quick expressions for oblivion. It was one of the notable evenings of my life.

The French children are fine, a joy to watch for their grace and independence. Why our good friends over yonder should have called them degenerate only the devil who inspired their spiritual pride can explain. And the women. How different their faces are! How full of character. Some of the country we passed through was very beautiful — rather like the Stroud Valley only far longer, and there was later a river, most serenely set in trees, long lines of trees.

We are of course trying to brush up our French, but it is not easy, for where we stayed the dialect was very broad, and instead of "Oui" they uttered a sound like "Waw".

The food in trenches is curiously arranged, apparently. I dont know whether the A S C steal it, but nobody gets more than a third of a loaf ever, and as a rule only a quarter. This is serious to a battallion that has innocently trusted to the army and spent all its money, before knowing how fickle and uncertain is the day of pay. Where everybody is broke there is of course a certain consolation of comradry, but O give me any other reason to be thankful for this spirit which binds the Infantry into a happy band of brothers. But who may resist French bread, and the inviting open door of cafés? Not I. I take my good thing where I find it, and excuse my weakness and extol my taste.

The night before we came in there was a heavy bombardment of these trenches so our debut narrowly escaped being extremely thrilling, but the telling of all this and much more must be postponed till that happy day when I shall hold the listener with my glittering eye and bore him to shrieks and titters of apprehensive imbecility. Après la guerre.

But these few days in the signal dugout with my Cymric friends are of the happiest for years. Out of the company to an extent we breathe the air of freedom almost forgotten. It really does not do for one who so much desires freedom as myself to think of the general conditions of the last few months.

A waste of spirit in an expense of shame. We are all sick of this continual ———— about (Pray excuse the language; nothing else but that word does justice to the Army ways.) And these boys here, so friendly and good to talk to are ———— O well, in agreement with us. War's damned interesting. It would be hard indeed to be deprived of all this artists material now; when my mind is becoming saner and more engaged with outside things. It is not hard for me to die, but a thing sometimes unbearable to leave this life; and these Welsh God makes fine gentlemen. It would seem that War is one of His ways of doing so.

Best wishes for health: Yours very sincerely   Ivor Gurney

Your going to London sounds as if your health was improving. I hope so indeed. It is a hard thing to have an active mind and be helpless. Yesterday in the trenches we found it so; our minds were active enough, and we felt sufficiently helpless. There was a trench mortar strafe, and we had casualties. As I was in a signallers dug out, a bombardment means little else but noise and apprehension — as yet. But a whiz-bang missed me and a tin of Maconachie (my dinner) by ten yards; a shower of dirt no more. Good luck to us all. I have been told that I may say that we are with the Welsh. They sang David of the White Rock, and the Slumber song, both of which Somerville has arranged. And O their voices! I thank God for the experience.

To Mrs Voynich   41.28

June 1916 (E)

Dear Mrs Voynich: I hope you are well now — from whooping cough and all other ailments that do afflict the wearied flesh, and able to play Bach, delight in meditation of your garden, or look after aliens, as most pleases you. I also am attending to enemy aliens, as you may guess . . . Being at this moment in the reserve trenches near Somewhere or other, after a stay in the front line and then in reserve. Here I went through the most amazing experience, it may be, in my life. We were told that our battalion was to go up for instruction to a Welsh battalion, and some of us feared a rough type. Well, up we went through the interminable communication trenches, watching the West when we halted, our minds filled with thoughts that are naturally the raw soldier's; reached our point, were detailed, and then ——— C. and I crawled into a candle lit dugout, and so met four of the nicest young men you could meet, possibly. They knew folk song. And one of them sang "David of the White Rock" and "A Slumber Song", both of which Somervell has arranged, and both beauties —

We talked later of Omar Khayyam, Borrow, Burns, Wordsworth, Oscar Wilde etc etc.

A most amazing evening, as you must admit. I had but 3 hours sleep the night before, but sleep was out of the question on such an occasion. Some of them came from Welsh Universities, one of them was a Yorkshireman. All of them good fellows, and as kind as could be to us new arrivals.

Most soldiers seem to think that the French are a lot of thieves; but that is probably due to the fact that we get paid only 5 francs a week, and that irregularly; and get anything from ¼ to a ⅓ of a loaf as a rule; and things seem dearer than they are perhaps, and thus feeling reacts against the keepers of estaminets. Up till now however such people as we have met have been very nice. Everything goes on as usual behind, and only just behind, the firing line. The children move gracefully, the farmers tend their fields, coffee is sold and beer in large quantities; and at evening soldiers stroll about under the lime trees in the shadow of ruined churches and roofs long ago wrecked — usually in a blind rage, it seems, by our neighbours the Bosches, only a few hundred yards away from where I write. We speak French well enough (C and I) to get what we want, but the talk here is fairly broad, I should say, and it is difficult to go much beyond that. Whether the faces of the French have changed with the war I cannot say; if not, then it was a horrible height of spiritual pride to maintain that the French were degenerate — or a very great compliment to the ancient state of France. There was a boy I saw — at the landing port — who stood in one of the most noble attitudes I ever saw as he watched us pass; and yet his face was not unEnglish. How is it that so few of us are dignified in appearance? Were we in the time of Tom Jones afraid of looking noble? Well, as the whole world sees, we can behave well enough; and the account of Beatty's squadron fighting against so great a superiority should stir us to all nobility, act word thought and appearance.

"Let's do it after the high Roman fashion,
And make death proud to take us".

This is a queer war though. Guns are going in the distance, and every moment there is the chance of a strafe (we have had one, not a bad one) yet the note of the whole affair is boredom. The Army is an awful life for an artist, even if he has such experiences as we had with the Welsh. Either it is slogging along uselessly with a pack or doing nothing but hang about after — or boredom or hell in the trenches. Very little between.

How different the life of Richmond, save in sickness! There are gardens here and a broad river, a sense of security and houses whole and not shattered, with blind eyes. And one can forget the present deeds of les Boches, with the high thought of old Germany. Well, Good bye and best wishes for all good fortune:

Yours very sincerely   Ivor Gurney

To HERBERT HOWELLS   3.27

[with two following letters in envelope dated] 21 June 1916 (P)

My Dear Howells: How are you all this long time? Be good, and write me a long letter full of meaty things about College; a real gossipy letter full of all the little things I want to know — what you are writing now; whether Sir Hubert is lecturing, and if so on what subjects; how Sir Charles is getting on with his new pupils, how everything goes; what the gossip of the tea-room is, though there must be few indeed left to carry on anything animated.

Well, here we are in France, and almost at once shoved up into 1st line trenches, but where I write is reserve, in billetts, and surrounded by some of the attributes of civilisation, but not many. Thank the Lord you had a weak heart, my crescent genius; you cannot imagine to what a length of nervous tension we are driven. The Chinese knew a little of torture, and had an inspiration named "Death by the thousand Cuts," but amateurs they were besides the Grand High Inquisitors who run the British Army; which, while "resting", has the natural aversion to wounds and death to a fear lest it should, by the anger of God, be left alive and physically fit to endure more of the same kind of "rest" — how it hurts a man with a sense of word-values so to misuse words! It is almost as bad as 3rd grade neurasthenia.

But supposing I come at last through all this complete in mind and body, there will be some memories will remain. Our first night in trenches was one of the most surprising things that can ever happen to me. We set out I suppose about the beginning of the afterglow, and went eastward with the usual thoughts in our mind — at least I suppose so. In the communication trenches, which were very long, we had lots of opportunity to look at the West, and remember what lay under Venus; as Wordsworth did in a Sonnet written on Calais sands, beginning "Fair Star of evening"; up we went, with now and again a bullet whizzing above us or a startling clatter of machine-guns in the distance; and then at last the trenches — 2nd and then 1st. We made enquiries, and then C and I crawled into a signallers dugout, and so made the acquaintance of 4 of the nicest people that ever you could meet — and educated. They were absolutely first rate chaps. Unlike some men out here, they didn't try to frighten us with horrible details, but gave us as much help as possible in getting hold of ordinary routine, and in making us feel as much at home as possible. I had no sleep for 36 hours. We talked of books and music. And they sang — Glory be — "David of the White Rock" and the Slumber Song that Somervell has arranged. What an experience! I have also got hold of an address of a man who is rather noted for his knowledge of these things. If there is anything left of either of us after the war I shall attend to it myself — if not, you will write to him and find out.

E Kemp
109 Madeline St
Pontyquaith
S. Wales.

He was busy at the time, and I shall most probably not see him again in France. Such a chap would not only give you his songs but give you other names of other singers also. Lest your pride in your name should become overwhelming, I must tell you that a day or two after, we were put in for instruction with a much rougher crowd. But most men look well in steel helmets, and they had the reputation of being a daring crowd. I have also had the experience of seeing a most beautiful city, about which you also must hear some day; perhaps visit. There is precious little jerry building in France, and all the village roofs are red like the Sussex Roofs, and in an easy walk from the front trenches all the normal life of farms and villages goes on as well as possible except for the shortage of men. They cultivate very well here too, leaving very little grassland.

Write me a letter old man full of news and Fashnable Fax and Polite Annygoats, as Thackeray called them.   Remember me to everyone: Yours ever   I.B.G.

To HERBERT HOWELLS   3.28

21 June 1916 (P)

Please have letter sent I havent any Envelopes
My Dear Howells: Your letter reached me just before going into
the trenches, where I read it last night with great pleasure, and, I
trust, profit. It was good to get a letter so gossipy, and remindful of
home, the R M C, and, not least, my friends — our friends. On
whom be Peace. (May it be soon on us also). I am glad to hear of the
new Quartett, and considerably flattered by the dedication, which is
the first of a considerable bunch in the future; from admiring
comrades, and worshipping disciples. If you could write a Quartett
inspired by Chosen, I can only conjecture how Framilode would
move you did you know it as I know it to be — the most magical and
fascinating of places. Then Crickley Hill, a magnificent conception.
Cranham, especially Portway; little Minsterworth, Redmarley and
the noble Malvern road. Someday perhaps. . . . But there is much
to see, and there are three walking tours — in France Wales and the
lakes, that simply cry for fulfilment. By a walking tour I mean
something accomplished without a pack — not carrying one's
possessions like a snail, at a snails pace.
    You are right about the Elizas. They need a String Quartett or
Quintett very badly, and should it be 1 flute, 1 clar:, 1 bassoon and a
harp? Anyway the news of their approaching production gives me
great pleasure. The selection of artists satisfies me wholly; and the
piano accompaniment is perfectly adequate. I look for a huge
increase of membership in the W.M.S. They are to be congratulated
on their President, and she on her taste, and all deserve completest
success. Please remember me to Idwen Thomas, who sang these
things so well — how many ages ago. Surely I am a different
creature since then? Ah, Howler, there will not be much the matter
with me a year after the Army sees my back. —
    'And joy shall overtake us like a flood
    When everything that is sincerely good
    And perfectly divine
with truth and PEACE and Love" shall shine once more on this
poor distracted Europe of ours. And the swiftness of the Russian
victories have given me much hope. In this connection, please O
please try and get last Sundays Observer (June 12th or there-
abouts). The leading article is a perfect exhibition of pusillanimous
twaddling and a kind of sneaking shamefaced hope that the war will
not last 4 years after all, as it might be — worked out on the
blackboard by fainthearted blitherers. I believe it will be all over by
September — even if I am over too. And that will annoy me; partly

because I feel that when I have renewed and trained my spirit there is work for me to do, and partly because the New England — the New World will be so terrifically interesting. Your faith in the Survival of the Fittest as exemplified in me gave me pleasure, and renewed my own quite strong hope, but when you go on to include so many others, I feel that there is not a dog's chance for any of us. Curious. Keeyurious. But anyway on that subject my mind is pretty tranquil, and on that subject (compared with others) rests, as in a harbour, which is Marcus Aurelius — a great old boy.

How do the girls behave at College now? Is there any new air of dignity on them — or do they frivol and sing Coningsby Clarke and Landon Ronald with the same delight as formerly? What do they talk about now? Do they like Bach better?

By the way, have you heard or seen anything of Elgars setting of Binyons "To the Fallen", that noble poem? How has he done it? Don't forget to reply to this. I envy any man who can set that properly.

"They went with songs to the battle, they were young"
    "As the Stars, as the Stars they remain"
"Age shall not weary them, nor Time condemn"
    "We will remember them"

These little scraps stick to my mind and thrill me. It is a great poem.

If you would hear anything of life at the front, I am afraid that at present I have seen too little to qualify my description of it as a damn dull life. It is for me — "an expense of spirit in a waste of shame" save only for the glorifying touch of danger. One marches heavily burdened, cursing ones Fate, from the rear circuitously to the front, reaches ones post, and hopes for fine weather. I am a signaller, holding on to that name by my eyelids and teeth, and that is an infinitely softer job than the ranks, which nearly drive me mad for its monotony, lack of elementary commonsense living, and for what men like you and I must feel as insults repeated continually. But it is much better out here than in England — save only for the "Rests". Which if they be rests, bear the same relation to Rest as you know it, as a demisemiquaver to a breve. However there is the great consolation of being allowed free in the villages to go where one pleases.

It is sweet to think what a revenge of Joy I will have on Life for all this. For all this grey petty monotony, I will gather all the over-strength of spirit, so hardly earned and force it, coax it, lead it to the service of Joy for ever. And as Masefield points out in his wonderful little book on Shakespeare, no mind but a supremely happy is able adequately to brood with Pity and Anger on Tragedy. From the mountains one must look in the valleys and know their secrets, not dwell therein.

> Sing Happy Soul, thy Songs of Joy
> Such as the brook sings in the Wood
> That all night has been strengthened by
> Heavens Purer Flood.

By the way, those Welshmen I spoke of were a *very* exceptional lot. It was originally mostly from Bangor University. Another lot we met with soon after were not of much account. Gossip I prithee. Gossip!: Yours ever   I.B.G.

To MARION SCOTT   41.26

22 June 1916 (G)

Dear Miss Scott: Still another interesting letter! Please dont expect such a one from me as the weather is very dull and sultry, and this is a small room with 8 signallers lying low from fatigue. However, interesting things have happened. We have come into reserve now, having gone through a strafe which a machine-gunner who had been through Loos said was worse than Loos while it lasted — which was for 1¼ hours. And it left me exalted and exulting only longing for a nice blighty that would have taken me away from all this and left me free to play the G minor Prelude from the Second Book of Bach. O for a good piano! I am tired of this war, it bores me; but I would not willingly give up such a memory of such a time. Everything went wrong, and there was a tiny panic at first — but everybody, save the officers, were doing what they ought to do, and settled down later to the proper job, but if Fritz expected us as much as we expected them, he must have been in a funk. But they behaved very well our men, and one bay filled with signallers and stretcher bearers sang lustily awhile a song called "I want to go home" very popular out here, but not at all military in feeling. The machine guns are the most terrifying of sound, like an awful pack of hell hounds at ones back. I was out mending wires part of the time, but they were not so bad then. 10 high explosives were sailing over the signaller dugout and the bay where I was in front of it. A foot would have made a considerable difference to us I think. They burst about 30 yards behind. Their explosives are not nearly so terrible as ours. You can see dugouts and duck boards sailing in the air during even in a trench mortar strafe (Toc Emma Esses — signallers talk). Theirs of course do damage enough, but nothing comparable. They began it, and were reduced to showing white lights, which we shot away, and sending up a white rocket. Floreat Gloucestriensis! It was a great time; full of fear of course, but not so bad as neurasthenia. I could have written letters through the whole of it. But O to be back out of it all! We had a gross casualties or more — some damned good men among them. Two chaps especially, whom I hoped to meet after the war. The writing in the latter part of this letter will be very bad — myself having come off the worse in a single handed combat with a bully-beef tin; but the bandage looks interesting.

Out of the window we can watch men making hay in a fashion reminding us distractingly of Home. They are easily in range of the smallest field guns. Les bons Francais! There is a delightful girl who with her mother runs a cafe in Laventie, evidently born to be the mother of dauntless men. Here follows

The Song that Signallers Sung and Stretcherbearers of C Company, when the great guns roared at them, and the Germans thought to attack.

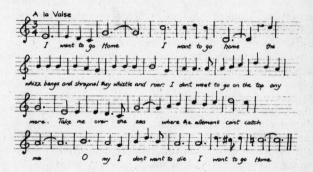

My dear lady, I am pleased with myself. They tell me I was nearly recommended for a DCM or something or other that was done chiefly by other men. But all through I had time to wish I had chocolate, and wonder whether so much baccy was good for me. I may be chronically introspective (and this is a shocking life for that) but as little fearful as a stolid cow. It has given me still further confidence that once I get back to work my mind will take proper paths and let me be happy. You see I dont expect to get knocked about much, and dont intend to go on bombing stunts if I can help. I have forgotten what my other letters contained, but anyway will repeat that your choice of singer and player for my songs gives me great pleasure. I would not wish any other.

I hope your health is still improving, still surprising the doctor. Keep on and hope like the BEF. Did you see R. Bridges Sonnett on Kitchener? Tray bong. And here is a poem on Pain by Morley

Roberts from the Saturday Westminster. It is a good poem I think woflille [?] and one worthy of the subject.

But O that G minor Prelude! It sticks to me in solemn moments.

I tell you what, mamselle; when I return to England I am going to lie in wait for all men who have been officers, and very craftily question them on several subjects, and if the answers to my questions do not satisfy me, they may look out for squalls. This is deadly serious. Talk of the need of "dithipline" wont suit me:

Yours very sincerely   Ivor Gurney

To MARION SCOTT   41.27

29 June 1916 (G)

Dear Miss Scott: Nothing to do — a signallers confession — so I start another letter to you, though there is very little to say — except continuous artillery action on the Western Front, which has up till now left me unscathed, and still able to see the fun of things — such as it is and they are. There are no exciting tales this time save of shells bursting uncomfortably near our billets in reserve. That was nasty, and made one feel as if les Boches were taking a mean advantage of us; but they are getting hell these days and dont seem to [sic] able to find our guns. Soon I suppose, the curtain will shut down on our Western doings and you will hear no more of our little gang for sometime. I should like to hear how my songs went and so forth, before we go over the top. It is an eternal mystery to me how I managed to write such sunny things when my mind was "covered with thick darkness as with a cloke". But as Masefield says in his book on Shakespeare, none but the serene of mind can contemplate tragedy and not be shaken. So that my turn for Tragedy will yet come, when my natural state of mind is Joy — "Freude, Freude" —

I hope when you were convinced that the little dust up in the North Sea *was* a victory that you turned to the "Sea Symphony".

> And out of these a chant for the sailors
> Fitful like a surge.
> Thou sea that sucklest the race in time, that
> Fate can never destroy or Death dismay.
> Indomitable. Untamed as Thee.

O the gorgeous stuff!
And
> Picked sparingly without noise by Thee, old Ocean,
> Chosen by Thee.

I shall be extremely rude to God Almighty if he takes me away from all his, just as I am breaking the egg so to speak. After dinner I am a clod; no spark is in me; but on fortunate mornings and after tea, I feel that there is stuff in me. But hold! Such thoughts are not for me. But only those of the Roman Marcus Aurelius and Epictetus the Greek, and our own Little Willy —

> "All places that the eye of heaven visits
> Are to the wise man ports and happy havens"

Only the eye of heaven dont visit us much now, and the mud is somethink chronic, and a nasty yellow in colour at that. Our dugout stinks of buried vittles somewhere. I myself am lousy — moi qui vous parle; and this majestical canopy fretted with golden fire is a washout in grey. But we go out to "Rest" in four days time, and the amount of work we shall have to do will keep me from thinking anything but strictly military thoughts, or thoughts which if translated into action would certainly bring me into contact with the military authorities. But up here I dont shave, and, in this weather, dont wash over often. But the Hun is at the gate, and Civilisation is a dream merely. I am quite sure that if man were left to himself, he would finally relapse into a most dreadful state of general disreputability, horrible to behold. It is the kindly influence of woman that has produced, or did produce so short a time ago, that crown and very top of civilisation, the oiled sleek and well-defined-shapely crown of the nut. The carpet slipper. The Temple Classics. The blanc-manger and all that is most lovely and of good report in our uncertain existence.

Only the Pipe is of man's own appointment, that dear rank foul companion of difficulty and danger, that goes with the great victory and the forlorn hope; that greets dawn with the sentry and the wide-eyed wakers after the strafe; that watches the sun down and the gnat like aeroplane sailing blithely amid bits of fluff — some dark, some cloud-white, some gorgeously crimson with the falling day.

That astonishes and annoys with its guggle the expectant lookers for death, and soothes with taste and smell the night-signaller tired of intellectual stunting with that horrid bore of Miltons, on Christmas Day. (Oh, but there's a perfectly stunning gun letting off Hell and Damnation {see the jump there?} a few yards away it would seem from the pit of my stomach, and I wish it would stop.)

Bored, Fed up, Full to the neck, is my motto tonight. And would that I were on a mine-sweeper (!!! Bang) earning more than a bob a

day, and though only a shipboy
  "and cradled in the rude imperious surge".
O Hell. What a noise! I cant write with that going!
Later
  After I finished that little scribble, I had to go up to the front line
for message running, and my first, or no — third — message, took
me out of the firing line just in time to escape the most hellish strafe,
which did the most incredibly small

[*A page-break here, but the discontinuity is more probably Gurney's
leaving an idea unfinished than there being a page missing or a
censor's deletion.*]

All heaven seems to be falling on top of us, and when it is all over,
our senior major, who looks as if taken direct from George
Morrow, reports "a little heavy gunfire", there are some dugouts to
put right, and in this case no casualties worth the speaking of.
  I am no expert, but it would seem as if there was absolutely no
comparison between the German explosives and ours. We get
frightened enough, but they have all the terror and a very good and
sufficient reason.
  And now I have your note and an offer to send a parcel — most
willingly accepted. Please send it in 3 days time after getting this. I
think that will be the best thing.
  Our men are still behaving well, and are still able to "gag" with
straight faces and to some purpose. For instance last night, after the
strafe had finished, some weary eyed signaller spoke the mind of
the dugout, "I wish this were all over". The man on duty, a nervy-
to-a-degree but plucky gagster, laughed at and loved, and one of my
beloved few who have kicked and still do kick whenever possible
against the Army pricks. "So do I. I've been sitting here 3 hours and
my behind is sore." An immortal joke, I think. But thats them.
Jokes in unexpected places. Our men will gag before the Judgement
seat and before the throne of Heaven, and not in the most refined
language either, and smoking a fag the while. Last time we were in
trenches to amuse myself I wrote a more or less, chiefly more,
obstetric Journal — The Somewhere in France Gazette, which has
caused great delight. But then, I always was a rude person, and
these things come naturally to me. Music and lewd nonsense and
using words. Well, I am summoned hence. Good bye:
  Your sincere friend: Ivor Gurney

Saturday
My beloved gagster has come a cropper and gone into hospital with
a breakdown. Another of my friends not to see for a space.

This was the result of a short but perfectly horrid strafe last night, and I feel depressed today, partly on account of a strained back caused by stretcher bearing last night — one of our best men; hit in many places but none serious.

Things have started to move. The big advance has begun and all things are now ready for the great Bust. On the top of that comes the news that the Russians have attacked Hindenburg and taken 10,000 prisoners — huge news, and soothing to my jumpy nerves. I need music, which means Bach, very badly; and wont be happy till I get it.

A fleet of aeroplanes on reconnaissance has just returned from a dawdle over the German front lines, with shrapnel bursting round so as rather to resemble the pin pricks on cardboard that one afterwards connects up with wool; reminiscence of childhood. Or thickly populated fly-paper. This is the ordinary manner of our aeroplanes at evening, who stroll over in the casual way that men use after dinner, smoking cigars and feeling pleased with themselves, not caring very much what the unimportant rest of the world think or do. A reassuring sight.

Gerontius has run very strong in my mind of late — the solemn and noble priests music especially

And

very beautiful that part. There is a bunch of glorious poppies perched as if they meant to astonish and delight one, on a little green knoll just back of the firing line. Blue through the rift, or one of Walt Whitman's letters from God.

To England — A Note

I watched the boys of England where they went
Through mud and mire to do appointed things.
See one a stake, and one wire-netting brings,
And one comes slowly under a burden bent
Of ammunition. Though the strength be spent
They "carry on" under the shadowing wings
Of Death the ever present. And hark, one sings
Although no joy from the grey skies be lent.

Are these the heroes — these? have kept from you
The flood of German beastliness so long?

Shall break the devil's legions? These they are,
Who do in silence what they might boast to do.
In the height of battle tell the world in Song
How they do hate and fear the face of War.

Ivor Gurney

To MARION SCOTT   41.30

5 July 1916 (G)

[*P.S.*] (This is the 9th. A green envelope doesnt seem to turn up, so here goes in the ordinary way.)

Dear Miss Scott: The parcel has arrived, and is being put to its proper use with the proper speed. The cake is excellent. Tray bong. J'en suis tres oblige. If you have not sent the other parcel by the time you get this do not trouble till you receive another F.P.C. The fact is, that in this last 6 days in the trenches, we had such a devil of a time that I felt that if parcels were to come at all — if tis to be done, then twere well it were done quickly. We were made a cock-shy of for the artillery, and so have really been a part of the advance. (One strafe lasted 2½ hours, and gave me a permanent distaste for such. We were under fire every day, and nowhere was safe. In the post where I was for half my time, there were twelve dugouts. Four have been smashed, the cookhouse a mere melancholy ruin of its former greatness, and the bombstore not what it was. Souvenirs are plentiful round there . . .

I hope you are pretty well now, and that going to the concert did not harm you at all. Your being able to be there sounds encouraging. Herbert Howells "programme" was quite charming, was it not? His English is usually tortured and topsy turvy, but that was clear and gets just the effect needed. I did not know my song was to be done. It was quite like old times to see "Sea wrack" down again. I must have heard the thing 4 times at least. But of course "The Twa Corbies" is a man's song, if there were any left to sing it, and thats all the comment SirCHHP will get when I write.
And thank you very much for the programme.

Well, the advance, or the preliminary advances has or have begun, and things have gone very well up till now. O may they so continue. There are surely great hopes now of an early advance. Up in the trenches one is liable to get only the big news and the wildest rumours. One needs good ones — of the latter, I mean — to keep ones pecker up sometimes. But the chaps stuck it like good ones, and I am proud of them. Pity it is that whatever happens to me, it will be difficult to meet them again. The world is large, but I do not want better comrades than these, and these are going by degrees.

[*Four lines deleted, presumaby by the censor, since "we shall be a minus quantity" is decipherable.*]

But look here about that parcel; and my pencil moves decidedly quicker at the thought of it.

Heres how (and Ive lost my well prepared curiously conned syllabus.)

Fowl. (since you insist on such a lofty height.)

Cafe au lait (Tin, you know?)

Cake. Stodgy and Sustaining.

Tommy's cooker and tin of refills (cant get them here somehow)

Lemonade crystals or powder or such like.

Chocolate *(Plain)   One book.*

Biscuits. *Oatmeal*.   cheap

Tin of Butter.

Any old *interesting* papers.

A candle or two (somebody's always short).

Acid Drops. Peppermint Bulleyes. Toffee or such.

And if you must leave something out, the fowl may be proscribed, on the ground that it is proteinous matter, and we get tons of such. If one desires to eat 4 pounds of meat a day tis easy done. But bread . . . Never have I had more than a ¼ loaf, sometimes less, and the tale of my woes on the subject has ascended to the Lord Almighty with no result, so I appeal to You.

I should have remembered about the matches. A piano would also be acceptable, but is not insisted on. One must not push about trifles. We could get some of this on reserve but not here so well. Part of the cake is lying on the first part of this letter so excuse grease marks.

You said, some time ago, that "Helen of Kirconell" would do well to set. She is a fine wench but too long and repetitious and her limbs too much in evidence to be easy in surrender.

"O Waly waly", I have designs on, but not yet. But have you heard Elgars setting of "To the Fallen"? Is it anyway worthy of the poem? I *would* like to set that! One of the best things I know "in memoriam".

Our sergeant-major has softened to all the world, and that includes even me, who went to him and asked him where the biscuits and cheese were; in a strafe; his mind being then set on less mundane matters. And so, in the trenches, I never shave, wash late in the day if I please, and wear horrid looking sandbags round my legs because of the mud. When the S.M. tackled me about looking so like a scarecrow — or rather . . . "Come, come, Gurney, look more like a soldier for the Lords sake". "Well, He doesnt seem to be doing much for *my* sake, and anyway I'm not a soldier. I'm a *dirty civilian*". He has taken to being more pious and is careful of the words he utters. Whereas I delight in expressing contumelious opinions of the Lord Almighty, and outlining the lecture which I have prepared against the Last Day. He is surprised that the "coal box" did not fall in *my* bay, but I reassured him that there was a worse thing laid up for me, and left him somewhat cheered.

But, in the name of the Pleiades what *has* a neurasthenic musician to do with all this? One looks at the clear West and the evening stars, and thinks of Minsterworth, book talk and music in the quiet room there; and then the guns begin; and after, one's friends are taken away, some still and some cheerful at a blighty.

O cuss it all though. I am glad to have been through it all, and will keenly enjoy telling others about it after.

And O the Somme — the valley of the Somme round Amiens! A delight of rolling country, of a lovely river, and trees, trees, trees. Apres le guerre, it must be that I write of the piffle under the name of Rupert de Motvilliers Fortescue-Carruthers or some such name, to rake in the good gold in exceeding abundance, to see the earth and the glories thereof, and develop a paunch. But for all these there is as yet no opportunity.

Well the weather has improved now, and I hope will give you a chance of getting strong and fit to do something of what you want to do. O Kind President of the Women Musicians — forward baggages that they are.

Some day I will write out on some dirty scraps of manuscript I always carry with me, my setting of Davies' "The Sea", which you would like, I think. Will you send me a penny manuscript book or some MS in the parcel — an extremely well devised one my committee say.

NO PROTEIN

is the soldiers motto. Another tin of café if you must, but no bully!

> Underneath yon auld dugout
> I wot there lies a khaki lout
> An' naebody kens what he does there
> But the ladye wha' sent the parcel
>   fair.

Your sincere friend   Ivor Gurney

Shrapnel makes a horrid clatter.
Trench mortars at a little distance sound
like footballs well blown up bouncing hard.
Coal boxes and H.E.s give a horrid crunch
quite like a back tooth coming out.

———————

To the Fallen (E.S.)
Living we loved you, yet withheld our praises
Before your faces.
And though our spirits had in high in honour,
After the English manner.

———————

We said no word. Yet as such comrades would
You understood.

———————

Such friendship is not touched by deaths disaster,
But stands the faster

———————

Nor all the shocks and trials of time cannot
Shake it one jot.
Besides the fire at night some grey December
We shall remember.
And tell men unbegotten as yet, the story
of your sad glory

———————

Of your plain strength, your truth of heart, your splendid
Coolness — all ended.

———————

How ended! And the aching hearts of lovers
Joy over covers.

———————

Glad in their sorrow, hoping that if they must
Come to the dust,

———————

That such an ending as yours may be their portion
And great good fortune.

———————

That if we may not live to serve in peace
England — watching increase —

———————

Then death with you, honoured and swift and high
And so — Not Die.

I B G

Here is a bit more, since the green envelope has not turned up as expected.

I hope the doctors have not forbidden work, or come down very heavily on you. You may be playing Bach at this very moment, now as I envy you the very possibility. This morning I was to have played hymn-accompaniments on the piano for our Wesleyan brethren, but suddenly they moved us, and there is filling sandbags instead; not an inspiring job though conversation may be easy and general throughout.

If you could come here where I sit, you would see little but English looking scenery, though flat and not of the best, and ruined houses, some still red-tiled, or partly so; some blind eyed and lacking scalps and others useful organs and appendages. War is a nasty job, and even a summer's morning like this cannot hide the evidences of war, even if there were no thumping of the guns to remind one.

Do you know anything of Lascelles Abercrombie's work? "Deborah" seems to me to be a very fine piece of work, more especially the first two acts, and he *can* write blank verse; rather of the type of "The Bishop orders his tomb at St Praxed's", or Yeats, in a certain mood. Here is a passage which may apply to us outcast art-lovers:

Deborah
"For us, with lives so hazardous, to love
Is like a poor girls game of being a queen.
What good are all these marvellous desires
That seem to hold life in mastery? They are
Dreamt things only. Men make no more of them
Than a hawk would make of a spiders mesh, when life
Is fearfully desiring towards death."

Surely you will agree that this is good clean blank verse, compact and truly English? It is quite a representative quote. There are lots as good.

By the way did you know that Howells has written a new Quartett — Miss Scott says a very good one — dedicated "To Chosen Hill, and Ivor Gurney who knows it.?"

To MARION SCOTT   41.32

27 July 1916 (P)

My Dear Miss Scott: Two days ago I wrote you a letter full of grumbles about different things, but was ashamed on re-reading it, and this is the outcome.

You write very interesting letters, and no one, either from the script or the matter, could guess that an invalid was their author. I did not know you had pain as well, thinking it to be an illness of weakness chiefly at any rate. I hope it is getting on satisfactorily and as rapidly as can be expected now.

Thank you very much for all the trouble you are taking and have taken about my songs. Evidently the performance would have fallen through had it not been for you and H N H, whom may the gods reward!

I am glad you like those verses. Here is another set. It is simply too much trouble to ponder and reconsider. These things have to be written rapidly out here. This life takes away one's virtue altogether, or seems to. A Wet Rag is solidity itself compared to my moral and physical feelings. (Crrunch! Jack Johnson on the right.) We moved very soon after I got your last letter, and it has got lost somehow, somewhere. But the other letter got here all right. Or is it the first I have lost?

It is good news to hear that Dr Allen has come across Howells, and I wish him the luck he deserves of it. I wonder if I shall ever hear "my" quartett? Or see Chosen Hill again? Somehow one never loses hope, and England may yet see me swanking round with long hair and a symphony under my arm. (Another Crunch. O Sound of Fear. unpleasing to a soldiers ear.)

I am glad the photograph has pleased you. Myself I knew nothing of it, save that it was taken in the afternoon, which is my chief indigestion-time; and nothing on earth could make me look cheerful then. But anyway it was taken a day or so after my Redmarley visit — a memory of great joy — and I probably felt more gay than I looked. Your offer of parcels is most grateful to me. *And* books. There is Nelson's 6^d Classics, Cassells 6^d National Library and 8^d Classics. And Everyman. Also Steads Penny Poets — a most useful edition — in which I would like Keats, Shelley and Tennyson, also Browning and Walt Whitman if you can; but these are out of print I think. Also I want a Supplement to the Golden Treasury in a small edition. There is one in Everyman, but a smaller would be preferred. You see the reason of my liking for the Penny Poets? There is no verse pleases me better than the best of present day stuff though. We may have no great poets, but poetry so saturated with the very spirit of England has not been written before. When I try to call up a certain Autumn Evening at Minsterworth years ago, and now worlds away, it is our younger poets who give me help. Shakespeare and Shelley also but not so strong. Keats is sometimes good in that way.

You must not think we never get bread. It is very seldom that we get less than a quarter loaf and sometimes it is a third. We are not quite so badly off as you seem to think. There is meat in great quantities, but one gets very tired of meat. O for a salad, green white and red, with real dressing, and proper bread and butter! It is a great thing to have few desires, and those easily satisfied, but when the best of my desires are in their very nature impossible to do anything with, the ground seems to fall away beneath one and leave one dangling in mid air above the pit. My moral and mental fibre is that of the old grandmother, without the advantage of quiet and an old age pension. Could I but think that either were to be obtained! (Here I must work in a page of my discarded letter somehow.)

The machine gunners manage to make their job interesting by "playing tunes" on their guns. As thus. After the ordinary casual shots and steady pour, one hears

∐ ∐ ∐ ∣∣ ∐ ∐ ˥ ᴠᴜ∣

which always sounds comic, and must, I imagine require some skill. Here comes the other sheet

The infantry have to make all their fun, but, bless their hearts, there is a considerable amount when one adds it up, but their musical taste is simply execrable, and they are given to singing the most doleful-sentimental of songs. One of the worst of which is a lamentable perpetration called "For he's a ragtime soldier", which they love to sing on the march after being relieved. We are all fed up. How fed up you must gather from the fact that anyone who mentions home is howled down at once.

(O, of course, do as you like with the memorial verses.) But Gloster, like Troy in Masefields poem, has become a city in the soul.

We sit together and brood till someone suggests some fitting way of dealing with the Kaiser. Then people brighten up and conversation becomes general, but not polite. The universal opinion out here is that the Navy has a soft job. One does not expect the Navy to agree, but do not you? Their dangers are mostly silent ones, and do not obtrude, and the great presence of the Sea is about them; and furthermore there is the great change of Sea and Land for them, who can, in a manner, return home every so often.

I came across Benjamin's people the other day, and was very much struck by their friendliness and childlikeness. We got on very well together. And what a physique!

I wonder what you will think of these verses; the first effort at rhymeless verse that my humble muse has managed. Be candid, I do implore you. It is my one intellectual pastime barring only this same of letter writing, and I am too fed up with other things to be annoyed at a slating. Why need you give me your own opinion? Why not call yourself Our Poetry Expert? Your letter would take on an added importance, and receive greater attention. O what is the opinion of the success of this offensive? Of course, we have gained ground, but is it a real success, answering expectations? And worth what we have spent on it? You will probably have been able to get some general opinion on this matter.

Today, one of our men received a packet of army cigarettes containing a lady's name and address, and got me to write a letter to her; which I did in my best, most high-falutin Stevenson-to-Mrs-Sitwell style. I wonder what she is like, and whether this is the beginning of a romance, or merely the beginning and end of a puzzle. Her name is nice; Margaret Black; and her address is Medway St Westminster. Perhaps she is heir to great estates, or perhaps she used to take in washing. Westminster is such an inclusive sort of place, and it is difficult to get much from the handwriting. Do I stand on the threshold of great events? If not, look out for a "Lonely Officer" in the Agony Column of the Times.

There is nothing but burbling in my mind, nothing but an empty ache for Maisemore and Framilode and such.

The Gazette I send will probably interest you quite a lot. F.W.H is my friend of whom you have heard. He is sometimes un-grammatical, but increasingly a poet, and the "Dorothy" you have also heard of — for her speed, her lovely great sail and most of all for her leaks: Goodbye   with best wishes

Your sincere friend   Ivor Gurney

Will you please send me a copy of Masefields By A Bierside. I want to set it. And M.S.

Little did I dream, England, that you bore me
Under the Cotswold Hills besides the water meadows,
To do you dreadful service, here, beyond your borders
And your enfolding seas

_____

I was a dreamer ever, and bound to your dear service
Meditating deep, I thought on your secret beauty
As through a child's face one may see the clear spirit
Miraculously shining.

_____

Your hills not only hills, but friends of mine and kindly,
Your tiny orchard-knolls hidden beside the river
Muddy and strongly flowing, with shy and tiny streamlets
Safe in its bosom.

Now these are memories only, and your skies and rushy sky-pools
Fragile mirrors easily broken by moving airs
But deep in my heart for ever goes on your daily being
And uses consecrate.

———————

Think on me too, O Mother, who wrest my soul to serve you
In strange ways and fearful beyond your encircling waters
None but you can know my heart, its tears and sacrifice
None, but you, repay.

   The Gazette will come when we are out of trenches

To MARION SCOTT   41.33

7 August 1916 (P)

My Dear Miss Scott: I have already written half a letter and lost it, but writing to you is less a trouble than to anybody almost, and that is a great compliment — I think — from me.

   Your parcels have arrived, and, though they must have cost some money, and trouble, I hope you will not think this was wasted: you have my deepest sincerest assurances that the pleasure caused by your kindness has been considerable. The days have been very hot lately, the lemonade very cool. And people in the bays sleepy before stand-to have taken great joy in peppermints and bullseyes.

   The Cooker is the observed of all observers; a marvel. And quite another and more sumptuous thing from what I expected. The reason I dared to ask for all these things is — we have been so busy and so much in the trenches, that it has been impossible to get these things ourselves, in the towns and villages. As for our canteen, the only thing one is certain of getting, is bootpolish, and perhaps batchelors buttons. This is an apology for having asked for so much.

   But now — the books.

   Shelley was very nice to get. Keats I havent touched yet. But O — Walt Whitman! I never dreamed he was so good. It is true that in most cases his poems are not really so much poems as raw materials for such, but dammy, it has amazed me to find so much in so tiny a book. I will go so far as to say that no present has ever given me so much pleasure; though that is not to say that a little boat and a month at Framilode would not be even more acceptable, but now I speak as one of the foolish persons.

   "Pip" is a jolly book, and full of good descriptions of sport, which I always liked. (O, what would a clean hit for four feel like now?) But there is [no] need to send me such — *unless you have already bought them for your own use.* One can only read them once, then hand them on. True, a lot of men see them. But Walt Whitman — why he has after some fashion renewed me, and while he makes one more unwilling than ever to die, noone can more feelingly persuade as to the beauty of Death. (But there is more in the lost letter which may yet be found. It will be wise not to repeat.)

While I remember. Cushy rhymes with bushy, not rushy. We have been having a quieter time lately on the whole, but never give the Boche much chance to keep quiet, and he returns the compliment. Men go one by one, some with nice blighties, some with the Eternal Discharge. But on the whole we are a cool lot. Some of us, including the subs, amazingly cool. I have an unresting imagination which never ceases to suggest danger, which when it comes, does not greatly affect me; but some of our men have all the gifts of courage, and humility with "fundamental decency" piled on the top. There is one little sergeant who is the unconscious hero of an epic, which will end with *his* duration, or the war's.

O what a lot! What a lot! But I would like a turn with some Scots we just met once. They were fine indeed.

It is difficult in these letters to interest you, and yet avoid trouble with the Censor. I would like to tell you where we are and when we managed to get more than a general mention in "the rest of the front", but it cant be. And on the other hand, humour and things humorous are either impossible to show in a letter or too long to write of. But there *is* fun, occasionally. What there is to see, and see with joy — is, men behaving coolly with white lips, or even unaltered faces. Men behaving kindly to one another. Strained eyes and white faces yet able to smile. The absence of swank of any sort — among the men. The English virtues displayed at their best and least demonstrative, and musical taste at its lowest, worst, I would not have missed it for anything, and wait for my Nice Blighty with satisfaction, pride, and trepidation, lest the Almighty may have misunderstood my wishes in the matter. They talk about a Trade War after this. Will not the fact that so many Englishmen have become masters of Life have a bearing on this, in spite of the calculations of our Economic Experts?

Since men who do so much for England have at last come to see what they love in Her, and what they would have Her be, and what they themselves desire to be — Since these men if they return are to do the work and to shape England anew, will they not have something to say on all the proposals for night-schools that are to make us the Swots of Europe, thereby dethroning Germany from that proud position, and all the schemes to make them merely the builders of a huge trade? Are we to provide statistics to please the heart of the "Times" Economic Supplement leader writer! By heaven, I think not! In my dugout there is placed very prominently a photo of a place that stands for delight with all Gloster men. It means a good tea, clean air, feminine society, a good row on a pretty stretch of river, Beauty and leisure to enjoy it; Home and all its meaning. I lead weary men into this commodious residence, and show them this pennyworth of poor printing. They cannot speak, or do so in such phrases as — "That hurts my cory." "My God, my God!" "What a life!". Or more explosively, "How *Long* IS this ═════War Going to LAST?" The first phrase is an obscure one to many, to me even. But our men use to say "That'll hurt his cory" when they would indicate that such a one will receive annoyance of some kind — from coming too late for tea, to just missing a Blighty. And here I break off for chocolate. Which having found I resume. Dont send any more books just now please. Unless (see previous underlined caution) they are absolutely not wanted and are meant to be handed round. And for the rest I must thoroughly steep myself in Whitman and the wonderful boy (comparatively) that is Shelley. He is rather too facile an exquisite poet for me as a rule. Though I know myself to be too grown up at present.

You send me an exercise book, which may yet contain my Collected Poems. But it was music M.S. I meant, to write out the "Sea" poem of Davies — and me.

My mind so takes that other letter for granted that I have forgotten to say, what the other letter said at length, how disappointed I was to get no letter with all this manna and nectar and honey. Other people may send parcels and letters. But *you* send letters and parcels, which is a prettier speech than deep emotion commonly drags from me. And indeed B Co Signallers are under the stress of deep spiritual emotion tonight. (It is 1.45 a.m. Aug: 1st) They started with cafe au lait, passed an hour daintily with biscuits and weak tea, and have only now finished their felicitations on the lemonade. They do not say prayers, I believe, nor know your name, save as Fairy Godmother; but were both these things so, you should be mentioned, yes, even in the Lords Prayer (amended version, on account of luxuries.)

And have I thanked you for the trouble you have taken about my songs? Was that in my *last* letter, or my *lost* letter? Well, you will understand the feelings of a youthful composer, making his bow; at a distance may be. I had almost resigned myself to never hearing anything of my own things. It is long since I troubled much about them; but here you come reviving my hopes and vanity in the most delightful fashion. (Squeals and moans from nose-caps) (By the way, the cafe au lait was hit by a shell splinter this afternoon. But luckily this was noticed and disaster averted by a mess tin.)

I could talk with you for hours, but blithering along in this fashion

on paper will probably bore you horrid. But please write whenever you can. Shouldnt I just like a talk on "This Compost" or "A Sight in Camp"; on the man who could write Bach like openings like "Word over all, beautiful as the sky"
or
"To the Leavened Soil they trod, calling I sing for the last."
or lines like
"They were purified by Death, they were taught and exalted."
No, I don't want to lose all this. There are so many parts for an ambitious young man to play, from disciple of Walt Whitman, lover of common men, to the composer of 9 (Immortal) Symphonies, all English every bar. And what about sailing?

My other letter has inquiries about your health. I hope to find it and include it with this — but if not, I hope everything goes as well as possible with you. If pluck could do it, you would long ago have been rudely and annoyingly robust.

May your phagocytes do their damndest, is the wish of:
Your sincere friend   Ivor Gurney

To MARION SCOTT   41.34

August 1916 (E)

Dear Miss Scott: The address on the label of the packet of M.S. is shaky and would not impress a real expert in such matters, but it seems to be yours, and so I guess that you are out of danger, and will soon be able to resume that correspondance which is inevitably fated some day to be the joy and wonder of my biographers. That is, if my biography is not fated to be one line in the casualty list, with the wrong number and a J. instead of an I — as is set forth on my identification disc. I hope you have not been having too evil a time of it though, and that this is the last attempt at dissolution for a long time. It would be a pity to depart now — when all things seem coming to fruition, and Mr Garvin becoming more and more optimistic in spite of the price of paper. Well, cheerio O. Ipshi pris, as the 2/5th say.

Halt of a day

I have just finished a setting of Masefields "By a Bierside", and this will come to you either now or when we get back out of trenches. I hope you will like it. I will praise it so far as to say that I believe there was never anybody could have set the words "Death opens unknown doors", as it is set here. The accompaniment is really orchestral, but the piano will get all thats wanted very well. It came to birth in a disused Trench Mortar emplacement, and events yesterday evening gave one full opportunity to reflect on one's chance of doing *this* grand thing. Did you see an article on Trench Mortar Tennis in Punch of a short while back? That is very good.

Last night I got letters from the whole Scott family. At least, they got here then, but did not reach me till this morning, having mysteriously been discovered in the Cook House. But everything is queer here. I feel like a cinematograph shadow moving among dittoes.

It is bad to hear that you cannot sleep. Read Dr Johnsons works, or Addison's, which are nearly as bad. If these are unutile then parts of the Excursion might meet the needs of the case.

The fear of death in sickness is widely different from that in a strafe. The most of us do not fear death very much. Hardly at all, in fact. It is hearing the shells and mortars soaring down to wipe you out, and the spiteful gibbering of the machine guns which *may* get you that does the trick. If a hypochondriac in the last stage of depression were to stand by a river, having fully made up his mind to drown himself when his waistcoat would come off; if a boy were to throw a brick at such he would dodge it. It is the same instinct that makes war dreadful, but by a merciful dispensation relieves the flat boredom of living among sandbags.

This letter is a spasmodic affair, and has already been interrupted 3 times, but we get on.

I have made up my mind to adopt that alteration you suggested and had already written a letter to Mr Dunhill to say so, but envelopes being na pooh, it had not gone. However, it shall go. The title should be To Certain Comrades (E S and J H.)

Mrs Voynich has sent me M Aurelius and Epictetus. The last is a game old boy, and I should dearly love to watch him in a strafe, but M Aurelius is a pious swanker in comparison, though he says some lovely things. Epictetus remains among the persons decidedly worth getting to know; perhaps after the next strafe.

If you were to send a parcel in anticipation of that happy date . . . . I regret to report that the signallers show signs of being, metaphorically speaking, fed up.

Keats certainly was no end of a poet. If he had lived? And Schubert? Well, no one can say. (If the violet were not so frail . . .) But from the little foreword to Endymion Keats would have been a fine man, and he left St Agnes Eve — a joy for ever. And La Belle Dame and the Cortez sonnett. He went "before his pen had gleaned his teaming brain", but there's enough to make a fine show in an anthology. Shelley wrote well too. Someday I must set "Rarely Rarely comest thou" and that Invocation which begins, white hot, with "Light of Life, thy lips enkindle."

Walt Whitman is my man however, and I want to write in music such stuff as "This Compost". Everyday my mind gets less sick and more hopeful someday of sustained effort.

What news! What a change since May! Let us unchain the optimists, and disport ourselves in the realm of the Ideal. In which the Germans must find increasingly their consolation, but not their rations. (Do you remember John Baptist's advice to soldiers?) I wonder whether any up to date fool will try to depict a strafe in music. The shattering crash of heavy shrapnel. The belly-disturbing crunch of 5.9 Crumps and trench mortars. The shrill clatter of rifle grenades and the wail of nosecaps flying loose. Sometimes buzzing like huge great May flies, a most terrifying noise when the thing is anywhere near you. There are better things to treat though, and among them are sunsets such as the last, which would have coloured my thoughts had it not been for the greasiness of the duck-boards. Life is an aggravation unless the duck boards are dry. (There are fine opportunities in an Ode to a Duckboard.) There was also a double rainbow — a perfect thing of its kind. But rainbows always look as if a child had designed them in crayon, garish and too shapely.

Please thank Mrs Scott and Miss Stella for their letters, and ask them how soon the War will be over. They forgot to say. Goodbye and best wishes for a quick recovery. This may have been what has kept you weak for so long. O, have you read any of the Askew's books? They are a feast of delight. There is one here with a gorgeous strong silent duke of Jovelike power. An amazing duchess of the most astonishing beauty, who, poor thing makes numerous abortive attempts at adultery. A patient but occasionally insupressive wife. Spiteful Cats galore. Latest dresses. Magnificent scenery. Snobbery and Indignant Virtue. Golly what a feast is the Tempting of Paul Chester!:   Good luck   Ivor Gurney

PS.

Today is changeable, rather cold and windy. I should have been out on the hills or riding round by Haw Bridge to Tewkesbury, if . . . . . short views, monsieur, short views! This letter will go today I hope, and find you getting on at a surprising rate. I am glad not to have lost a most interesting correspondent. I recommend to you a book which was reviewed in the Westminster. It is a book of (French) poems by Marcel (?) Claudel. A poet whom France has just recognised as he is. What was quoted was very fine to me. He speaks of his dead countrymen "set in the ground like corn". A most beautiful way of reference to the number of deaths and the virtue thereof. The publishers are the "Editions de la Nouvelle Revue". Paris, or something like that. The price is 1 franc for 3 poems. I feel sure it is worth getting, and he is a man of whom, so one tells me, much will be heard. I wish I could hear Howells best work, my Quartett.

I hardly think of music at all, but stick to books. My friend Harvey who is now a lootenant in this battallion has just lent me his "Spirit of Man"; and I am now browsing therein. Masefield is quite right, "Life is *too wonderful* to end", and the better part of me is on fire adequately to praise it before I go. O please excuse the dirtiness of the M.S. but mud abounds here, and I always manage to find more than most people. And it is a horrid clayey muck that sticketh closer than a Flag seller.

On rereading my letter, I find myself thinking that my references to Mrs Scotts and Miss Stella's kindness in writing are rather curt. This was not intended at all.

> The careless writer
> And swift inditer
> Often omits
> To fill in bits
> Would make the prophetic obscurity
> of his meaning and writing lighter.

To HERBERT HOWELLS   3.26

August 1916 (?)

My Dear Howells: How's a' wi' ye? I hope you are going strong on the Muse, and that ideas flow strong. Do my share as well, do double turns; for I tell you that here I feel altogether out of place — as if in some horrid long-drawn out dream that will not vanish. Your letter was a very generous one, and cheered me up, partly to feel that one so frank should have such gifts. You *must* do well, must do great things, for you have self discipline and staying power besides all the rest, and a high ideal. Continuez vous, mon ami! It is hard lines not to be able to hear my Quartett, for Miss Scott is the author of the good news that it is your Best Work, and this means a lot to me for I remember very well what your Concerto was — is. Continue my child.

I have had rather a blow lately, and need music to express my feelings, and let off steam. F. W. H. is almost certainly dead, and with him my deepest friendship, as far as that does pass with death; a very little with me. He went out on patrol alone, and has not returned, an unworthy ending for so fine a spirit, who should have died, if his destiny were to die in this horrible anonymous war, hot in the battle, in some hopeless-brave attack. But this was not the purpose of the Will for him, and none can say well or good to it; but it is bad to see one's friend to go from one's bodily touch with so little sign or cause for pride. What he would have done with his life it is hard to say. For he was a spirit absolutely beyond the reach of any earthly power to satisfy. Restless, set on other things, discontented in a fashion both evil and very good, but increasingly good, and less and less evil. He had all the gifts save only serenity, and whether he could have attained that is solely the question. Peace to his spirit! Someday you must remember him, if that is not possible to me, for not many knew him anyway so well as I and his generosity, and his heart of kindness to all men. His flaw, his only fault of nature was that cursed one of introspection; that and that only. Not a bad fault as towards other people, but a great misery to ones-self. However my dear Howler, I feel convinced that could I only get back to the work which is mine I could myself get rid of most of it in no very great space of time.

These are great days, my son. Against a huge evil there has risen up a huger force of good, and the world, knowing itself to be saved, must endure the utmost misery for the sorrow necessary in and inevitable to the fighting of evil. It is doubtful whether artists can gain a full enough view of all this drama for generations yet. Do not attempt anything that your spirit does not feel bound to meditate upon, but go your own way in trust and clear confidence; for you were born to a great end. Probably also to great difficulty and discouragement, which will merely be the cause of a greater achievement, since you are what you are — a brave spirit. If the Will designs to blot me out before I can do also what I would — I am content, but may such gift as is in me descend on you, and make your love of Earth and Men deeper. I wish no more. Which will show you that my mind is cleaner and steadier, than heretofore. Death would have no vestige of terror, if this only could be granted; and if not, well you are big enough, it seems . . . . . .

You will be pleased to hear the Glosters continue to do well, and are taking honours and getting commended more than any other battallion in the division. The note of our men is not cheeriness. It is ordinarily a spirit of comradeship, sustained and real. Not much laughter, but many smiles. A hunger for the news of the end of the war, and an unflinching determination to stick it until Our Peace is obtained. No kind of hate of the Germans, but a kind of pity and wonder mixt — on account of the terrible power of our explosives, and their detestation of the German mind. A fixed grey-coloured nobility of mind that will last longer than hate and fury, for it is subject to no after effects of exhaustion or lethargy of spent force.

And O Howler! The French women and children! What features! What carriage! What pride of race! And the young Frenchboys who come home on leave are soldiers of a proper appearance. We are obviously civilians in uniform, but they are the real thing. And no Frenchman or Frenchwoman has been in the least discourteous to me at any time. In England, if one went in to a public house, one would have to be careful of one's language, careful not to offend people. Not so here. One just talks — and there you are.

Write me another letter, old man, meaty and full of news, with special reference to our revered Benjy.

Goodbye. A la bonne chance. Au revoir et bientot:
Yours ever   I.B.G.

To MARION SCOTT   41.35

24 August 1916 (P)

My Dear Miss Scott: I hope you are still improving, and getting on as well as becomes an English woman in these times. You may have written to me, but I am at a hospital miles away from the lines to have my spectacles and teeth mended, and to drink as much coffee as my interior may be induced to receive. Unfortunately we are kept within the camp, and one's efforts are necessarily confined in their sphere. Anyway there will probably be your parcel waiting to go into the line with me, when the time for return comes.

Do get on well though, and write me those interesting letters which are a part of such joy as I can get here. They are the proper kind of letters too, properly commixed of news and intellectual brilliance. Continuez, mon ami, or rather m'amie (I suppose.) I am writing in a canteen, temporarily transformed into a lecture room, subject being Prussia, the soldiers listening very attentively. Would they have been so attentive 3 years ago? I wonder!

The thing that fills my mind most though is, that Willy Harvey, my best friend, went out on patrol a week ago, and never came back. It does not make very much difference; for two years I have had only the most fleeting glimpses of him, but we were firm enough in friendship, and I do not look ever for a closer bond, though I live long and am as lucky in friendship as heretofore.

He was full of unsatisfied longings. A Doctor would have called it neurasthenia, but that term covers many things, and in him it meant partly an idealism that could not be contented with realities. His ordinary look was gloomy, but on being spoken to he gladdened one with the most beautiful of smiles, the most considerate courtesy of manner. Being self-absorbed, he was nevertheless nobly unselfish at most times, and all who knew him and understood him, must not have liked him merely, but have loved him. Had he lived, a great poet might have developed from him, could he only obtain the gift of serenity. As a soldier, or rather as I would say, a man, he was dauntlessly brave, and bravery in others stirred him not only to the most generous recognition, but also unfortunately to an insatiable desire to surpass that. His desire for nobility and sacrifice was insatiable and was at last his doom, but his friends may be excused for desiring a better ending than that probable, of a snipers bullet in No Mans Land. There is only one thing to make me glad in all this, which is — that I saw him a few hours before he went out, and he lent me his pocket edition of Robert Bridges "Spirit of Man", a curious collection, but one well worth having, and a worthy memory of my friend. I need no such remembrances; if the Fates send that I live to a great age and attain fulnesss of days and honour, nothing can alter my memory of him or the evenings we spent together at Minsterworth. My thoughts of Bach and all firelit frosty evenings will be full of him, and the perfectest evening of Autumn will but recall him the more vividly to my memory. He is my friend, and nothing can alter that, and if I have the good fortune ever to meet with such another, he has a golden memory to contend with. A thing not easy.

I am anxious to hear what you think of my setting of Masefields lovely poem. Do not spare criticism. Once I could not write away from the piano; that was written in the front line. Indeed I am becoming fit for my job — by which, as you know, I do not mean fighting. Our front has been fairly quiet, but that term will not exclude raids or bombardments, or the unwelcome irritations of Trench Mortars. These things often make me horribly afraid, but never past the possibility of making jokes; which must be my standard of paralytic fear. (I tell you, should we return to the R C M, it will not do for Sir C V S to act the python to our rabbits. We live in holes but only for protection against Heavy Artillery, and his calibre I fear is not as huge as other more modern calibres.) Tell me something about our College people.

O horror! Mr Dunhill sent me the proof, and after the bother of coming from trenches it cannot be found. Please let him know the *only* alteration is the one you suggest —"an ending such as yours etc Not the very trite schoolboy alteration of the second All ended to How ended! Or at least, let him do so in proper journalistic style with

all ended . . . .

HOW ENDED!!!!!!
or something of that sort. Printed in red, with vari-coloured exclamation marks; and a huge sforzando fff in brackets; with a foot note to emphasise the point, and a mention thereof in the editorial; also an increase of price for the Magazine Supplement — my photo with a huge laurel printed thereon.

These are great days now — in England. But in France, they are either — awful or — dull. Ours is the latter lot, which means less horror but also less chance of a blighty.

I still expect to come through, but then, who doesn't? — out of the line

"Our Cheery Wounded." You dont say!

Mr Garvin ventured to speak of a 15 months possibility last Sunday. But the French papers have a more optimistic opinion, when they condescend to hint at it. Gustave Hervé does not think she can last another winter. O that it may be! Anyway, we can stick it, and will, since now we understand Fritz and his cloudy soul.

Goodbye and best wishes for Exuberant Vitality:

Yours very sincerely   Ivor Gurney

To MRS VOYNICH   46.32.3

28 August 1916 (?)

Dear Mrs Voynich: My twenty-sixth birthday finds me at a Clearing Station having my teeth attended to. I wonder where the twenty-seventh will find me? I hope — in England; consuming such wonderful chocolates as you sent me. They were very tray bong, and deserve mention in dispatches. You are to be envied, being near cliffs and the sea. I do not care for skylarks — you may have the whole tribe, but your telling me the French name for them came in useful a day or two after, as we marched past an Estaminet with "Alouette" printed for all the world to see and wonder at. The French are a lovable lot, and a holiday in France; a walking tour especially; could not be bettered as a cheap escape from war-thoughts, if there are any, just after the war. (Aprés le gore, our men say; as a joke, and not a bad one.) The French are so courteous, so easily interested, and obviously such a fine-tempered race, that j'en suis fervent. It is possible to imagine them destroyed, but not conquered. We are probably the finer and more miraculously achieving, when we are put to it; but the French will be sooner stirred to great ends than we — as allies we are ideal, and have a suitable enemy to call out our best. And how well and lovingly they build! France will not erect ugly little tinpot churches all over her tiny towns, but will have one great church worthily built in an open space. Our men do not speak well of the French towns, but all their comminations and cursings come down to the simple ground-objection that there are no picture palaces. They will remember the quiet grace of these farms, and towns and villages when, apres le gore, they reach their own badly built, evilly conceived, wilful-carelessly planned conglomerations of houses, and see vistas of grey depressing slate roofs, and terrible fever-visions of desirable villas.

Well, the thought of la belle France has run away with me somewhat. I hope you are much better now, and at least able to write, and please yourself in creating. Do you so much regret leaving Richmond? All London save only the City and the Embankment might, almost, fall through to hell without a word of regret from me. You surely cannot mind being far from (Cobbett's) "Wen", since there is Dorset, or some such county to live in? But perhaps it is that friends cannot get at you so easily, and that is a strong objection, even though I might feel that with a pound a week, one might live in France for ever, and use one's friends, and think of them, merely as things to write to and pour out one's impressions upon. I hope this indisposition does not weaken you much; and that it is merely indisposition and an illness taken in time — even over by now; but that is much to hope.

You must have gathered from all this rigmarole that up till now I have been able successfully to dodge flame and steel — even nice blighties have eluded my anxious search. There is something that one ought perhaps to be grateful for, in that my mind is very much more serene than it was and my health altogether better. Perhaps two years . . . . .

My best friend went out on patrol some weeks back, and has never returned. I am glad to say that we accidentally met on that morning and he lent me R.B.'s "Spirit of Man". Mine for always I suppose now. Unless that event occurs which will dissolve such rights of ownership, or desire; For it is a good book, though very far below what it might be. Why all that Shelley and Dixon, and Hopkins or what's his names of the crazy precious diction? About one third of the book is worth having, some of it foolish merely. The Greek stuff is sometimes nonsense. The French trite and dull. Where is Wordsworth, Stevenson, Whitman, Browning? And why not more Tolstoi? The Yeats things are good, but he has omitted rare stuff, as Kathleen ni Huolihan, the Fiddler of Dooney. One would not expect Bridges to include any Belloc; he is an old man; but the book would be better for it. You are right about M. Aurelius. He is mostly a washout. The only thing truly worth preserving is the "Dear city of Zeus" passage. Epictetus has humour and more courage, but it is a waste of time to read more than the Manual. The whole of E: is there, save the "custard with a hook" sentence. Anyway, are all of them, Whitman, Christ, Epictetus not included and summed up in the mind of Bach? Perhaps not some of Whitman, but add Beethoven and there you are. Having read these two philosophers once, it should never be necessary to read them again. They have one "tip" to give, for which I thank them, and so — farewell.

Rondel (is it?)
on next page.

Nor flame nor steel has any power on me,
But that its power work the Almighty Will.
Nor flame nor steel has any power on me;
Through tempests of hell fire I must go free
And unafraid, so I remember still
Nor flame nor steel has any power on me,
But that its power work the Almighty Will.

(Yes, I note the two "powers"; but perfection is not a thing I value, but only Truth and Beauty.)

A French-woman told me that les civils expected the war no more than we did, and that les civils say, that if there were a God, he would go into the Trenches and finish the War. Les soldats think otherwise; and anyway, to see the French faces and to look into their eyes, is to be sure that whatever France thinks she thinks she will have no part for ever in the Prussian type of Atheism or religion. What news! What a time to live in, and, if it must be as a soldier, What a time to die in! And for what a cause! Il faut a ècraser les barbares, and then perhaps les barbares will remember and serve Europe again after their own great fashion. But a thousand years might well run before even the charitable forgive, especially as Germany will so easily forgive herself; if she ever manages to reach that spiritual height. However we propose to try to help her there . . . . . Au debout de 1917. Hé quoi? (If there is such an expression.) With best wishes for present and future health:

Yours very sincerely   Ivor Gurney

To MARION SCOTT   41.38

13 September 1916 (P)

My Dear Miss Scott: Thank you for your letter and the postcard, which is very fine, and you are to be envied; the more so as, both from your writing and matter, you seem to be getting better. Well done, and stick at it.

Here am I beside a French canal, watching the day, and remembering with an ache what Glostershire is in such a season as September, and with whom I usually spent the best of it — with Will Harvey. The sunsets and afterglow are lovely now and behind their joy lurks ever the fear . . . . which I cannot put aside, as it is my only hope to train my mind to think of such things for the music that one day may come out of such a saturated mind, full of sunsets and the smell of earth. Well one must pay something for being born in an heroic age. An age of continent shaping, when foundations are set afresh.

I am out of hospital, just out of it, and going into the line very soon, for which I am not sorry, as the chief delight in the Army remains for me the coming out of danger, which means in this connection reaching a place commanded by every sort of gun except trench mortars and field artillery; however they let us alone, for which mercy God and German fear of reprisals be thanked. I see by the French papers that Prussia is about to call the boys of sixteen to military service. Surely this is the last straw; the women will hardly stand that, and a copy of a broadsheet entitled "Hunger" now being circulated secretly, a most significant document if authentic.

Peut-etre six mois, peut-etre moins. But that should do the trick. And to hammer them too hard to let them retire without disaster; in which connection please note the glorious bit of luck in having Hindenburg being made chief! France has suffered badly enough, but the faces of the women show one how very far off she is from yielding. They do not adopt men's costume, or get photographed by the "Daily Mirror", but do the work, and say nothing, cultivate every square inch of the ground that needs it, smile and do their hair prettily.

Last night I saw the queerest way of catching fish that ever was. We were walking by the canal noticing how many fish were on the surface, and it struck us they might be ill. We met some Frenchman who said "Oui" and "malade" and "usine" which explained the matter. One of them then let down a string with a noose at the end dangling from a stick, so that the noose was just in the path of a young pike drifting in an aesthetically lazy way down stream, and yanked him out with a bash. It was very funny to see, and gave us thoughts of trying the same game on the Germans. Fancy yanking Hindenburg out of the front line one fine unsuspecting morning! The French stoves are worthy of this crafty way of catching fish: I must draw a diagram of one for you. Not a scrap of heat can be wasted. They take up room, but as the French dont litter their houses with useless stuff, this doesnt matter much.

You may be right about the extra bar in the song, very likely it is so. About binding the song more closely, that may be so too; but I cannot alter it out here. I need to play things over and think — for the present — about alterations; and then leave it, and return. Anyway it is good enough. The repetition of that figure in the orchestral version would insist bar after bar on a different thread of the counterpoint, or at a different octave as

then at an octave higher and so forth, with trumpets especially at the loudest with accented notes. The piano version can be made significant enough. There should be another bar at the beginning — the C major chord to be played twice. You please me in saying that it gives you the impression of looking down at a bier. In my mind I saw a picture of some poet-priest pronouncing an oration over the dead and lovely body of some young Greek hero. No song writer ever wrote a better phrase for Beauty than the one at the beginning. At least I begin to fulfill some part of my desire — to see and tell the ultimate truth of things, and especially of the primal things; what H. Belloc calls "Sacramental".

Yesterday, some misbegotten fool took all my books and burnt them. They were in a sack and too near other rubbish sacks for safety as it seems. This includes the French war songs I had promised. You will have to wait for them till I can get back into "rest" again. We are just going up again and will be on business for a little while now. Old Pepys is a great man, really a great man to be so absolutely interested in everything interesting. Of course he is funny, but that is not the final impression left by the book. While in hospital I had a lot to do with a friend of mine in the R.A.M.C. who visited Tolstoi about 1902, and loved him very much. He flew into a tremendous passion with an American Pastor who was dilating on what America was doing for the poor. Curious that even an American pastor should choose such a subject for a long discharge of gas. In hospital there was a Warwick man who described in the gravest tones, how a German officer on a raid against them while bombing dugouts, bombed the bomb store and blew himself to bits; an event which seemed to me very funny indeed — for War.

If Howells gets called up it will probably be for clerical work only, and may we not think it? not for long. It is probably bluff anyway.

The article in the Times Literary on the Navy was very good. Noyes isnt bad, but no more than that, and "Drake" never impressed me. I read a great deal of Kiplings Fringes of the Fleet in a shell hole, during one of the most annoying times we have had. It was during heavy fatigue, and the Bosches spotted us and let fly with heavy shrapnel and 5.9^s.

Just received two delightful letters from Shimmin and Mr Taylor, who turned up trumps with a letter about mountain climbing. Curse me though, they both talk about Bach in a most disturbing manner, and remind me there is another world but that of war; a thing one usually realises, when the bottom of one's mind seems to fall out suddenly with the horror of it all. But those times are very rare. Thank the Lord. Sidney says you are getting on wonderfully; perhaps his operation means permanent health for you. CheerO!

In books, after a careful survey, I find myself reduced to Wordsworth's Excursion, and a few blitherings from the "Pastor" have reduced me to a state of "wet" melancholy. ("Wet" is B.E.F. for half-witted.) I bought that book from a 2^d box in Putney, and the excruciatingly mild engraving at the beginning alone is worth the money; but not to me. It is lucky that some of my books were distributed, and can be begged back. But alas! Walt Whitman and Browning are na poo. However there is a luckful wight that has W.W. him must I cajole.

Books recommended for an invalid

By Land and Sea — Tomlinson

Dumas Memoirs

Huckleberry Finn. Tom Sawyer. Roughing It. (Mark Twain)

Nicholas Nickleby. Pickwick.

London Voices — Keble Howard.

A Book of Stories by Andrieff (?) not very long published. (Or the author might begin his name with a V. Pretty indefinite) Tolstoi's Short Stories, especially the Prisoner in the Caucasus. Stevenson's Wrong Box. New Arabian Nights. Kidnapped. Treasure Island. Davies "Autobiography of a Super Tramp" and "Beggars". All these, or nearly all, if you belong to a library. Arnold Bennetts "Buried Alive" "A Great Man" "Those United States". "Paris Nights" Yoshio Markino's books — a Japanese Artist in London especially. Up in trenches we are not to be allowed to send any letters now. So write whether you hear or not from me:

Yours very sincerely   Ivor Gurney

To Marion Scott   41.39

29 September 1916 (P)

Dear Miss Scott: Today the R C M magazine has come, and so I
have renewed old memories; but, O, curses on my losing the proof!
Bad grammar, bad punctuation. The bad grammar is, if I do not
mistake, the result of a correction by one possessed of more blue
pencil than wits. "*Nor* all the shocks and trials of time cannot" — O
Lor! Thank you very much for the letter and book, both of which
were very welcome. It is not ingratitude that makes me say now that
the second half of Walt Whitman is probably the best.

Ah, dear mamselle would you were only right in what you say
about my health and work! The sad fact is that I do not know what it
is to feel well, and what work I do has to be done in spasms very
quickly over. But — were I to get back now at once, things would
very quickly improve.

It is good news that you are still getting on well. Keep it up. Also
that Howells has been rejected again. He has sent me two part
songs; words by Blake. One of which is absolutely and perfectly
exquisite — the "Shepherd". This is truth and Beauty. It is not *quite*
perfect, some day he will see that a little more might have been got,
but always he must feel a pride in it. And what restraint! A
wonderful thing. The other is pretty, and clever; hardly much more,
but delightful to listen to.

I had an interesting letter from Mrs Voynich today; she also is
doing well, it seems. Please let her also see the Masefield setting,
though when you please, at any time. My letters in future will not be
so long; by special request of the Censor; but do not you stint.
Perhaps in my next letter I may talk about Aeschylus, but not in
this. Going into the ranks is a strenuous change from signalling. I
shall feel much better for it, having become horribly unfit and
fed-up with all things. Thank you, yes; I am better now.

Allow me to indicate that with my change of occupation and of
the season, a corresponding tendency towards substance rather
than luxury in such parcels as you might feel inclined to send . . . .
(A mine of ours has just gone up. Nothing much.)

   Cafe au lait is a necessity.

Would you mind sending a copy of Binyon's To The Fallen? I
might have a shot at that, though not easy to make a song of.
However I might try.

I saw a scrawl on a barn door a few days ago. It will interest you, I
think.
"Where is my wandering Boy tonight?
                    Neuve Chapelle" (and date.)

Thats all, and pretty grim at that. The Autumn sunsets are *very* disappointing. The land is low and exhales mist, which blots sunset and night skies. It spoils even Orion hanging high over the parapet at stand to in the morning. Good bye. With my next letter you shall have F W Hs book. Ah, his name is a part of Autumn — and a Gloster Autumn,— to me. And the falling of leaves has one more regret for me for ever: Yours very sincerely   Ivor Gurney

To MARION SCOTT   41.41

8 October 1916 (E)

Pas de contraband/Lectures pour tous/De la musique De la litterature etc etc etc

My Dear Miss Scott: We are in rest, and at present I myself am in quiet, with a sore foot that has compelled a little respect, so here's a letter. I do not know whether the packet sunk the other day had any of my letters on board, but hope not. There will be bloody fighting if the Germans sink our parcels; if you have sent one I have not received it yet, let us hope frightfulness has not been carried to so extreme a limit. All the things you send arrive in good condition, thank you; and the coffee tablets sont plus convenables que le café au lait. I find now that I have forgotten to ask about your health (of which H.N.H. reports most favourably) and your sisters; but the reason is that I take your letters as they run.

You will understand however that I *do* hope everything goes well with both of you. H.N.H. says you look like becoming stronger than ever. Trés bien. I expect to hear the same news of Miss Stella soon, who I expect, as an energetic person, is tired of being sick, by now.

I am sorry to have forgotten the punctuation of "Strange Service". Everything I do is done in a sort of determined fury after doing nothing, and something is always omitted. Comma after "Service", after "beauty", after "ours", after "being". Should it be "*your* uses consecrate"? (I cant help the bad grammar.)

Thank you very much for the trouble you are taking about these things. I must admit it would please me to see my verses in Osborne's book. Now I have reached your corrections of my punctuation, and approve. You may always alter things like that. As they say in plays, I rely on your discretion.

Vehews on the Setting of Poems

Really, I havent any. If I can set "La Belle Dame sans Merci" well, the reason is; that there is something in me of Keats able to live in the same atmosphere as that in which he wrote his poem; only — being musician, to have told my thoughts in another language. They must not be Keats thoughts only, but mine also. It is not always necessary to read a poem through to start setting it. When one reads in Elroy Flecker —

"High and solemn mountains guard Riouperoux".

One may start there at once. Sometimes it is necessary to be wary and forethoughtful, as when setting "I praise the tender flower", but that is a difficult poem — to set it adequately is a "stunt," I think. So is to set "By a Bierside". It would not do to try to set anything very big, like "By a Bierside" at once, perhaps: But who knows? I had only the first two lines in my mind, or perhaps three; when I began to write, and did not finish till my idea was complete. I did not trouble about balance or anything else much; it came. And after 5 years or so, I will write sonatas in the same way. The points of vital importance are

(1) A *Poem*; that is a collection of words that have inexplicable significance, and gives one visions and vistas.   And

(2) You. (the right "you".)

Being almost devoid of patience, I am always in a hurry to get the first verse done, but that is a thing Time will correct, I hope. You see, all this amounts to "I dont know", and one usually has to be satisfied with that for an answer. N'est pas?

Last nights sunset was a thing would have stirred the devil of War to fine emotions and intangible longings. Gods mind stirred from its late gray calm, and sprang to life in great masses of clouds and streams of colour against a windy-clear West. Even a soldier might be moved.

The Verdun victory is a very great one, do you not think? The Marne; the Thiepval — Contalmaison — La Boisselle day-: and Verdun. Belles victoires! By the way, do you know anything of a General Bohem, or of Notre Dame de Bohem. The girl at the farm here claims proudly a descent from this man who came to France "after a Revolution". Please do find out if possible. It would please her very much, and they are nice people. They asked if the English speak much of their dead, and were astonished, almost incredulous to hear it was not so. I saw in "Public Opinion" a sort of article on the spiritual attitude of the men out here, which was very good.

The truth is, as Hardy says, that the English fall back on stoical fatalism; and whatever it is they believe, it is not Christianity. They go to Church, and desire something spiritual, but it is nothing the

Churches give them. They are fine, but self-reliant not relying on God.

This is a pretty place; flat, with some poplars, and always the same cultivation and red-roofs. Never a vulgar building to be seen, as usual. And O, the twilights of late! Que Dieu soit loué! Of course, Minsterworth has been in my mind; and with Minsterworth, Bach and F W H, whose book the Doctor — in Spite of Himself — has lost. God reward him! But how good to see poplars against the clear west! There's a great Autumn wind raging outside, and freezing my feet in this barn. "Le Matin" and "Le Petit Parisien" flap about helplessly, and the chickens feathers ruffle up. A day to love, and to walk the Cotswolds in.

How the leaves must be flying on Cranham, and up and down and round in swirls on Portway! Painswick Beacon will stand as high and immovable as ever, and Birdlip too; I can do without them. But O for the wild woods and the leaves flying!:

Your sincere friend

Ivor Gurney

Robecq

Apres le guerre is over, the minds of English boys
Will turn to thoughts of England, as a lover to his love,
Where peace is crowned and shining, with never a battle noise,
And death not screams above.

And we shall drink our fill of a never fathomed quiet,
Love among friends deeper far than before,
War shall be the battle of winds and woods in riot
Or seas on sandy shore.

Some may desire forgetfulness of any thought of France.
Some wrapped in home thoughts of France will not reck,
But I shall ever dream how the poplar shadows dance
In the sun at dear Robecq.

———————

Now I must love her because she brings me near
To thoughts of my own home, leagues on leagues away
But then — for that Robecq for beauty must be dear
For her fair fresh look of day

Strangely made are we, flesh and spirit soul and body
One lagging backwards, one aspiring high
But Robecq is part of this whole strange compounded
Until the day I die

———————

To MARION SCOTT   41.42

10 October 1916 (P)

My Dear Miss Scott: Your letter of one sheet with the good news
of your sister has just come; I am glad that affair also is turning out
well. Perhaps Europe, like you two, will be "better after it". (Have
you seen the reviews on Maeterlincks latest book?)

Yes, you are right; weather and trenches no bon at present.

I am sorry not to acknowledged your parcel, for which thank you
very much. The sweets solaced the night hours of many sentries.
The ration was three acid drops. (Further reference to further gifts.)
Another lyrical masterpiece next journey. This letter is dangerously
long already. Did you read G K Cs review of Masefields "Gallipoli"
in the Observer? O, it is a noble piece of praise. There are giants in
our land, and in France; by the line he quotes of Peguy (?) Thanks
very much for L.B. Not *too* easy!

Yesterday, I found a letter to you from me in my pocket, which
must be at least a week old. I know, or think I know that one was lost
which was meant for you, and rewrote it. I hope to goodness it is the
lost one in my pocket and not the rewritten. It has a reference to
Neuve Chapelle.

I had a letter from Mrs Voynich a week ago, which gave great
praise for a thing I sent to her. Have you had it?

>   Nor steel nor flame has any power on me,
>   Save that its malice work the Almighty Will;
>   Nor steel nor flame has any power on me;
>   Through tempests of hell fire I must go free,
>   And unafraid; so I remember still
>   Nor steel nor flame has any power on me
>   Save that its malice work the Almighty Will.

Which is all very well; but what about Mud and Monotony? And
Minnies and Majors?

Your Naval officer was very cautious. The French papers are,
also. But the extracts they give from German papers, and the
comments on the Chancellor's speech, give one to hope much. If I
had £20 — a large supposition — I would bet the end comes . . . by
the end of November 5£. By Christmas £10. By End of Feb £15 and
by August £20. You will not convince me that such already panicky
losers will hold out long. If Hindenburg has reserves Rumania will
hear of it soon. If nothing happens — then no reserves. I am not
convinced that we could not get through at the Somme, if we chose.

You must be enjoying Hindhead now. No Man's Land is in the
last degree desolate, and nothing could seem sadder than the old
willow tree I shoot at during Stand to. There are no Germans and

one must shoot at something at Stand to. It was partridges that a corporal discovered two days ago. He shot 3, but as he had to wait till evening again, the rats got one more than he did. No bon.

Trench dialogue

Cook drops bacon in the mud.

   (Cook). — ! — — — !!! — !

(Passer by, sympathetically) No bon, eh?

(Cook). Compree me explique no bon?

(Passer by.) Na pooh fini, eh?

Cook Wee, no — bon at all.

———————

Such accomplished linguists our gallant soldiers have already become.

Or. *Trench Dialogue* no 2

Entitled *Rations*

    Missing, apply ASC

Prometheus Unbound (off duty.) General expletives.

Chorus (Sympathetic silence)

Prometheus No Bon! No Bon!!

Chorus Dont compree.

Prometheus Compree no grub?

Chorus Whatt!!

Prometheus. Compree no ——— grub?

Chorus (dejectedly) Me compree. Wee, Wee. (Goes off to spread the news.)

Prometheus HE comprees! *And* me.

———————

These are the real Trench dialogues. The Spurious may be told by their unlikeness to these models, so Greek in their perfection of form.

Harvey's book is too much in request here to send it yet. Bide a wee, s'il vous plait.

May I request that your next parcel be more substantial with a cake and some sort of paste. Anchovy lasts a deuce of a time.

    Summer is over
    And the delicate taste
    Of the sweet and dainty lover
    Is turned to the common desiring of fish paste

Will you send me, sometime, the 6^d Edition (Nelsons) of Wild Wales? Or that which once was 6^d. It is a wonderfully companionable book, and long, beautifully trench-fittingly long; although one skips so much in Borrow.

Best wishes to you, and for the quick return to health of *all* the invalids: Your sincere friend   Ivor Gurney

To MARION SCOTT   41.45

25 October 1916 (G)

My Dear Miss Scott: I am very glad you both go on so well; please
continue, and continue to please. (I had written "breathe", because
they are talking about gas-drill behind me). We are in reserve now,
living in huts, and harried by inspections and the awful crescendo of
brightness in buttons and buckles. This last is most dreadful to me;
surely if any deserve blighties it is musicians! Captain Barnes has
one. O lucky, lucky beggar!! "Wild Wales" has come, (yours is a
good joke) and has already given me great pleasure. If one has the
gift of skipping, it is a most companionable book — full of interesting people. That poem of mine was meant for a triolet — but I know
none of the forms; not even the sonnet, to say off at once,without
hesitation. However, what I wanted to say goes all right in its
bastard form, so let it stand, but O for "serenity"! Your own triolet
was very neat I thought.

I am sorry to hear of the accident to Sir Hubert, which is bad
news, since he is so little able to stand shocks.

The Binyon poem is too long, too big, I fear, for any setting I
could give it, but perhaps, perhaps . . . . . .

. FWHs books seems to have disappeared in the lending. But bide
a wee. Before I start my usual discussion, let me ask you not to stop
writing, if you do not hear from me, as there may be little time for
writing for a bit.

I promised to tell you something of the life in trenches. Our last
orders were as follows. — from Stand to 5.30. Stand Down, clean
rifles 6.0. Breakfast 7.30. Work 8.30–12.30. Dinner 1. Tea 4.30.
Stand to 5–5.30. Stand Down. Then Ration fatigue. Listening Post.
Sentry. Wiring-Party. Some of these last all night. One is allowed to
sleep off duty — but not in dugouts. And the average, now the cold
weather has come, and rain, is about 3 hours sleep. Out of trenches,
there are parades, inspections, chiefly for shortages; and fatigues.
RE, Pioneer, and Ration fatigues for battallions in the line. The life
is as grey as it sounds, but one manages to hang on to life by
watching the absolute unquenchability of the cheerier spirits —
wonderful people some of them. After all, it is a better thing to be
depressed with reason than without.

When confronted with a difficult proposition the British soldier
emits (rather like the cuttle-fish) a black appalling cloud of
profanity; and then does the job.

A pal of mine just returned from England — Cheltenham in fact
— tells me that the people there are quite resigned to the war lasting
another year and a half; and also quite resigned to any sacrifices we

may be called upon to make. Tres bien! It is the war spirit, also Zeit-geist.

The weather here is melancholy, except for an occasional nippy morning of bright sunshine.

Bad news from Roumania and good from Verdun and the Somme. I suppose this war will appear much about the same as Christmas 1914, till the trumpet sounds and the walls fall! It seems like a Sunday Pictorial serial, also. Please tell me the opinions of any responsible people who open their mouths to you. Howells memory does him credit, and makes me compliment. I am not sure you are not right about the figure being repeated after "Death opens unknown doors." It may mean a couple of extra bars. About the extra bars that Howells finds — I should need a piano to find that out. The 4 Es must stand, even if the lady should need 4 trumpets to back her up. She is supposed to make a row like a brass band there. This only is admissible beside the repeated notes and it is from an unwilling writer

It is most grand

Compree?

They have loaded us up with all sorts of extra clothing for winter — leather jerkin, vest, body-belt, Lord knows what all. I am afraid books will be too much of a responsibility and encumbrance. Anyhow "Wild Wales" will last me for months and months. And there are the Greek plays. "Agamemnon" is very fine, and the man does know how to translate. I suppose that Blackie is that Greek professor whom Stevenson sat under, and who professed years after never to have seen the young man's face. I wonder how RLS would have come off in the Army, had he lived now and been fit. Very queerly as a whole, I fear.

Well, may both you and your sister continue in the right paths now, and be blest as you deserve. Sickness no bon: Dinner up. Me down. Moi explique that Anglais soldier plenty fond of dîner. Not necessarily Army dinner though, for his thoughts float fondly back to the days of long ago. Yesterday we had pudding: clammy lumps of cold damp flour congealing and hanging together strongly by the force of malice. Goodbye best wishes:

Your sincere friend   Ivor Gurney

To HERBERT HOWELLS   3.16

30 October 1916 (P)

My Dear Howler: Yours was a nice comradely letter to receive;

and of a good fat satisfying length. It was good to get it, and I can stand many such without a shrink (if there is such a word.) First let me congratulate you on having got rid of that tiresome Arts exam, which is a fine thing to be rid of. The rest should be very easy to you. By the way since you have taken French, have you read "Le Malade Imaginaire"? That's great fun, and easy to read.

Now to take your letter bit by bit.

Yes, F W H, is well, but hungry. Tray Bong! No more to be said, except — since I am freed from supposing him to be na pooh, I have only to worry about not being na pooed myself, in order to meet him again.

All nonsense about the rhythm of war! Dr Davies has said that the noise of the guns etc etc. But then, it is only what one expects him to say. Some of the guns have a fine noise; but nearly all is of an insensate fury — too savage and assertive to be majestic. The noise of a Minnie hitting the ground is of a most horrid nature. One does not realise how sensitive the earth is. A "dud" shell may be felt easily a half-mile away. And then the outburst of a minnie explosion! The earth spouts up to a great height, and dugouts rock. It is a horrid sensation to hear a shell coming over you. If it is anywhere near, one feels it in the back of the neck, until it bursts, perhaps 25 yards behind, or even 50. Up till now however, we have not experienced the biggest shells; that being a pleasure to come.

A mine explosion is like a minnie-concussion many times magnified. The ground jumps exactly like a nervy person in a fright, the dugouts rock and the candles fall. Our Co has gained a piece of parchment for steady behaviour in trying circumstances of the sort. (An uncommon honour.) Very lights are very beautiful affairs, especially the German, which glide up in a perfect arc, and burn perfectly also. It is embarrassing to be in No Man's Land waiting for one to fall, as it seems, on top of you. To stand up at wiring, like living pictures, is more interesting than amusing, when Very lights begin to fly.

(O, in future, numbers of Brigade and Division must *not* be mentioned in addresses.)

I am glad Dr Allen is properly impressed by you, and hope that Oxford will soon have a chance of hearing "my" quartett. It was very interesting to read about the dons and so forth. Their cobwebs and superstitions. The subjects they set aside for essays.

You say pretty things about "By a Bierside". I cannot agree with you about the repeated E^s. Somehow they will have to sound like an immortal challenge after the recital of deaths damages and wrongs to man. If the Es are impossible then

It is most grand

It *is* a surprise to hear that Elgars symphony is to be done. It has all the faults you mention. And all the good points, too. Yet

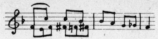

is a phrase of joy (from the 1st movement) which often recurs to me.

Your account of evenings at the Taylors sticks pins all over my inner consciousness. In the language of the 2/5. It hurts my cory, whatever that is. S.S. has probably received a letter from me by now. But O for Clifton Hill! We have to form hard places – callosities – in our hearts against such thoughts:

Yours ever   I.B.G.

To MARION SCOTT   41.48

7 December 1916 (P)

My Dear Miss Scott: I have written a whole letter to you and lost it. Let me write a scrappy one now to tell you that I received your parcels (both) and letters at odd dates, and that they were all of the greatest comfort and assistance. The post is most irregular but things arrive. As for writing letters — there was a whole fortnight passed without a chance of sending a letter off and little of writing one.

On all verse questions I ask you to judge. Do as you please, and thank you for the trouble you are taking about it all. All I have sent you is my own, use what you like for the R.C.M. Magazine.

Please, please send the socks. They ought to be just the thing.

I hope you are all getting better and feeling able to work to some purpose. How does your book progress? As to the sentence of mine you wish to use, use it by all means. I could write a book on the sentence, which I have forgotten — almost. How would this do. "The true aim of the artist should be to perceive the divine significance of tiny things, that rightly seen, "link one in some way to one's immortality" as Hilaire Belloc has said. What has the pedant to do with firelight or the morning blue? He is merely playing with the machinery with which other men have striven to express the inexhaustible wonder of life –– That is equally seen in the huge Alps and the small violet. In the wide sea and the tiny rain-pool." There is so much to say that, in this letter, I cannot find room. Permit me therefore characteristically to indulge in a monologue.

My dear friend, we suffer pain out here, and for myself it some-times comes that death would be preferable to such a life. Yet my chief thought is that I have found myself unfitted for Life and Battle, and am gradually by hard necessity being strengthened and made fit for some high task. I suffer so because of my self-indulgence in the past, and some part of my temperament. This thought upholds me, as it upheld Peter in "War and Peace," and I try to accept whatever comes with patience — to take it with smiles is years away from me — and to feel that I am fulfilling God's purposes. The task is hard and myself weak, but the thing must continue, and may leave me ready to accomplish some great work for which I am intended. All this is to say — that I blame myself much more than I used to, and pray for patience.

We need it too; in face of the Rumanian news. Whatever can be the reason of so surprising a disaster? It beats me completely.

I have received no letters for a few days being in a Rest Station for cold in the inside, going quickly now. I will write again in a day or so to say more than can be said here. Please keep on writing; your letters are my chief link with music and my real life; and it is a great help to feel that my work is not altogether forgotten. // I do not know what those lighters you sent are like. As I was coming to this station I left them with my unfortunate companions to use. We had had no bread for a week. Send substantial things please now; we are out of civilisation. Standard Bread? Yes if you please.

Another letter very soon, but it is very cold in this tent, and I must walk about. I hope that this cold weather wont hurt you and your sister. You deserve to be well by now, and able to do what you want: Goodbye with best wishes

Your sincere friend   Ivor Gurney

To MARION SCOTT   41.49

15 December 1916 (P)

                                                        No letter for days.
My Dear Miss Scott: I have received all your most interesting letters, and now the two parcels also. Thank you very much for all. We need something of the kind now — now that the land is a sea of mud, and thoughts as grey as the weather. I wish I could remember all the questions you have asked me. However, as to the verses question, decide yourself. "So hot my heart desires" is legitimate enough, and the line is not original probably. Compare A E Housmans "How soft the poplars sigh". Or hundreds and

thousands of other such. About everything else, do as you please; not caring overmuch for correctness, but setting more intention on colour and the conveying of truth. "How hot my heart desires" is nearer fire and passion than "So hotly my heart desires." In "Strange Service" — "and uses consecrate" may stand. I *never* keep a copy of such things. I get them off my chest, and send them to you. So it is wise in you to quote in full when you make suggestions, for I could not repeat "The Fire Kindled" as you have it for any money. Only — I remember the end, which was that poem's reason for being. Did you see W B Yeats reviewed again after so long a silence? By Heaven, there must be some fine verse in that book. "Suddenly I saw the cold and rook-delighting heaven", absolutely electrified me. It was glorious to read it. (Quoted in full in the "Sat: Westminster") If you have not read it, I will send you a transcript in my next letter.

Really, we have little time for writing letters lately, and if any were written the officers would not receive to censor them. So my chief pleasure vanished; and as for music! After "Death opens unknown doors", your suggestion that the chief figure should be used is probably right. Anyway

Sketch for H N H

As to all publishers arrangements — that shall be in your most kind care, and thank you very much. All I have sent you hitherto is mine, only. I want badly to write an "All-Hallows Day" and "A Salute", but cannot get time to think, and am not big enough for what I want to say.

I hope your book goes on well, and that you are strong enough to take joy in the writing. As to my sentence you wish to include, I am afraid that my sentences are too hurried and altogether-scribbled to bear quotation. Wait till next letter. Or "What the artist needs is not so much technique, as a greater appreciation of beauty so generally overlooked. Why should not the violet be considered as the chief work of God visible to us? And yet it is the bunch and the coloured vase that must make up most people's mental idea of that lovely thought of innocence. The Artist must learn to feel the beauty of all things, and the sense of instant communion with God that such perception will bring. "To feel Eternity in an hour". Blake knew that to attain to this height, not greater dexterity, but greater humility and beauty of thought were needed. And the composer must judge his work by this standard — that his work be born of sincere and deep emotion sufficiently controlled by the intellect to be coherent and clear. And if his thought be deep and worthy, who shall say it will not shape its proper expression? Which is not quite want I want. Do as you will.

Tonight we have had cafe au lait, our little circle; seated round a tiny hut fire; surrounded by the abomination of desolation and by day depressed by the sight of a piteously ruined church tower; once a glory. And amazed by the sight of a hanging statue. The weather is grey, but thank the Fates! not rainy, and we are grateful for this small mercy. Please go on writing in your usual fashion; your letters giving me great pleasure; and dont expect any regular reply from me. None knows what the next day might bring forth.

———————

There is some chance of leave soon.

———————

After all, my friend, it is better to live a grey life in mud and danger, so long as one uses it — as I trust I am doing — as a means to an end. Someday all this experience may be crystallized and glorified in me; and men shall learn by chance fragments in a string quartett or a symphony, what thoughts haunted the minds of men who watched the darkness grimly in desolate places. Who learnt by the denial how full and wide a thing Joy may be, forming dreams of noble lives when nothing noble but their own nobility (and that seemed tiny and of little worth) was to be seen. Who kept ever the memory of their home and friends to strengthen them, and walked in pleasant places in faithful dreams. And how one man longed to be worthy to celebrate them in music and verse worthy of the high theme, but did not bargain with God, since it is best to accept one's Fate when that is clearly seen.

———————

This has been discovered, and is now to come to you.

I am on a temporary job now, as I may have told you, and consequently have a little more time to myself. But there is no sun, and the whole outlook is depressing.

No letters have yet arrived (Dec 9th) but perhaps tomorrow. If I send a F.P.C. with nothing at all crossed out, please send to me Pte Gurney attached to Sanitary Section, 61 Div.HQ. Or please do so in any case. Perhaps my letters have been returned to England. If so please send 'em again.

———————

It will not take long to forward letters if I am recalled soon. The sign of recall will be, everything crossed out on a F.P.C.

———————

What news of Rumania! What a tragedy! No words can show what a disappointment this is to all our hopes. How — how has it happened?

Good-bye and best wishes for all good things and health most of all: Your sincere friend   Ivor Gurney

To Marion Scott   41.55

11 January 1917 (G)
Sent with "In Flanders".

My Dear Lady of Courtesies: Here is what is meant as a courtesy from me; I hope you will be able to decipher it. This valuable fragment dates anywhere between April 1916 and now. Or is it September or August 1915? Goodness knows. However, here it is, cast up with the flotsam and jetsam in more or less permanent form, with — Wae's me – another orchestral accompaniment, dammit.

Well, it drew me out of lethargy for a space, and was no more trouble than an ordinary fatigue. Surely, it reflects the words?

But on the other hand, ought there to be a figure to bind it together? And (my usual thought) is it Oldfashioned? And though undoubtedly music in places, is it Immature? Or will its freshness carry it off? *Is* it fresh? My Hamlet-mind revolves its usual course — From the desire to set, to — the being too lazy to set, to — Self Castigation, to — The Beastly Bother of Setting, to — Half Disgust, to — Carelessness, to — Will it be Elation? All is Vanity, and until another decries my stuff I care little for it. Please do not trouble about the Binyon verses; I having just received a copy. Beautiful stuff, which must be cut; and where? And altogether rather difficult to do. Wait till I have had a month with the 48 and the songs of Schumann and Schubert and the often heavy Brahms. "What! is *that* The Great Song —? Then let Me Show Them!" Then starts the afore-mentioned round. — Heaven forgive me for my envy-inspired motives! I write from anything but Joy in the Making. More monologues!:

Your sincere friend   Ivor Gurney

To MARION SCOTT   41.55

18 January 1917 (P)

My Dear Friend: Thank you for your letter and the trouble taken in writing out those poems — most interesting to read, but not seeming to me to be great. I like the "Dying Patriot" hardly at all; the Old Ships has some very fine stuff in it.
"Set the crew laughing and forgot his course" is very suggestive — gives one an Odyssean feeling and visions of blue seas, golden sands and tanned men bathed in a light of old adventure. And the end of course is beautiful indeed; Brangwyn in verse?

I wonder whether the three sets of verses, including "Communion", have reached you. It is doubtful whether the book, if book it comes to be, can ever have for title "Songs of the Second-Fifth", since there is so little of the battallion in it. The number of things mounts up — it is over twenty now.

By the way, do you know much of Yeats verse? If not, it will very well repay you to read "Poems" (his first, I believe) and "Poems 1905" (I am not sure of the title.) In the first he is often annoyingly mystical and fluffy haired — if you understand me — but still; there is the close of "Countess Cathleen", The Fiddler of Dooney, a Slumber Song, and other things not clear in my memory. In the second, the plays On Baile's Strand, and "The King's Threshold" will lift you bang right out of yourself. Theres the man who can write blank verse, fluid poetical and English all at once. Also a song called "Kathleen na Houlihan" is very good. These two are all I could get hold of, of all Yeats books. (O Abercrombie! what would you be without Yeats?)

Have you read Synge's Aran Islands, Deirdre of the Sorrows, Well of the Saints? I can recommend these. His other things I do not know so well.

Masefields Everlasting Mercy is well worth reading. So is "Pompey the Great" they say. Wilfrid Gibson has written shoals — but see the two books of Georgian Verse.

Thank you for what you wrote about F W H. I have written to his mother quoting some of it

Song

Only the wanderer
Knows Englands graces
Or can anew see clear
Familiar faces

And who loves Joy as he (Who loves fair joy as he?)
That dwells in shadows?
Do not forget me quite,
O Severn meadows.

Your brown bread parcel came three days ago on the 7th. It was tres bon. Bread and biscuits first rate and most acceptable; particularly as the rations did not turn up one day. How good it was to get bread not dust dry to eat. What is in the stuff to keep it grateful to eat?

West Country

Spring comes soon to Maisemore
And Spring comes sweet,
With bird-songs and blue skies,
On gay dancing feet
But she is such a shy lady
I fear we'll never meet.

Some day round a corner
Where the hedge foams white
I'll find Spring a-sleeping
In the young-crescent night
And seize her and make her
Yield all her delight.

But theres a glad story
That's yet to be told.
Here's grey Winters bareness
And no-shadowed cold

O Spring, with your music
Your blue, green, and gold!

> Come shame this grey wisdom
> With laughter and gold.

———————

All these lispings of childhood do not prevent terrific strafing on the left, where Hell is apparently combined with the angry gods to make things thoroughly uncomfortable. On the whole, we do well to be here. The proper soldier's morality is in general to do what his comrades would do; in the case of Soft jobs to stick to them.

I say, I would like to get hold of some of Verhaeren. He seems to have hold of an artistic dogma that is my foundation stone, and perpetual starting point — that simplicity is most powerful and to be desired above all things whatsoever. Not to be afraid of modernity of theme is again another great virtue. Well, another man to read on leave . . . . (and Stacpooles "Villon" too.)

Would you mind telling me candidly sincerely as possible, what you think of my things were they collected in a book and compared to F W Hs? Personally, I think there is nothing of mine so good as "Flanders". And also, perhaps, "If we return", but outside those, I think my things are better on the whole and more poetical. Do you think there is too much regret in mine? His book has a fine spirit, is mine too much the confession of being unwillingly a soldier? Is there too much of a whine? I would not be out of it — right out of it — for anything: this gives me a right to talk and walk with braver men than myself and an insight into thousands of characters and a greater Power over Life, and more Love. But if I get knocked out — with the conviction sometimes of being able to write the finest sort of songs — then "deevil a ceevil word to God frae a gentleman like me." But it is not good to let this appear since the forfeit of Life is paid by the noblest so often. After all (I take pride in it) there are not many chronic dyspeptics writing verse at the —. I think this is a title of Pride, and gives me excuse to be a little selfish.

Henderson's declaration to the Tribune's reporter was a fine one. Surely we are really first Ally now, at last? France must be first in honour, but more depends on England than on any of us now. And the Tsar's proclamation to the Army and Navy — what a stroke! O it is a great time, and pain is the price thereof and in any case a damned hard time for musicians.

What shall we do? Combine a picture palace with a church job? Or dress as a monkey and turn the handle? Or dress up as Germans to tour in a band?

Behold I show you a mystery. We shall live by correcting each others proofs, in a Home for Mutual Admirers:

Your sincere friend   Ivor Gurney

Book progressing plenty bon?

To MARION SCOTT   41.56
21 January 1917 (P)

My Dear Friend: Thank you for your two letters; including one
that had gone astray.

H N H is a faithful friend to lug my comps: round the country a la
Commercial Traveller; it may mean an extra couple of lines into the
"Gloucester Citizen" notice — with luck. I am sorry to hear the cold
has pulled you back a little, but that should not be unexpected.

It surprises me that you like "Song and Pain" best. It seems the
least of those three. However, Compree this?

Time and the Soldier
How slow you move, Old Time;
    Walk a bit faster!
Old Fool, I am not your slave. . . .
    Beauty's my master!

You hold me for a space. . . .
    What are you, Time?
A ghost, a thing of thought,
    An easy rhyme

Someday I shall again
For all your scheming,
See Severn-valley clouds
Like banners streaming.

And walk in Cranham lanes,
By Maisemore go. . . .
But, fool, decrepit Fool,
You are SO SLOW!!!

And this

Influences
When woods of home grow dark,
    I grow dark too,
Images of strange power
Fill me and thrill me that hour
        Sombre of hue.

The woods of Dunsinane
   I walk and know
What storms did shake Macbeth,
That brought on Duncan's death
   And his own woe.

Strange whispers chill the blood
   Of evil breath.
Such rumours as did stir
Witch and foul sorcerer
   On the lone heath

No power have these on me;
   I know too well
Their weakness to condemn.
Spring will exorcise them
   With one blue bell.

How many do *you* think the book will need? It will include the two
sonnetts already printed in the R C M Mag, and, if you have it, a
Christmas Carol I wrote some time ago. As to the arrangement, if
you will let me have a list of what there is — when the time comes —
I will write one, and you can correct it as you please, who have the
copies. Sidgwick and Jackson would be tray bon. There will also be
a Preface.

      Later   19th of January.

O tis cold! but this barn is pretty strawy, and my oil-sheet is over
my legs, and I go straight on. Merely through boredom I have
turned out another masterpiece today. Also having seen the
Observers appreciation of Ledwidge's description of the robins
note as being like tiny cymbals, I looked for a robin, found one,
heard it — and dont agree, altogether. He must have thought a lot
to have written that description — it being too out of the way to be
spontaneously observed. Now please turn back to the back of page
one, where further grace will flow from my pen.

I think everything you have sent me has arrived now. There are
no stragglers left. Binyons verses, for which I thank you are here
also, but — O I need a piano; though two verses are pretty well
settled in me. For the sum of one franc I got an hour on a faint toned
piano yesterday; but that was not good enough, and there was no
Bach, my fingers were stiff and my mind wandering allways . . .
there was not much pleasure in it; even though it was my first chance
of hearing "By a Bierside", which contains even more of
"strangeness" than I had thought. (As to orchestration, if it comes
to that H N H has absolute yea-or-nay-say.) By the way, what did
Ernest Walker say of my songs, if indeed he said anything?

Poor Folk

1

We wonder how the poor get on in England,
Who wonder how the troops get on in France.
We're better off than many folks in England,
Although we've got to face the Great Advance

2

We've troubles too — the mud, beer not worth drinking,
Sleeping in filth, and feet forever wet;
But women be all night thinking and thinking
Thoughts that they hug with fear, and would forget.

3

We waste good food at times — Why some poor people
Work day and night for what we'd never miss.
Lengths of land and water to cover a steeple
To keep it from them . . . Yes, a bad thing, this.

Oh when at last there comes the Judgement Day,
I'll ask of God some questions that he must
Answer me well, Or I'll choose rather to be
Some free spirit of Hell, or merely dust.

As how the poor who fight so well in France,
Die with a smile for England in some ditch,
Seem never really to get a proper chance —
Their wars and justice made for them by the rich.

———————

Well, the Soft Job is behind me almost now; we are away behind
the line, and going back to the Batt: may mean leave soon. And the
full joy of leave in Blighty will be tasted by me when that is
sometime gone, more strangeness than Joy lies in the present of
such things. And yet — Hot baths — breakfast in bed — tablecloths
— books — late reading — Bach — Great walks — Renewing
friendships — Talks of books — hunting second hand bookstalls —
a sight of St Pauls again and to lose oneself in being in
London. . . . . Strange that should [such?] things should not always
be; and stranger that a stroke of the pen may give these back again,
though but for a short time; now I hope you will not feel the cold too
much and soon will meet a Spring February alive with shy smiles. O
to see "Severn valley clouds like Banners streaming." These are no
vapourings but the mere truth. They are as galleons to the London
wherries, or huffles, as I think the real name is. Au revoir —:Your
sincere friend   Ivor Gurney

O surely the book would do best to appear before the end of the
War?

To MARION SCOTT   41.57

1 February 1917 (P)

My Dear Miss Scott: Yes, back with the Batt; and doing the old
dreary work, purposely designed to the breaking of hearts that the
mud could not break. God reward the old sweats who run Army
training in some suitable fashion of agony!

I have not had a letter from you since two came together — one a
returned letter (O the name of the Sestet is "Serenity") But that was
not long ago. We have shifted about a lot since then but this is a
permanent stay, I think, for some weeks. The Black Prince did
some stunt not far away, but one is too fed up in the Batt: to take
walks for historys sake.

By Jingo but it is cold! The cocoa dregs freeze in the messtins in
this old house, and most of us sleep almost in full kit. Somehow our
contrived Chimney is not a success, and the smoke is occasionally
overpowering. But what of it? There are six Gloucester-or-near and
one Northerner, and on the whole despite the appalling language
things go very smoothly with the crowd of us.

There is Ozzy, who has the sweetness of an angel, the Stretcher-
bearer corporal; certainly of Welsh blood, and certainly one of the
nicest of men. There is Don, never depressed, a corporal who
mocks at all things military, and keeps his place because of his
pluck, and would certainly have no stripes in the first B E F (Old
Sweats Gang.)

Ac Emma, who is Brigade Bomb Store keeper — a lance corporal
of extremely great powers of profanity.

Jem — who is really a nut. An old schoolmate of mine. Rather
like Dick Swiveller in talk, and most india-rubbery as to feature.
There is always laughter where Jem is, and usually at the Army.

Joe who is a lance corporal and Military Medallist. Also a bore,
and the cleanest, most willing burnisher and brusher up in all the
Company. (Curse him!) but a good sort. And Dicky, a small
Northern corporal of terrific energy and pluck, with the most
wonderful eyes. His face shines with courage and chivalry, but as an
old pit hand, his language. . . . is not to be taken seriously.

O, a good lot. And it will be nice to meet them in the after days,
and talk over our past miseries together.

There is no Literary Supplement this week. Too much cleaning
has dessicated my poetic vein. But that's not to be wondered at — I
must have turned out about 15 in the last two months.

How are you all now? This weather is cold but the sun is a gift to
men tired of the grey skies and mire. At least there are hard roads

here and promiscuous trees, and French beer and some sort of cafe, and eggs and chips and a canteen.

The letters from Sir Hubert (and Sir Charles?) did not reach me. I'll write to them and ask them to send them again. Herbert N Howells Esq shall also receive a letter, but I believe I have answered his after some fashion. Likewise the Hon: S.Shimmin.

It is extraordinary how tame-looking the Germany prisoners working on the roads are! And a joy to notice how untamed the French. But to tame the French would be no easy job; the Bosche would have had a rough time of it. Men, women and children always the same — that is, always different.

Ah, but this sunlight, this cold, and these elms remind me so vividly of Minsterworth, and are so sharply different to the present business that I cannot get used to them. They and I are out of place. Goodbye and all good wishes: Your sincere friend   Ivor Gurney

To MARION SCOTT   41.60

3 February 1917 (P)

My Dear Friend: The boys are nearly all asleep — eight of us in a room, say, 14 feet by ten, with a large stack of wood, a fireplace and equipment. Outside it is bitterly cold; in here, not so bad; and good companionship hides many things. A miner, an engineer, a drapers assistant, a grocer, an Inland Revenuist, and a musician among them ("Retreat" sounds)

Firelight

Silent, bathed in firelight, in dusky light and gloom
The boys squeeze together in the smoky dirty room.
Crowded around the fireplace, a thing of bricks and tin
They watch the shifting embers, till the good dreams enter in

That fill the low hovel with blossoms fresh with dew
And blue sky and white cloud that sail the clear air through.
They talk of daffodillies and the blue bells skiey beds
Till silence thrills with music at the things they have said.

And yet, they have no skill of words, whose eyes glow so deep,
They wait for night and silence and the strange power of Sleep,
To light them and drift them like sea birds over the sea
Where some day I shall walk again, and they walk with me.

———————

But O, cleaning up! I suppose I get as much Hell as any one in the army; and although I give the same time to rubbing and polishing as any of the others, the results — I will freely confess it — are not all they might be. Today there was an inspection by the Colonel. I waited trembling, knowing that there was six weeks of hospital and soft-job dirt and rust not yet all off; no, not by a long way. I stood there, a sheep among the goats (no, vice versa) and waited the bolt and thunder. Round came He-Who-Must-Be-Obeyed. Looked at me, hesitated, looked again, hesitated, and was called off by the R.S.M. who was afterwards heard telling the Colonel (a few paces away from me) "A Good man, sir, quite all right. Quite a good man, sir, but he's a musician, and doesn't seem able to get himself clean." When the aforesaid RSM came round for a back view, he chuckled, and said "Ah Gurney, I am afraid we shall never make a soldier of you."

It is a good thing they are being converted to this way of thought at last; it has taken a long time. Anyway the R.S.M. is a brick, and deserves a Triolet.

> He backed me up once;
> I shall never forget it.
> I'm a fool and a dunce
>   He backed me up once
> If theres rust I shall get it
> Your soul, you may bet it
> Yes, all sorts [and in?] tons. . . .
>   He backed me up once
> I shall never forget it.

(Triolet form quite forgotten. Please let me have it.) I fear there will be little writing till this tyranny be overpast.

I am glad you are pleased with your first Chapter, and shall be very interested to see it someday, Someday. Meanwhile le permission n'arrive pas, Curse it.

I left the soft job only to get leave, and if the fates have landed me into an orgy of cleaning without the leave. . . . May the frost have their potatoes, as Don says.

I am interested to see how you compare poetic forms to musical. It will mean what I love anyway – a Good Jaw.

Please dont expect anything of any setting of mine of "To the Fallen" until after the war — and after that. You see, most of my (always slow) mind is taken up with trying not to resist Things, which means a passive unrhythmical mind and music. Wait till I know Wagner and Bach thoroughly, and have a better digestion.

Jem tells a tale of how he wore one of those sachets until he found that, though the rest of his clothes were pretty good, the sachet was quite — athletic. But toujours le gagster — Jem.

Fire went out long ago, while I was hammering out "Firelight". It is too cold to think, write or read. Then sleep. O if I could but dream such things as would mean escape for me. But I never dream, one way or the other. Please excuse writing:

Your sincere friend   Ivor Gurney

To MARION SCOTT   41.63

Received 7 February 1917 (E)

My Dear Friend: Your great letter was received with joy this afternoon, and I sit up late by a candle, well within reach of a wood fire cunningly stolen, to show you I appreciate your criticism and praise.

Also, your putting aside your influenza to make so huge an effort in epistolatation, or whatever the word is, (Epistlery, Epistolification, etc). I am sorry you are sick; even though there is some excuse to be found in the severity of the weather. Cheer up, the operation will make you or break you I feel sure, and flu might be anybodys fate.

Thank you for all the pretty and stern things you say. I relinquish "Framilode" with pleasure; if there is a whole after-the-war for me, little enough verse will I write again — most, *most* probably, I know which is my chief game. "Time and the Soldier" I think will improve on you: it is W. H. Davies, but stronger; and one of my best. You are right about the roughness of some of my work; there is no time to revise here, and if the first impulse will not carry the thing through, then what is written gets destroyed. One virtue I know little of – that is, patience; and my mind is Hamlet's a wavering self-distrustful one, though quick and powerful at its times. Will Peace bring me peace, though?

The four line thing was impromptu. Would "The Dawn" suit it as title? "Serenity" you have received. The first line is "Nor steel nor flame has any power on me". Alack, "Friends" has not arrived! My grief; but still there is a chance of leave. What I said about trying to get a soft job is absolutely sincerely meant. Two years in the ranks, almost 9 months in France, is quite enough for one who loathes the life as I. Who has better right? And who desires Glory less? But the chief reason is, that no man in the company would blame me, but only envy. And anyway, here I am still, though at present in a haven of peace as odd job man at the canteen, which suits me very well. Only, it is undignified to go to frantic lengths for such a job.

[Rough version of "Pain" followed by]

Pain

Pain, pain continual; pain unending;
Hard even to the roughest, but to those
Hungry for beauty . . . Not the wisest knows,
Nor most pitiful hearted, what the wending
Of one hour's way meant. Gray monotony lending
Weight to the gray skies, gray mud where goes
An army of grey bedrenched scarecrows in rows
Careless at last of cruellest Fate-sending.
Seeing the pitiful eyes of men foredone,
Or horses shot, too tired merely to stir
Dying in shellholes both, slain by the mud.
Men broken, shrieking even to hear a gun . . .
Till Pain grinds down, or lethargy numbs her,
The amazed heart cries angrily out on God.

which is also an impromptu — the first of Sonnetts 1917, 5 of them,
for admirers of Rupert Brooke. They will make good antitheses;
but the note of the rest will be quite different; this being the
blackest.

It must be late — I will fill a last pipe, and finish this.

It would seem that "Flanders" *ought* to have some binding figure,
and yet — I think it is all right there. But what of the change from D
to D minor, B♭ minor, C minor, in about 3 bars? Ask Herbert
please, and give him my best wishes and kindest regards when you
see him.

I must to sleep. Goodbye: Your sincere friend   Ivor Gurney

O, it is west Country not County.

To Marion Scott   41.64

14 February 1917 (P)

My Dear Miss Scott: Now we are nestled in a village under a huge
rock; or so it seems, after much regular country. The place reminds

me of Birdlip and Crickley, but O tis ruddily cold. The fates have been kind to be, and still leave me as canteen attendant; which means that though freezing one has time to oneself, and are off those confounded cleaning parades, which so gnaw at my life.

How are you and your influenza now? There can be little gadding about for you anyway, yet who knows what February may bring — that sometimes is so kind and smiles like Spring. Well, good luck to both of us, as I fancy cold is little good to either. And your book, tient-il? If you can sit up and refound musical literature, things will not be so bad; it would be like a Nice Blighty, which I do most heartily desire the Lord to send myself. Anyway do not get too ill to write.

I hope the rest of the family is tres bon, and appreciative of the "fine nipping air". And Herbert how is he? There is some slight recollection in me of having written to him. I wonder whether it is correct. (Yes, it is).

There is more literature in this letter, but not yet. The literal translation of the pretty name of this place is The Star, and there are earthworks all round, remains of 1870. Soon we go up again to the trouble; soon Fritz will be hurling high explosive compliments at us with gusto, and we close to the parapets. Well, tres bien, if there is no soft job, the hard one must do, but the first is better.

The title of the book I would prefer to be "Songs from Exile, or Songs from the Second Fifth" as subtitle. That is the real title, and besides, the second needs writing up to which I am unwilling to do.

Home-sickness

When we go wandering the wide air's blue spaces,
Bare, unhappy, exiled souls of men;
How will our thoughts over and over again
Return to Earth's familiar lovely places,
Where light with shadow ever interlaces –
No blanks of blue, nor ways beyond man's ken —
Where birds are, and flowers; as violet, and wren,
Blackbird, bluebell, hedgesparrow, tiny daisies,
O tiny things, but very stuff of soul
To us . . . so frail . . . Remember what we are;
Set us not on some strange outlandish star,
But one love-responsive. Give us a Home.
There we may wait while the long ages roll
Content, unfrightened by vast Time-to-come.

Servitude

If it were not for England, who would bear
This heavy servitude one moment more?
To keep a brothel, sweep and wash the floor
Of filthiest hovels were noble to compare
With this brass-cleaning life. Now here, now there
Harried in foolishness, scanned curiously o'er
By fools made brazen by conceit, and store
Of antique witticisms thin and bare.

Only the love of comrades sweetens all,
Whose laughing spirit will not be outdone.
As night-watching men wait for the sun
To hearten them, so wait I on such boys
As neither brass nor Bosches may appall,
Nor guns, nor sergeant-major's bluster and noise.

These Sonnetts. For England. Pain. Homesickness. Servitude, and
one other; are intended to be a sort of counterblast against
"Sonnetts 1914", which were written before the grind of the war
and by an officer (or one who would have been an officer). They are
the protest of the physical against the exalted spiritual; of the
cumulative weight of small facts against the one large. Of informed
opinion against uninformed (to put it coarsely and unfairly) and fill
a place. Old ladies wont like them, but soldiers may, and these
things are written either for soldiers or civilians as well informed as
the French what "a young fresh war" means. (Or was it "frische
(joyful) Krieg". I cant remember, but something like it was written
by the tame Germans in 1914.) I know perfectly well how my
attitude will appear, but — They will be called "Sonnetts 1917."

"Friends" is with me, and is as a friend. I love the book and have
written to Gibson saying so. He is a man who would well be worth
meeting. Belloc, Masefield, Yeats, Gibson, Kipling, Tomlinson —
O have you read Tomlinson's "By Land and Sea"? It is a travel
book about S. America. Bon, in the extreme. What do you think
now of Germanys chance of collapse . . . . ?

I hope I have not offended you anyway by my outburst about
"The Fire Kindled". I had thought it better in my mind than it really
was, and the shock made sparks. Some of it I dont remember at all.

Go on and prosper and be kind; and tell me when to turn the lyric
tap off. It spouts freely at present, but I desire to see my only book
of verse in the dignity of print.

Meanwhile, Mamselle I am your most obliged servant and
sincere friend   Ivor Gurney

To Marion Scott

14 February 1917 (P)

My Dear Friend: Thank you so much for your letter of the 5th of Feb: I think everything of yours has come so far; quite a lot came close together, comments on song etc etc It is still intensely cold here, but the sun is warm (when the canteen attendants see it anyway) and the afterglow is always beautiful.

The order of the Battallion work is someways as follows. Reveille at 7. Parade at 7.45 for some footling inspection, but always clean as to chins and buttons and boots. Parade again at 9 for the sort of drill recruits do, this lasts till 12.45. In the afternoon, usually nothing. Every other night, night operations of some comic sort. Lights out at 9. Most of the spare time till now has been in cleaning, always cleaning equipment. For anyone with more sensibility than the yokel it is a life infinitely full of pain. Whether the wind blows gales of icy needles with the temperature below zero; always the same. And no fires now, in most billets: From this, you will gather that "Rest" is merely a technical term. If you will take the trouble to copy out all those things one by one, please do so, and thank you — but dont write shorter letters because of it.

I shall be content if you attend to all matters of punctuation and merely ask my opinion on doubtful points. The name, as I have said is

Songs in Exile
or Songs from the Second-Fifth

The first poem will be To Certain Comrades; the last poems, the five sonnetts. (Perhaps an Envoi also.) Any poem you think needs correction, send on, and fear nothing. And mix up things as you please, for I know you can be trusted. The (pretty long) preface is nearly ready, please get it in unless they firmly refuse to have it. But — if you do all this, punctuate as you please, and take no notice of any marks of mine.

"Under the Greenwood Tree" is perfectly charming, and very Shakespearean in feeling I think. Hardy is a marvel.

I see Tolstoi's "Cossacks" is published in the Worlds Classics; how good the review in the Times was! Do you not see some likeness between Tolstoi's sense of beauty and that of Beethoven? So constantly do I feel the two in company . . .

With these beautiful days it becomes more of a loss to feel music and books so far away, and my county. And the days slipping past so quickly in which I ought to acquire technique and get rhythm into

my mind. Once I get back, for a while I will simply reek songs; mere exudations; while I study hard Wagner and Rachmaninoff and the Russians; also the 3 B's and Folk Song for pleasure; and Chopin for piano technique. But, Time, you are so slow,
and hold the secrets of doubtful things not yet disclosed.

You will please supply indignation to the description of the ordinary routine here; and understand why the words are calm . . . Yet we are most volunteers and not prison-conscripts. Toujours le même, I believe, everywhere now. And nobody seems to care, as the song says.

Good-bye and good-luck with the influenza:
Your sincere friend   Ivor Gurney

To Mrs Voynich
41.61

February 1917 (E)

Dear Mrs Voynich: Thank you very much for your letters and parcel — which came in rather a God-forsaken place where bread was most difficult to obtain; one had to lie in wait for it, with plots.

You are very lucky to be so successful with your work; it makes me heave sighs like a Stokes gun to think of it. And to walk in nights of storm not controlled by any military authority, free to set Villon to music or watch the moon as your desire leads you. O to feel my hair — longer than now — blown by big winds of the Belloc kind. (See "On a Great Wind"). And to see

"Jagged Malvern with a train of shadows".

What is the cheapest edition of Villon? Is there one in Dents French series (after "Everyman"?). Or one smaller still? There ought to be something cheap in paper, some common French publication.

What difference will America's attitude make? They say today that she has declared war, but the paper only speaks of broken relations. Que le guerre fait finir bientôt!

You hold me for a space — What are you, Time?
A ghost, a thing of thought — an easy rhyme.

And I shall once again,
For all your scheming,
See Severn-Valley clouds
Like banners streaming,

And walk in Cranham lanes
By Maisemore go. . . .
But, Fool, decrepit Fool,
You are S O S L O W ! ! !

Round us here are earthworks and impressive earthworks that I
thought were ancient Gaulish; but today un petit garcon m'informait
that they were of Soixante-Dix. So my dreams of old battles have
partly evaporated. There is a big rock here, and the village nestles
thereunder. Some of this country is well worth painting; but not like
Cornwall, and Blighty is a far dream.

Go on and prosper in your work, for it is nice and encouraging to
know that someone is hard at it. As for leave . . . Congestion is the
only talk now.   With best wishes:
Yours very sincerely

Ivor Gurney

To MARION SCOTT   41.65

15 February 1917 (P)

Preface

This book stands dedicated to one only of my friends, but there
are many others to whom I would willingly dedicate singly and in
state, if that did not mean the writing of 40 books of verse and
dedications; a terrible thing for all concerned . . . So that under the
single name and sign of homage and affection, I would desire such
readers as come to me to add also — To my Father and Mother; F W
Harvey, (also a Gloucestershire Lad;) Miss Marion Scott, whose
criticism has been so useful, and she so kind; in spite of my
continued refusal to alter a word of anything. The Vicar of
Twigworth; H.N. Howells, (and this is not the last time you will
hear of him;) Mr Hilaire Belloc, whose "Path to Rome" has been
my trench companion, with the "Spirit of Man"; Mr Wilfred
Gibson, author of "Friends", a great little book; many others also;
including Shakespeare and Bach, both friends of mine; and last but
not least — 5 Platoon, B Co, 2/5 Glosters; who so often have
wondered whether I were crazy or not. Let them draw their own
conclusions now, for the writing of this book it was that so distracted
me. . . . This is a long list, and even now does not include old Mrs
Poyner that was so jolly and long-suffering; not my boat "Dorothy"
now idle in the mud; though a poet sung of her full of glory at
Framilode.

Even as I write the list becomes fuller, farther extended, yet a
soldier must face pain and so it remains shorter by far than might be.
I fear that those who buy the book (or, *even*, borrow) to get

information about the Second-Fifth will be disappointed. Most of the book is concerned with a person named Myself, and the rest with my county, Gloucester, that whether I die or live stays always with me; — being so beautiful in itself, so full of memories; whose people are so good to be friends with, so easy-going and so frank.

Some of the aforementioned people I have never had good fortune enough to meet in the flesh, but that was not my fault. I hope they will forgive my using their names without permission. Ah, would they only retaliate in kind! That is however not likely, as I never was famous, and a Common Private makes but little show.

All the verses were written in France, and in sound of the guns, save only two or three earlier pieces. May well be indulgent to one who thought of them so often, and whose images of beauty in the mind were always of Gloucester, county of Cotswold and Severn, and a plain rich blossomy and sweet of air — as the wise Romans knew, that made their homes in exile by the brown river, watching the further bank for signs of war.

Compree. Ballad also
Ballad of the Three Spectres

As I went up by Ovillers
In mud and water cold to the knee,
There went three jeering, fleering spectres,
That walked abreast and talked of me.

The first said, "Heres a right brave soldier
That walks the darky unfearingly;
Soon he'll come back on a fine stretcher,
And laughing at a Nice Blighty.

The second, "Read his face, old comrade,
No kind of lucky chance I see;
One day he'll freeze in mud to the marrow,
Then look his last on Picardie.

Though bitter the word of these first twain
Curses the third spat venomously;
"He'll stay untouched till the War's last dawning,
Then live one hour of agony.

Liars the first two were. Behold me
At sloping arms by one — two — three;
Waiting the time I shall discover
Whether the third spake verity.   Feb 1917

Not so bad eh?

By Gum, what will All the Good People of Gloster think of the Ugly Duckling they have hatched? There will be Some Surprise, what with one thing and another if the Tome appears. Roll on that time as soon as possible. Good luck with the Flu:

Your sincere Friend Ivor Gurney
Sunday night

To MARION SCOTT   41.62

17 February 1917 (G)

My Dear Friend: Here we are, back in our little holes; with strict instructions not to show our heads above ground; in Reserve in fact — deucedly uncomfortable; and expecting to become still more so. To get to this haven of rest we had a 6 hours march with twenty minutes halt, perhaps. So, as you may imagine, there is no literary supplement this week. Nobody has any water; there may be none for 12 hours or more, and bully beef and biscuits and a little bread provide the wherewithal for philosophers and soldiers to exist. For God's sake write letters, no-one knows how long this will last. Well, long enough I have existed upon hope, and why not now? And why should we not be cheerful, since this is better than the first line?

Farewell, Canteen, thou not un-appreciated, but not over-appreciated Home to me: thou wert at zero too oft, but there was freedom in thee and a fairly interesting occupation. Fare thee well. And only the day before yesterday, I was asking myself whether I ever should be able to write a good long movement, or how long it would take! O Evening Dreams!

Sir CHHP[s] two letters have arrived, and are very nice too. But niceness makes me yearn.

Sidney's sister also came up with a good one: (I hope she wrote with cleaner hands than mine).

You see, I am so over-wrapt up in myself, that there is little thought left for other people, but all the same it occurs to me that you are sick or sickish with influenza. Soon I hope your book will begin to swell in spite of all drawbacks, Flu or Female Musicians; and soon I hope, too, to be able to see it myself and let fly torrents of praise or vituperation. Duggy Haig seems pretty confident, and Germany must be having the worst sort of time; but O books of any kind seem a long way off.

As for my own — "Friends" is with a Trench Mortar Man. "Wild

Wales" and R.Bridges "Spirit of Man" are with me. The rest are in the care of a Frenchwoman at Laventie, and someday I must send for them. Anyway, who could read 'Aeschylus' now? "Under the Greenwood Tree" is with the Sigs.

Harvey's book is now known to be with the Brigade Major, so there is a chance of getting it still.

The French are on rations now, and their soldiers dont like it — the only drink about here being wine at 4 francs the bottle. They are a much more cheery lot than ourselves though; I cannot say what they are like in trenches, but out — they are quick to smile and move about quicker than we. All the German prisoners I have seen anywhere save at Havre seem very tame creatures and not at all savage creatures.

In the mind of all the English soldiers I have met there is absolutely no hate for the Germans, but a kind of brotherly though slightly contemptuous kindness — as to men who are going through a bad time as well as themselves. Occasionally — as last night — you get nasty remarks about Lloydd George "Fighting to a Finish" — at home but not often. The whole thing is accepted as a heavy Burden of Fate. I have never been able to accept anything that way myself, and can only envy those who have such an attitude. Best luck with all sickness: Your sincere friend   Ivor Gurney

To MARION SCOTT   41.68

23 February 1917 (P)

My Dear Friend: Soon we are to be at work again — after the Rest — that is we go into trenches; for myself there are not many regrets, for Resting is a tiring business; and though being shelled is not pleasant, yet the escape from death gives in itself some slight interest in life. Anyway, Spring's first signs cannot be so far off now, and the cold relaxes a little. I hope you are progressing towards health now. Do you not get sunshine? There is hardly ever a cloud here, and the sun shines its very best sometimes. April will dispel the last sign of illness in everybody save les Allemagnes.

I am glad you like "Firelight", and as you say it ought to be popular.

If a full stop is substituted for the semicolon at the end of line 2, verse two, the sense will be clear, I think. Bluebells', it is, not, bluebell's. If you will send a complimentary copy of the RCM.M to Miss M Hunt, 54 Wellington St Gloucester that will be very bon;

also another, if there is a spare one to Mrs Chapman, St Michaels, Castle Hill, High Wycombe, Bucks.

I dont think there is any need to send me the original of "The Fire Kindled", I not being enough interested really. What I want to do with this book is

(1) To leave something definite behind if I am knocked out
(2) To say out what Gloucester is, and is to me; and so to make Gloucester people think about their county
(3) To have *some* good stuff in it, whatever one might say about the whole.
(4) To make people realise a little what the ordinary life is.

Anyway it was good fun, writing; and gave me something to do.

"Hail and Farewell' I think will stand; it is impossible for me to try and perfect these things, save after 6 months of life in peace and beauty. Would you prefer (the first draft):

> But I — the fool at arms,
> Musician, poet to boot,
> What joy to me, what charms
> In this salute?

You are right about the dots in "Pain"; alter as you think.

As for the "Elizas", your choice is all right, yet I rather wondered you should leave out "Orpheus" and include "Under the Greenwood Tree", but this will not worry me. Herbert's letter has not arrived as yet.

As for leave, that is possible, but probable? Soon? Je ne sais pas.

I am sorry you have lost a good friend, and by so foul a thing as cancer, and hope you will not feel separated too much.

Never yet have I lost any real friend, and so it is a guess to me how another may feel, but Death is a very little thing, so long as dishonour does not lie there.

I wonder how FWH has got on in his prison lately . . . My thoughts of England are first and foremost of the line of Cotswold ending with Bredon Hill, near Tewkesbury, and seen with him. Or the blue Malverns seen at a queer angle, from the hayfield, talking when War seemed imminent, and the whole air seemed charged with fateful beauty. For illness I can feel strong sympathy, but Death means not much to me. Either I do not care much, or care a great deal and am not separated.

"To the Poet before Battle" is all right. Alter line 12 of "Afterwards" to —

"The troubled heart shall know a presence near".

The first word is "Those".

Here are two more with this, one of which you may have already received; I send it again being doubtful.

As for the evening of "Firelight's" concoction, I will do my best to find out; it was about two days after I returned to the batt:

It sometimes puzzles me what you find to interest you in my letters, since what is not verse, is either about verse or myself. You support all this very bravely, and deserve better things: but so much it means to me to cling to verse, the one interest (now cafe au lait is not possible) left to me in life, and so good to talk about it, that I fear you will have to suffer yet more.

All I can think of is — What an unholy waste of time this is, what a lot I have to learn, and how long it will take me to learn to write one good sonata movement; to satisfy C.V.S.

As for my comrades — after the war I can be interesting about them, but not yet. Goodness knows I am fond of them — some of them; but I cling to life by deliberately trying to lose myself in my thoughts of other things; trusting to some innate pluck in me to save me at moments when pluck is wanted. This is not the way to make a soldier of oneself — just the opposite in fact; and increasing sensibility must balance the advantage gained by concentration of thought on other things. But though I were sure of saving my life if I altered, and losing it did I not, still I should be the same, having set all on the future.

Forgive all this egotism, and may your book and you progress cheerily. Continue, flourish and triumph, and put up a little longer with my cockeyed epistles. With best wishes:

Your sincere friend   Ivor Gurney

                    Afterglow   to FWH

Out of the smoke and dust of the little room,
With teatalk loud and laughter of happy boys,
I passed into the dusk. Suddenly the noise
Ceased with a shock; left me alone in the gloom,
To wonder at the miracle hanging high
Tangled in twigs, the silver crescent clear —
Time passed from mind, Time died; and then we were
Once more together, in quiet, you and I.

The elms with arms of love wrapped us in shade,
That watched the ecstatic West with one desire,
One soul uprapt; and still another fire
Consumed us, and our joy yet greater made —
That Bach should sing for us; mix us in one
The joy of firelight and the sunken sun.

                                            Jan 1917

Praise

O Friends of mine, if men mock at my name,
Say "Children loved him".
Since by that word you will have far removed him
From any bitter shame.

To MARION SCOTT   41.69

4 March 1917 (P)

My Dear Friend: Here is an odd letter written with the filthiest of hands but the best of intentions. The mail has not arrived for two days, but tomorrow may bring something from you.

Today I have been thinking of what might be instead of what is. The conditions for us in support are not so bad as in the front line, because one can move about, and we manage to get a fire going with damp wood. The thing is to suffer things without a sense of revolt; to accept as much as possible. And to forget the past — unless in the way I try to view it; as a means to write songs. And if I come out of this alright, there are two priceless lessons learnt — the first, that the price of almost anything that one desires worthily, is only Pain, ("only agony, and that has ending") and the knack of getting on with people, which I have developed out here to a much greater extent than heretofore. So I fix my mind on these two possessions of mine and think what they will mean to me in the future. Long ago I decided that to accomplish what I wish was worth a great deal of pain and was ready to undergo it. Perhaps the last 6 years will be found sufficient by the Master of Beauty, and he may think fit to set free in me unknown forces of beauty to gladden men as some have gladdened myself. With my heart comforting itself with these things I try to accept mud and cold feet as prices, prices; and wait for my repayment. And if a soon end is meant for me, and my hopes are destined not to be fulfilled here, then though disappointment lies in that and very keenly. Yet who can say what lies beyond? Only — waiting for ever, and hardships, and doubt are heavy burdens — and may the time be not long.

Now I feel better, having "unpacked my heart with words", though music would suit me better — the G mi Prelude in the 2nd book for example. Or my book of "English Preludes" of which only the name is yet in existence; even of thought.

There are no more verses; the sonnet "England" not having taken shape, and anyway that needs quiet and comfort — but chiefly quiet.

You see this letter is all about myself, but you must have learned to expect that by now, and let me but once out of this little of my thought shall be said in words; and there will be things beautiful and comfortable surrounding one to absorb the mind.

Nevertheless, though this is My Letter — so to speak — I will spare a word to say that it will please me greatly to hear you are well out of your sickness, and well on with your book. O to answer a query — I have no certain Dearest Prelude. Perhaps the E major 1st book (*my* arrangement — NOT Bach's) or the C major or G minor or A♭ or F major from the 2nd Book. I do not know the B♭ minor (2nd book.) Surely the 48 is the wisest of all the works of man? It trains one like the noble touch of Pain; yet who could understand Bach without having suffered? The song at the close of Masefield's "Good Friday" is beautiful, is it not? I saw it in the "Times".

Good-bye, and best wishes: Your sincere friend   Ivor Gurney

To MARION SCOTT   41.71

5 March 1917 (P)

My Dear Friend: Thank you so much for all your kindness. And I am delighted you are able to scrape and bow again — this is very good news. I hope to receive more of the same kind now the warmer weather — *should* be here, but of course it *is* warmer, though not comfortable. There are an enormous number of points to answer, and I will try to get through them straight away as they come up in your letters.

Very well — a baritone for "By a Bier side". You are right about "For England" and "Home-sickness". I will alter "For England". "February Day" I may think it worth while to alter and keep.

Does it matter very much if someone has used the title "Songs from Exile"? How would "Remembered Beauty" or "Beauty remembered" do? I shall wait a little and think, for a good title is important. "Songs before Dawn". Anyway, you have a perfect right to do what you like, except alter. You may cut out anything you think is not worthy if there are enough things to make up the number. At present it is too cold and muddy to write. Perhaps in a fortnight . . .

Preface

The name of dedication is Margaret Hunt. The name that puzzles you is Mrs POYNER. (Sidney knows her.)

"Gloucester people" are the two words omitted.

Name to be signed at end of Preface is Ivor Gurney. I write B in my name only because I like writing Bs.

———————

"To certain Comrades" may stand as it is. The lines should be printed so that the initial letters are under each other.
Compree
    Living————————————————
    Before————————————————
    And though our spirits etc
Punctuate as you please all the way through the book — but never too much. Curse the pronouns; my feet are too cold.

Do as you please with the merely pretty "Carol", but it would do to dedicate to Micky Chapman. So let it stay.

I want to write my last Sonnett, but that refuses to come, so much is there to say.

The grammar of my book is, technically speaking, often shaky. Never poetically. I say what I want to say.

Sidgwick and Jackson first.

Elkin Mathews second, is my best chance and choice. If these publishers cannot sell, then none can.

There is a lyric in my mind — just the beginning. "Starlight in Water".

Starlight in water stirs the secret dreams;
Starlight in water;
Starlight in water troubles hidden deeps;
Starlight in water.

———————

Goodbye and good luck and thank you.

Another letter soon perhaps. May it contain the last sonnet and the correction of "To England", also "Poor Folk".:
Your sincere Friend   Ivor Gurney

To MARION SCOTT   41.76

7 March 1917 (G)

My Dear Friend: Still in trenches, still in the mud, and watching lucky — and some unlucky — people going out with trench feet, and men almost weeping for exhaustion and sheer misery, stuck to the knees with some distance of torment still to traverse. Why do not I fall ill? God knows! The soul in me is sick with disgust, and hospital now would be a good stroke of business. The unfortunate part of it for me is that the ordinary and best way to face these things, is to face them; whereas my mind, by inclination and long training can only try to turn away and remember such things as a certain Spring evening at Minsterworth when all was gold save the shadows of golden trees black on the ground of orchards: and FWH. was with me.

Here is the Alteration. Will it do?

Where never the late bird is heard to sing . . .
And (or for) England's image must indeed be slow
To fade. How shall dull her sombre glow
Of Autumn sunsets, or the fire of Spring?

Song of Pain and Beauty

O may these days of pain,
These wasted-seeming days,
Somewhere reflower again
With scent and savour of praise.
Draw out of memory all bitterness
Of night with Thy Sun's rays.

And strengthen Thou in me
The love of men there found,
And eager charity,
That, out of difficult ground
Spring like flowers in barren deserts, or
Like light, or a lovely sound.

A simpler heart than mine
Might have seen Beauty clear
Where I could see no sign
Of Thee, but only fear.
Strengthen me, make me to see Thy Beauty always
In every happening here.

Please write anyhow. When we get back in rest, I may be able to think more clearly, and see exactly what I want to say in my final sonnett. And O, for the days when, with cigarettes, biscuits and milk all round me, and a good fire and a piano, I shall joyfully attempt to say what is in me in music.

I am glad they are going to do my two songs. Vaughan Williams wrote me a friendly little note, in his queer writing. We are to know each other afterwards . . . Afterwards; toujours apres le guerre.

They are shelling this place, but no-one takes any notice, being too fed up. Fires are forbidden in daylight, but it is better to die by a fire than live without one.

And as for snipers, who cares for those. Why yesterday one of our heavies landed 6 shells about 30 yards on our left, just behind our own lines. Cheerful Tommy Atkins takes not much notice; it is only a Bairnsfather incident: Yours sincere friend   Ivor Gurney

I hope the violin is progressing?

To HERBERT HOWELLS   3.5

11 March 1917 (G)

My Dear Howler: Your appointment pleases me immensely, and when the letter reached me, in a crowded dugout, full of men weary of labouring in the mud, it was as light in the darkness. How well I remember that exquisite Close with the Cathedral so delicate and yet so strong soaring like a pure desire. It gave me hope also for myself that one of my friends had had good fortune — the pleasure was a little selfish, so far selfish; and I thought how I might return to College and come down one day to see you, full of joy at work accomplished and anxious to see yours. And "Lady Audrey's Suite". Of course you deserve all these things, but your getting them must nevertheless be received with welcome at the start. Well done! go on and prosper; and take all the joy out of life you can. It has been very good of you to score and rescore my songs; I could wish for no better hand. Do as you will with them in the details. You know how hard it is to settle tiny points away from a piano, and particularly for a slow minded cuss like me. You have all my trust. But, old chap — aint my song pure Gloster? Standing off from it, I can see the whole plain and the tiny dear places — orchards, roads winding through blossomy knolls — as clear as they really seem in that crystal air. The memory has comforted me in the long blank spaces as if it had been the work of another.

The verse tap has not been running very freely lately, we having had the longest time so far in the line and in the most appalling mud. Well it cant last for ever, and a determination and fixed will toward Beauty such as mine must have its reward somewhere.

Yes, the writing was R V W^s, and a nice letter it was too. Nothing much to tell you of it, save a wish we should meet after the war. A hope which I share, as you may think.

By the way have you read Cobbett's Rural Rides? I think you

would like it, though just an itinerary undertaken for the sake of agriculture. But its quality of English would please you. The more letters you write the better I shall be pleased. Miss Scott's letters are most valuable things to me, as they talk of all the things I try to remember, and so give me something to feed on. And she is a most valuable critic although I take so little notice of her advice. I hope someday you will set a cycle of my songs, or at least, a group of songs; I hope they attract you that way. And a couple of guineas a time from a successful composer is not to be sneered or snorted at . . . . And all the while I am thinking about the Close, and you set somewhere in it, and Bachs majesty and passion filling the nave . . . O take double joy for my sake, and tell me something of it that I may share again. Goodbye and best wishes. Please remember me to Dr Alcock: Yours ever   I.B.G.

To Marion Scott   41.78
23 March 1917 (P)

My Dear Friend: Things are beginning to move, and no one knows when may come the next opportunity for writing. I have just received your letter of March 11th, and a rumour hastens me on to answer it. Your letter to Osborne is a model of tact, business-method, discretion, savoir faire etc etc Do not consult me about these things, but do as your far more experienced judgement may lead you. But dont I wish he had some later ones!

I am glad that your article has been postponed, and you set free to do as you will for a little. And it is good news that you are able to play sonatas again, and with a sympathetic pianist. It gives me a feeling of sharing your good-fortune to read of it; may your strength increase and give you hours a day of it.

Concerning Verse
Requiem no. 2. Either comma or dash after "England's".
Requiem no. 3. 3rd line
For these were slain, so strangely still reclining.
Is the "Song" worth reprinting.

The "homeward-come" in verse 2 the last word in line 3 is a-quiring. Should the word "could" in "Acquiescence" last line but one, be "can"? (I don't care for any of these things much. Just padding.)

Well, that finishes the replies to your letter. One parcel of yours I have received — not yet the other. All the letters have arrived and all given pleasure. O to return to England and my friends! Such joys are there as are dangerous to imagine at present; not all at once will my mind and body become sound, but it cannot be so very very long before Joy becomes "used to me". And as for piano technique, 3 weeks will give me all since my brain is so much clearer.

The new state of things entered upon by the German retreat may mean little letter writing. This is the reason why I hasten to reply, though never have I felt more acutely the inadequacy of words. Last night and this afternoon have been so beautiful that my mind has been filled with Blighty thoughts. But consider what a queer past I have to look back on! Either I am a great musician or a chronic neurastheniac! There is nothing outside it, for the visible world is hardly to be seen by me unless music hallows my spirit with beauty and toughens it by the necessary work. You will be glad to hear however that as a personality I am rather popular in my company. It pleases me this, as so I know myself nearer Walt Whitmans perfect man; equal to shepherd and President; equal and familiar. O the joy to be able to go into a little Cotswold inn and drop into conversation with the nearest man! And that, compared with my tongue-tied shyness of 3 years ago. And if not here, then in the Shades I will be friends with men contemptuous of the fate to which some Power has doomed them, jovially drinking in some phantom pub over doubtful takes and unprintable denunciation of the Infernal NCOs.

You patient correspondent, though you make no complaint, how should you not be tired of the continual self-analysis which makes up the bulk of my letters! And yet those letters are the safety-valves of my discomfort. It is a cheap amusement — grumbling — pleasing the writer and leaving the reader to read or not as she pleases. I absolve myself therefore from half the blame, take the other half if you please. Once I etc etc there will probably be little of discontent in such few letters as I may write.

We have all been overeating to make up for our three weeks in the line, and indigestion has brought a mood of spiritual blight — penitence for unknown faults, elegiac, moribundish, Symphonie-Pathetiquish mood. O but one night walk round Cranham would dispel all this. Will you please keep on writing though you may not hear for a bit. And as for that final sonnet . . . . Bless you, there is not a patriotic man in the whole BEF. And how should I — poet, musician, fool-at-arms . . . . . ?

Goodbye and many sonatas, Unless I write very soon, more verse-books off: Your sincere friend   Ivor Gurney

To MARION SCOTT   41.79

29 March 1917 (P)

My Dear Friend: It is too dangerous to move towards my valise, where your letter lies, there being too many men looking for seats, and the fire being too comfortable.

Your apologies for your letter were not needed; it was by no means a dull letter; but your thinking so seems to show that you must have been tired or not well when you wrote it.

I hope you are well however — as well as can be expected, and expecting to become still better.

The news that my poor versifications are to be shown to RB: gives me no pleasure at all. I did not want technical criticism, being quite aware that good stuff does not come out of such a one as myself in a hurry. It would need quiet and continued thought — whereas the things are finished as quickly as possible: often finished at one go. Things like the "Signallers Vision" are meant to appeal to such people as are in this room with me — not to the experimenters in Greek metres. However your second letter having arrived, and the chance of an interesting meeting for you being there made apparent — all I will say is, that at present there is neither Time nor energy to do what might be done. The final sonnet seems fated not to be written; we being on short rations and hard work. Thank you for copying out Drinkwater's poem, which makes me feel small. It is beautiful; someday I will drown myself in such.
(This is March 24th by the way).

I am afraid one of my letters has got lost. Have you received some verses beginning "O may these days of pain"? If not, directly you say so, I will write them out again, being rather proud of them.

———————

Well what thundering interesting things are happening now! O if I but knew German! Lots of newspapers, some quite late have come my way; and a book of short stories about Military Life — supposed to be humorous "Simpllicimus" "Berliner Tageblatt" etc etc. There is no room for souvenirs, as the opportunities for getting them later will probably be only too numerous. You cannot imagine the amount of work behind his lines; he must have worked very hard.

I hope you heard my songs on the night, and will be able to tell me of the extraordinary effect they had on the audience . . . . How strong men wept like children etc.

Our mails arrive very well still. I hope they will continue to bring your letters, though my replies may be short and infrequent. I enclose something which looks like a complete description of a German private but dont know. I found also about a dozen pc^s, one of Nuremburg, which provoked sadness that we must never visit Germany. Anyway the place I want to visit now is Blighty. "Blighty is the place for me" as the song says. Goodbye, Good health and Good luck: Your sincere Friend   Ivor Gurney

To MARION SCOTT   41.81

25 March 1917 (G)
5 April 1917 (P)

My Dear Friend: This, the next night to that in which I last wrote — (Doesnt that sound pedantic?) seems to offer opportunity for writing; so here goes.

Today we have been salvaging above swamps and a canal, both a heavenly blue in the clear sunshine; and that was warm as the day went on and the sun went down the sky. This poetical start means nothing — digging and short rations leave me little energy for writing; hanging on to my companions' courage I strive to forget what has been and might be; and leave such thoughts to the marches and late evening.

But here's an emendation for "Firelight"
"Till Silence thrills and murmurs at the things they have said."

It is a hard life the soldiers — especially for one given to dreaming. It is strange to me how great a part the mind plays in every affair of the body. Always concentration is the secret; and where there is usually concentrated dislike . . . . How would Hazlitt have got on I wonder?

I see in todays Daily Mail that food regulations are to be made more stringent. Is it really serious? Or a right precaution? What a time our poor villagers must be having! I dont like to think of some of my Framilode friends, to whom the price of bread is a real distress.

I think that verse in "poor Folk" may stand. I find it difficult to alter, and the sense is clear — just space and its difficulties to make food of no avail.

Mrs Harvey has just written me one of her charming letters, in which the good news comes that F W H is getting his parcels, and that his book is in the 4th edition.

There is a blazing fire going in this partially ruined house every night; no dislikable man; common troubles; and common subject of conversation, grub, Fritz, and Blighty — (I cannot imagine why there is not a huge capital G there!) and we rub along as well as can be expected. What an education it is for me — and would this last moralisation were but truly felt!

As for leave, it is a dead thing till October. There is no chance of it at all. But even the thought of Nice Blighty haunts the mind.

Here is a little tale for you.

One of the finest little pocket corporals that every breathed went out on patrol, mistook his direction in the dark, and was shot when about to enter the enemy lines by mistake. His fate was unknown for a fortnight or more; but here in these changes one has discovered a grave with a cross, Corporal Rhodes, 2/5 Gloucesters. And so certainty comes, and a momentary warmness towards Fritz; who must have loved his beautiful face and thought of his own beautiful youth wasted in the tragic tomfoolery of war.

I hope your book goes well in the midst of whatsoever distractions may surround you. Perhaps before so many months I shall get a look at it, or hear you playing confidently the great musings on Life and High Praise. Soit.

Your sincere friend   Ivor Gurney

I believe the long line in the Song of Pain and Beauty is quite all right. It is like 3/4 after 2/4

To MARION SCOTT   41.81

26 March 1917 (G)   [*same envelope as preceding.*]

My Dear Friend: Another letter has arrived, again very welcome, and again keeping me in touch with the things that mean life to me.

It was kind of you to send those things to be read. Who knows? through all the exalted names connected with my book, perhaps I might perform the incredible and make money out of the book.

Well, it is nice to hear of people liking these things — it pleases me in this waste of living.

My last letter that reached you did take a time. Everything is upset. The canteen is empty save of cigarettes. Rations are very scanty; we are all as weak as rats and bad tempered. And hardworked.

But

We have managed to make quite a nice billet out of the gaping remains of a room, and, there being any quantity of wood, have had huge great roaring fires to sit round. The remains of our platoon is very chummy; noone quarrels, though arguments are fairly common in high voice. And after all, though we have our troubles, they are woes in common, and the little better and more grub arrived tonight is a common joy.

Next to me is a man of the 7th Gloucesters who was wounded when that splendid battalion got cut up at Gallipoli. I dont think it will be ever possible to tell you much about these people, but they are all part of me, stored up in the novelist part, and an influence to fulfill my music with humanity.

By the way "In Flanders" was not written in the trenches, but at Crucifix Corner, if you know where that is.

I am afraid the final sonnett does not stand a chance of getting written. The sooner the book is printed, the better I shall be pleased. In that case Sonnett 5 will stand thus

> England The Mother
> (then at the bottom of the page)
> This sonnet will not shape itself, probably
> because there is too much to say. I hope however
> to say out my thoughts in music — someday.

This is to get 5 pieces corresponding to Rupert Brooke's. It is simply not possible to screw anything out of myself at present.

This is a barren land, of flowers, that is. Once it was rich cornland, and is not much scarred by shell holes; but O my county; what tokens of your most exquisite secretest thoughts are now appearing under the hedgerows. On the march not many days ago we passed a ruined garden, and there were snowdrops, snowdrops, the first flowers my eyes had seen for long. So I plucked one each for my friends that I so desire to see again, and one for Gloucester-shire . . . .

What has happened to the Times Literary? It does not arrive now, though the others come as usual. Has it finished?

That list of books is cancelled just for now. The "Spirit of Man" still accompanies me, though past its best days.

Mrs Harvey has just written me a charming letter. Will is well, and getting his parcels, and well on with a new book, thank Goodness; so that is good news of him. The Minsterworth rabbits are having a luxurious time in my absence . . . .

O, your two parcels arrived all right; unfortunately when we were paid and could also get biscuits; but for all that they were most welcome. The cooker things have been most useful not in cooking but in starting fires when wood was damp. We expect they will be more useful soon. Mr Scotts parcel has not arrived, but these things are very irregular. (By the way, your first parcel was waiting when we arrived after a four hours march from trenches. Nothing to eat . . . and to see that waiting is as a great revelation of light.)

Please thank Mr Scott for taking my things to be read. I hope their success gave him pleasure. How is Miss Stella Scott getting on? Well, I believe; she looking a capable lady altogether. I hope your domestic affairs are not too dislocated. A talk with Mrs Scott on

Russia would be very interesting now; and as for your Audrey, I have never been able to forget her, and her Puckish smile. With best wishes: Your sincere friend   Ivor Gurney

To Marion Scott   41.83

1 April 1917 (G)

My Dear Friend: This is the right day for such a business, if it were not so bitter, and surely a fest-day should not be so dull? Well, here it is, and fatigues are over, and this queer billet echoes and re-echoes with the sound of tin whistles and mouth organs, just issued; and the lilt of some Scottish tunes our crack players are rollicking through make life a little alive and worth living. The billet is a family mausoleum owned by a duke and spared among so much ruin because payment has been made to the Germans — 17000 francs, they say.

I am sorry to hear you have been unwell, ill, again, and rejoiced to know you have got over it so much more quickly than a few months ago would have been the case.

You have had far worse weather in England than in France, where there has been quite a lot more sun than with you. Much of the severe frost was absolutely clear as to the sky. This morning was quite beautiful, though it turned to rain later.

I hope by the time this reaches you, you will have started spurted with the Spring, which must be somewhere near by now.

Thank you very much for the accounts you have given me of the performance of my songs. It interested me and bucked me up very much. But Mr Taylor seems remarkably like a dam-fool; it was good of you to wrestle with him, but difficult to convince a man who held such "movie" views on the "Bierside" ending. The first part of the song is of course a rhapsody on beauty, full of grief but not bitter, until the unreason of death closes the thought of loveliness, that Death unmakes. Then the heart grows bitter with the weight of grief and revelation of the impermanence of things — Justice and Strength turning to a poets theme. But, anger being futile, the mind turns to the old strangeness of the soul's wandering apart from the body, and to what tremendous mysteries! And the dimly appre-hended sense of such before us all overpowers the singer, who is lost in the glory of the adventure of Death. But thats all summed up by asking what the foremizzentopmast did I write "ff" [for] if it were as this Taylor man suggests.

I will think about your suggestions as to "Pain and Beauty" but do not yet agree (The "or" in verse 2 should be on line 5, Is it?) The long line should have something of the same effect as the 3 line in Fitzgerald's Quatrains.

We have not had so bad a time lately, nothing like trench conditions, at any rate, though hard work and not enough food (or at any rate, food not seeming enough) have made us all weak, and upset our insides. I should put this down to the peculiarities of my own stupid constitution, did not men of farming and similar trades also complain. I believe a great deal is due to the dulness of the life, which makes every one look to meals more than ordinary; but anyway they are bound to work us; it being as certain as anything that only going keeps us going. We should all relapse into neurasthenia were we not driven. Considering everything, especially the callousness to certain things such a life must develop, the men are marvellously good to one another, and surely much finer than ever they were, bless em.

I am glad London takes a more optimistic view of things than Mr Garvin — who has always been in the right when things went wrong, but not right. I remember his dolefulness about last May.

Lord, what a hell of a row in here, and what a crush! But I remember how quavery your writing was, when you were sick and still wrote. And not any of the alarums and excursions shall disturb me. But were I only at home ransacking books for verse to set. The baccy parcel arrived last night, and we were all most grateful; everybody was short or bankrupt; and the cigar things were most grateful to us stranded wretches. (They are singing "Annie Laurie". O the joy of it!)

I fear I can send you no money yet, but if you would send the paper covered National Song Book, and the small selected Browning in Walter Scotts edition they would be most useful. The latter is 1/6 I believe. I believe "The Spirit of Man" is sucked dry for me, and my thirst for good verse, and short, is very strong.

The day has been springlike on the whole, and last nights sky was gloriously tragic; I sang "In Flanders" to myself, facing the West, alone in a lately ruined house, spoiled by that unutterable thoroughness of the German destruction; and was somewhat comforted thereby. That has all been said for me in "In Flanders". What you said about the sense of being out under the stars, in "By a Bierside" pleased me very much. The scene of "In Flanders" is obviously Coopers Hill. O times! O saisons, O chateaux!: Goodbye for now: Your sincere friend   Ivor Gurney

To Marion Scott   41.80

2 April 1917 (G)
11 April 1917 (P)

My Dear Friend: Tin whistles and mouth organs still going hard, and we waiting for dinner and moving afterwards, for a company of ours took two more villages last night, and we shift also of course.

We have been hard worked, but still and all the same, this open country work is far preferable to trench life. This place is quite pretty, very pretty; and this morning I saw, at first dawn, one mystical star hanging over a line of black wood on the sky-line; surely one of the most beautiful things on earth.

I hope by the time this letter gets to you you will be trotting about in real Spring sunlight; it is cold here as yet, but no man may foretell of Aprils whims.

I told you of the death, a little time back of one of our most looked to corporals. Well, that was before the advance. About a fortnight after the movement started, we heard his grave had been discovered; and after tea one evening the whole company (that was fit) went down for a service there. Quite a fine little wooden cross had been erected there: the Germans had done well: it was better than we ourselves would have given him; and on the cross was

> "Hier ruht ein tapferer Engländer,
> Richard Rhodes", and the date.

Strange to find chivalry in sight of the destruction we had left behind us; but so it was. They must have loved his beauty, or he must have lived a little for such a tribute. But he *was* brave, and his air always gallant and gay for all his few inches. Always I admired him and his indestructibility of energy and wonderful eyes.

I am sorry to hear about the shortage of pianos, that may affect me and my tinklings.

April 4 or 5th.

I thought we were going over the top tonight, but it has been postponed — a state of things which will inevitably lead to soul-outpourings. My state of mind is — fed up to the eyes; fear of not living to write music for England; no fear at all of death. Yesterday we had a little affair with a German patrol, which made me interested for 5 minutes; after which I lapsed into the usual horrid state of boredom. O that the Nice Blighty may come soon! I do not bear pain and cold well, but do not grumble too much; so I reckon that cancels out. One cannot expect to have everything, or to make one's nature strong in a week. It snowed like anything yesterday, but today has been quite beautiful, and I have strolled about chatting of Maisemore Wood and such-like things of beauty. Your Kampote blocks came in very useful — what were left of them, and a warm drink now and then is salvation indeed; after the drink I settle down to think of the delightful cosy comfortable teas I will have one day, and of the music to follow; trying so to forget my feet. What an April! Well, we have had some bon fires not so many days back.

My dear friend, it has been very kind of you to write to my friends as you have, and I know they are grateful. It is something to know that my father realises his trouble and sacrifice have not been all wasted. He has been only too good always; especially considering the difference of our temperaments, and my long wasted time. Surely my life must lead to something. Surely the apprenticeship has almost passed?

I am afraid there are no poems again. The conditions are against it, but, thank Goodness rations are better now.

My friendships are mostly queer ones, and this is queer, but believe me, a very valued one. You have given me just what I needed, and what none other of my friends could supply to keep me in touch with things which are my life; and the actuality of which is almost altogether denied me. Well, perhaps it will not be long before I am back again, and having tremendous jaws about your book, and seeing you get stronger, and watching Audrey grow up, and seeing what her smile grows to be. Here we are called up. Goodbye: Your sincere friend   Ivor Gurney

Next day

Our Q M S has told us that the 61st are mentioned in despatches. Is this true I wonder? We have risen a little in our own estimation if this is so; one does not wish to belong to a washout division. This morning was beautifully sunny, and daisies are poking their heads out here and there — without steel helmets! O the Spring, the Spring! Come late or early, you must give hope ever to the dwellers in the house of flesh. How does your frail tenement get on? I hope it is warmer and sunnier with you now, and you playing on your violin, revelling in sunlight of earth and music.

To MARION SCOTT   41.85

14 April 1917 (P)

My Dear Friend: Well, I am wounded: but not badly; perhaps not badly enough; as although kind people told me it meant Blighty for me, yet here I am at Rouen marked "Tents". I do not yet give up hopes, but very few boats have been running lately; none at all for some days; and the serious cases go first of course. It was during an attack on Good Friday night that a bullet hit me and went clean through the right arm must underneath the shoulder — the muscles opposite the biceps, to describe them more or less accurately. It hurt badly for half an hour, but now hurts not at all; I am writing in bed with the arm resting on the clothes merely. Well, I suppose your letters will be lost to me for a little; please send them to me when you receive them.

I hope you are well now, inspite of the awful April weather.

There is a gap of two days between the writing of the two pages. I can send you no address; we are being shifted about too much, and everything is doubtful. Apparently the hospital boats have been and are almost completely held up, or else I might have had a chance for Blighty; though there is no real damage done to my arm, not enough to please me.

Alas! Alas! There are hardly any books here! And the life is made up of hanging about waiting to be shifted again. Now if I could find some real hard reading to do – something to distract my mind, all might be well; or if I had some MS and a few books of verse, I would turn out something in spite of the flatness of my mind. O well, hopes are not yet gone.

Will Harvey is getting all his parcels, and has a new book of verse almost ready. This is good news; and it will be very interesting to see the difference between the two; for of course there will be a difference.

Though this Spring is cold and unclement, I cannot keep out of mind what April has meant for me in past years — Minsterworth, Framilode, and his companionship. And my sick mind holds desperately on to such memories for Beauty's sake; and the hope of Joy. "By a Bierside" came from two evenings above all others; one most magical afterglow at Framilode when I was alone; and the evening before I rode in late to find England had declared war. Great billowy clouds hung over distant Malvern, and the poplars, black against the glowing West, sang music onto me, which someday I may fit myself to sing to others — but not yet; not in these conditions, when Pain rules so much and so continually in the sight of one who bears Pain hardly, supporting his courage by other examples. Still more analysis! Yes, but you are kind and infinitely patient and it does me good to "moan", as the Army word is.

My total cash is 3½d, so you see that in spite of my credit of about 175 francs, I can buy nothing in the way of books. Two Daily Mails will finish my literary purchases. So, if I can send you an address, please send me some small books of verse, and Tolstoi's Cossacks

(Worlds Classics – Pocket Ed.) I wonder whether at last I might try Housmans "Shropshire Lad"?

I will write again in half a shake:

Your sincere friend   Ivor Gurney

(I write with my perforated arm, so you see not much is wrong.)

To MARION SCOTT   41.82

17 April 1917 (P)   *[Post card]*

Dear Friend: Still at the Base. No certain address. No certain tomorrow. No luck. No money. No damage to my arm, save a hole. Yet, had the boats been running, I might have got to Blighty. I will write a letter tomorrow. I hope the weather has been as good these last two days with you as with us.   I B G

To MARION SCOTT   41.84

April 1917 (E)

My Dear Friend: Well, and how is all with you, in spite of the cold and clammy wind? I hope that your day includes hours of violin and book-making by now, and begins to resemble your desire a little. O well, the Victory which seems imminent should help you a little. This writing is pretty shaky — more from cold than anything else, though my fingers are rather stiff today. The orderly told me in confidence it might be three weeks before I was in training again: So there is time to write yet.

What news though! Today peeping surreptitiously on another man's paper, I see the French have got 10,000 prisoners, which must hurt Hindenburg slightly. And soon perhaps Spring will gain her victory and flaunting glorious banners sweep the last rearguards of winter in flight to the North.

How is my distinguished coadjutor H N H? Bless him, he with you have made my tiny triumphs possible. Did Sir C H H P really say my song was the most tragic thing he knew? If so, what an enormous praise! I shall be very proud of that, if it is so; and could desire no other or higher praise.

To resume next day. A kindly doctor has given me a weeks No

Duty, and there is a recreation room with quite a lot of old mags, and a few books; so I shall manage to exist, but O for some hard head work and long walks.

Yesterday someone was playing the rather good piano in the Recreation Room — toshy stuff played quite well. It was difficult to stay in the room with so many desires awakened and so poorly satisfied.

> Music pours on mortals
> Her beautiful disdain.

which is one of the few scraps of Emerson worth knowing; and I got it from the Times L.S. which arrives no more, since apparently Northcliffe will not bother with small fry. Would you mind sending me your copy unless you keep them for reference? It is a valuable thing and the extracts are stimulating.

This is a most beautifully situated camp — surely there can be no harm in saying what so many people know, that the 55th Inf: Depot is at Rouen — and there are some very noble pines not far from this tent. I hope to get a pass out of them before I leave here, and to see so historic a place of memories; was it not here that William the Conqueror saw his future wife washing in the courtyard?

Last night after lights out I had a long talk with a Cotswold man lying next to me — of his ambition to be a gardener; of Cotswold gardens; of the beauty of those churches; of certain jolly old masters-of-life there; of old songs; of the joy of life there in those homely and friendly-seeming houses of grey stone with so wonderful an army of flowers round each. I could hear music that I should make mixt with the older music respiring from his talk — language of Shakespearean comedy — and set myself to wait a little longer, and perhaps not so very long either.

I hope you are getting well, even if only to enjoy the warm weather when it comes. After all the cold and wet are hard on German spuds as well as Allied. But I should like some verse not yet known to me, especially as there is a good chance of being here 3 weeks or more. With all good wishes:

Your sincere friend   Ivor Gurney

To HERBERT HOWELLS   3.18

24 April 1917 (P)

My Dear Howler: How are you now, my dear collaborator, in your quiet Cathedral close, so far from the noise of War, but not its influence? I also, but with a souvenir in the form of a bullet hole in the upper arm. This would have got me to Blighty in happier times but there was no luck for me — here, at No 55 I.B.D. and hanging about regretting the wasted days, which might be filled with so much, so much. I hope you are forging ahead on some new thing or other, and well and not too occupied on other business. These are holidays, you should have some time to yourself now: have you been to Winchester yet? Or, in a smaller way, have you rummaged those second hand bookstalls in the street, not far from the Cathedral? I myself bought nothing there, but rummaged nevertheless; later buying several 6^d Nelsons at a book-shop not far off, before the return to servitude and the bleak plain again.

Is the time far off when we shall meet, and discuss all these things in a proper fashion? What does Hindenberg think, I wonder? And even more important, Nivelle and Haig? Well, we are all starving now, tout le monde. Soon the troops will be collecting up scraps of bully for the folks in England, "Comforts for Civilians", "Remember the Kiddies" and so forth. As Punch's lieutenant wrote "I seem able to think only of Europe and my belly — nothing between", and here there are only old mags; and toshy novels to read; not that my intellect is fit for any thing much stronger. But O those damned Minsterworth orchards, and what they might be singing to me! I am glad you climbed Robinswood. Coopers Hill is better, but then one cannot have everything. Good bye:

Yours   IBG

To MARION SCOTT   41.88

30 April 1917 (P)

My Dear Friend: Your letter of April 18th – 22nd and the Cossacks etc have arrived, and that is all I have had as yet. More may arrive for my address has been left at Con: Camp and sent to the Batt. Let em all come.

I am sorry you have had such a queer and inconvenient illness; after all, German Kultur or the results thereof may very well cause an Englishwoman to break out in spots. What will you do? Can you get a kind of permission? The blessed nuisance of it all is that all substitutes go up in price like rockets in the air. And this morning, 40 big ships reported sunk. We shall pull through, I have no doubt, but it is a mess. This morning the doctor has given me Duty, which will tell you what the official verdict is. Apparently the beastly bullet hit absolutely nothing at all profitable — and as to escaping serious damage, I am too near to the event to feel grateful.

Sunday

I am supposed to be on Church parade but owing to the fact that my ripped coat has not been replaced, I am here writing this letter.

Yesterday evening the two Poetry Reviews and the Times Supplements arrived. Thank you very much, especially for the first, which is just what England needed — a magazine devoted to the interests of weak but sincere verse. Local poetry, local poetry is Salvation, and the more written the better. And how good to get such beautifully printed stuff out here.

I am very sorry to hear about Sydneys illness and will write to him at once. Poor chap, he has not had the happiest of lives, but after the war he will probably have gained wisdom, to limit his desires, and to accept facts, thereby gaining the fullest freedom possible.

I knew about the Carnegie business, and have written about it I think. It gives me great pleasure that H N H should gain even so little a recognition, but when is the Concerto to be done again? Also the publication of the London Symphony is the best of news. About Bantock I am always sceptical. He is diffuse and ineffectual, and needs a great deal of material to make any effect.

(Oh, yes, my number is 241281 now)

I suppose all your plans are held up; your book tugging at the leash so to speak, but not getting on. It is a thousand pities, but there you are; the better weather ought to make a large difference to you, whether you stay in London or go to Dorset.

"The Shropshire Lad" and the MS have also been gratefully received, but once again I feel rather incapable of setting them. Such precise and measured verses are too easy to set, do not give the scope that R. Bridges songs offer one. One can only set them, say, a little better than Hermann Lohr or Maud Valerie White can; for their abilities are quite up to setting such poems. Compree? By the way, my subtle mind infers from the silence about R.B: that his judgement was not favourable, which does not surprise me. Such a master is not pleased with the amateur.

Does not the Poetry Review go for Abercrombie though! I am rather glad, hating by nature the obscure, and, pace Mr Masefield, being doubtful even of Sir Robert Ross.

So Edward Thomas is dead. This is a great loss; but this I think I have already written about.

"The Cossacks" is good stuff. Thank you so much; when one has read (Yes, I got hold of them) such a parochial masterpiece as "Esmond", and such a thin finicking piece of work as "Travels with a Donkey" within three weeks of this book, it gives ones national pride a severe shock. One may put the case as — Tolstoi might have preferred mans life in the open air to that of a writer, but Thackeray that of a clubman — a Thorough Gentleman. Dickens had twenty times his genius, and but for humour, he was small.

The "Poetry Review" may start me writing again; such imperfection in print is most encouraging. Please rush my book into print as soon as possible. If that sonnet can be done, it shall be. But continual disgust has sterilised me. However Spring really has been here for ten days now.

With all good wishes for health etc:
Your sincere friend   Ivor Gurney

To MARION SCOTT   41.89

4 May 1917 (P)

My Dear Friend: Your letter of April 24th is here to answer, and this morning "Responsibilities" has turned up. It is too generous of you really, and of course far too good a book to keep out here; so that directly I think they have put me on a draft I will send it back to you. The glance at it seems to show it an immensely interesting book, obscure, and unaccountably failing and only just failing to be great poetry time after time. What will the next one be like? Is it Transition or the end of him? After the War I shall be only too pleased to resume possession, but as to taking it up the line that is not possible.

I hope you are getting fit now — bedroom life must be terrible in these blue and momentous days. You have had a rough time since the similar days in August 1914. Perhaps you have been affected by some evil in the air, some potent and maleficent influence. Who knows? I dont believe it, but then this is only a letter, not an affidavit. The Herrick poem is very beautiful, and makes me long for the time when after a long tramp out towards round and about Staunton and Corse — on the way to Jagged Malvern, I shall return tired and full of memories to set up singing in my mind — and then Mr Herrick, we shall collaborate to some purpose.

I see Austen Chamberlain gives no official hope for peace before November. Then surely, having collared the guns, we shant be long?

Also another kind friend has sent me "Soldier Poets", in which there is precious little of value but much of interest. Julian Grenfell's "Into Battle" is of course easily the best. Geoffrey

Howard's "Without Shedding of Blood" E Melbournes "Before Action", "Back to Rest". Victor Ratcliffe's "Optimism". Robertson's "We shall drink". Sorleys translation from "Faust". The curiously alive and unequal "Charge at Neuve-Chapelle. The last two verses of "To My People" of Wilkinson's. (Have you seen any verse by a man named Sassoon? I remember having seen quite good stuff.)

You may send my things to Erskine Macdonald if you wish. The "Poetry Review" is a first rate pusher. Why cannot I write now? Dont know, but I believe after this long frowst and feed up, the line will give me beacoup ideas. No more strength had I than some decrepit rat, or seemed not to have, when we went up for the attack. But since being here, I have cherished my belly most generously, too generously some time, and hope to have a little spare energy for a month. In future however, I refuse absolutely to have any parcels sent. It is absurd and impossible to ask for them. And now the warm weather has come, we shall do very well.

After another dip into Yeats, I find myself still more impressed. It is not a great book, there are not more than a few things that one will remember; but it is a most valuable book for a young poet, most stimulating, swift and high-hearted. And though one cannot deny its occasional obscurity after reading "Soldier Poets" it seems strikingly original; though the strain is occasionally apparent of the care that roots out the obvious and worn phrase, and will not be too easily pleased with first sketches. You will find that when I come to work again, I also shall show much greater scrupulousness than before. It was simple lack of energy that kept me from revision, and the only method possible to me was to write for a minute or two at top speed, refrain from tearing it up, and return to the charge after some space of time. It wont be so, afterwards. Will you please accept the grateful dedication of "By a Bierside"? I dont think it would have come to birth but for you, and your receptivity, and the chance of its getting a hearing through your insistence. And as to verses, there would probably be a very small crop had you not seemed to expect them from me, especially so as F W H is in Germany.

O Robert Ross or whatever his name is — the Poetry Review man — is all bosh. Pope or Gray in the solidity of his good lines — ungoverned transcendability. A type of a different kind from Ella Wheeler Wilcox, but no better. Give me Walt Whitman.

What do you think of George Butterworth? The friend of Vaughan Williams ought to do well, but toujours I am sceptical about the lasting value of most English music. It is the ploughing of the ground, the preparing, and while one is grateful, there is too much as a general thing of excellence that so many clever people arrive at with their well trained intellects and healthy minds and instincts.

Tonight to the pine wood. But to the bath house now and to wash clothes, etc etc.

Tomorrow I start training, a good thing. You get frightfully slack doing nothing: Your sincere friend   Ivor Gurney

To MARION SCOTT   41.90

9 May 1917 (P)

My Dear Friend: I hope you are doing fairly well now — today is the first cold day for some time, and judging by the way the long-frozen trees have flourished in it, invalids should do pretty well; and the Gardens are not so very far from you.

All this week I have been down for training at the Bull-ring, as they call it — Napoleons parade ground, a bare white sand and shingle space set among hills and surrounded by pines. It is a fine place, but a nasty job. Perhaps I may be here for another week yet, and then up to the chance of Glory and another Blighty, a real one this time. My arm is quite well now, curse it.

Do as you will about my book. Will

"To Certain Comrades
              and other Verses" do?
as a title, I mean. Not so bad, I think.

I had a letter from Sidney the day after I wrote to him — a plucky calm letter. It over now, the second operation, I suppose, and he steering a clear course if a slow one towards health. Anyway, he stands a chance of escaping all this, which is a good thing.

The things I like best in Yeats, as yet, are The foreword in italics; the Grey Rock; the Two Kings; September 1913; To a Friend; the Witch; Mountain Tomb; To a Child Dancing; Memory of Youth; Friends; Cold Heaven; (as you may imagine). That the Night Come; a Coat; A Woman Homer sung; The Consolation; No Second Troy; Reconciliation: King and No King; The Mask; Upon a House Shaken; These are the Clouds.

Jolly good stuff these, and excellent chiefly for young poets interested in method.

Monday

Yesterday I managed to get to Rouen again, and was for a brief two hours and a half my own master. It really is a fine town, and a great rock which stands smiling and huge just out of the town and on the river is very impressive. I did not go into the Cathedral, whose iron spire struck me with increased horror; a dreadful thing. St Ouen has a very much finer spire.

Look here, did I give H N H the declaration of "By a Bierside"? I seem to remember something of it; and if this is so, I am afraid you must try and live without it. Cuss, I do get mixed up so in my wandering mind.

Still nearer to the line now — which may come any day. All kind of rumours fly round as to the actual whereabouts of the Batt: but noone really knows.

I have been reading Conrad's "Chance", only to get tired of all that analysis, and not being able to get to the end. "The Mirror of the Seas" is Conrad's best, as far as I know. Otherwise Kipling infinitely surpasses him. Conrad is a good artist, but to me seems not to have much original genius. (But our acquaintance is not extensive.)

Now I am about to steer off for my chess-pupil, who has beaten me in one game — the first! On Saturday I satisfied my vanity by flummoxing him completely, may it be so again.

I hope you are getting better now. Cant you get some kind of dispensation, or absolution from maize?   With best wishes:

Your sincere friend   Ivor Gurney
Please keep on writing

On second thoughts I have decided to send you the enclosed doleful production. You see I have shaved now, but cannot smile to order. I believe however that my ordinary expression is somewhat happier.

                                                                    I B G

To MARION SCOTT   41.94

18 May 1917 (G)

My Dear Friend: "The Observer" has just come, and J W Gs remarks on the probable length of the war (almost certainly true) seem to lead me on to write a letter — to have a good moan in sympathetic company. It is the bloomingest nuisance that a thing so well intended as the Russian Revolution can so upset things.

I hope you are getting properly well now, and have had a look at the pink and white world outside London — that you are beginning to enjoy yourself, in short.

As for me, I am back with the Batt: alright, but the Batt: is back also, practising attacks. (Tòday I was twice a "casualty" . . . Is there anything in it?) So there is no need for anybody to worry just yet; as the present is taken up by the process of Feeding you up, preliminary to serious business. (This process is noway related to excess of food.)

I am glad that my song had not been dedicated; it should have become yours anyway. Also that you are pleased with the little photograph. I may as well tell you that the expression is not intended for determination but for carelessness instead of the ordinary grim desperation.

Outside here men are cleaning up their equipment for sheer want of something to do — a dreadful state of mind, only possible in the Army.

By the way, how is that young boy violinist and composer of whom Sir Charles and Herbert thought so highly? Noone has mentioned him to me. Where is that Welsh girl who sang my Elizas once? I ask after her because of the kindness I bear to the Welsh by reason of Herbert, the 13th R W Fusiliers, Borrow's Wild Wales, and, also, herself whom I liked. And of course Mrs Harvey is Welsh.

If the Bosches hit an arm off me I will get the largest pension I can and go tramping the country, sleeping rough or with strange and wonderful tales attracting hospitality. And the first walk I take shall be Dymock, Newent, Ross and into Wales, to end at Chepstow after meeting names met in Malory; names known it would seem a thousand years ago in some forgotten life stronger in charm than their realities of houses and trees, almost. These journeys must be made alone for the greater part, for friends are often busy, and who will hire an actor to make up as one's friend to act the part, to have learnt "the probable range of subjects", and to "quarrel by the book"? No, they must be solitary for the most part, but only the fool is sorry for that when nothing but his foolishness prevents him finding friends at each resting place, and, if the wind is moving, between them? The modern composer must be a church organist and exalt forms and ceremonies all his days, not for bread (for that would be some excuse) but to wear a boiled shirt, and not to disappoint snobs. Looking at this blossom, it seems to me his choice is not a poetic one; for though tramps have been called lousy, the use of the term implies that there are some free, but who is free, of Britains army? (The Navy is alright, I suppose.) Who will deliver us from the body of this death?

You may like to know that in that mausoleum in which we slept two months ago, there was concealed — something which has sent the whole shute to glory. Good thing it had been set for a long time. Best wishes: Your sincere friend   Ivor Gurney

To HERBERT HOWELLS   3.22

30 May 1917 (P)

My Dear Howler: So you've been and done it! Shall I congratulate
you? I dont know; since before me there seems to lie two fat
biographies, both of Herbert Howells.

The first opens at a passage

"At this time the composer's powers, already great, were
doubled by the most fortunate act of his life: the engagement to and
subsequent marriage to Miss Dorothy Dawe; a singer of miraculous
endowments. From this time onwards his record is one blaze of
great works and huge accomplishments. The first 14 symphonies,
the great (Sanscrit) Te Deum, for the opening of the new lavatory in
the Dead Language Section of the British Museum; the noble
setting of the genealogies in the Old Testament; of the great
Bradshaw Opera, the epic of railway life; and the whole of his
masterpieces up to Op 462 which begins his Middle Period, was
inspired by the remarkable lady whose exquisitely chiselled nose
rendered beautiful sounds which otherwise would have been
painful; for she preferred to sing through this organ only. etc etc

And

We must here, with regret, but extenuating nothing as is our
business as honest chroniclers, set down the record of the sad fact
that blighted this great life; that drove a despairing man to the false
comfort of spirituous liquor, and that of becoming a Plymouth
Brother; bleared his eyes and upset his digestion; and in a word set
his feet on the dark path that was to lead him to spiritual damnation
as Harmonium Professor at the Royal College of Music. He became
entangled in the fatal web of fascination spread by an unknown
contralto of doubtful attainments and tone quality.

———————

O there's more of it, but I'm off up the Line tonight, and cant
bother.

Still, O the best of luck to you my bonny Herbert and Dorothy,
Dorothy and Herbert; may you be blessed as you deserve, may you
arrive at all felicity. And may I arrive soon and share it.

Carnegie ought to give you a Free Library for this.

But why dont you write to me? Your letters are as light in the
darkness or as a third of loaf instead of a quarter, up the line. And
you must have other news.

And look here; I have totally forgotten whether I dedicated "By a
Bierside" to you. If so, it is hereby reft away from you and given to
Miss Scott. If I had given it you, old man, please don't mind; Miss S:
seems glad to have it, and you can write your own masterpieces

dedicated to yourself, And she has been as good as gold about everything. And if you are angry, write to say so; you wont get anything out of it but to give me pleasure by your letter — up the line, where there is little pleasure. How is the amiable Benjamin? O God, what would a reunion mean, down in that basement tea room! What would it mean to talk about things that interest me once again, and to talk freely?

They have give me a new number and badge of servitude —

                    241281

I hope all goes smoothly and not too busily at Salisbury, whose close must be a wonder most high at present. Best wishes to both of you   Yours ever   Ivor Gurney

To MARION SCOTT   41.97

4 June 1917 (P)

My Dear Friend: Fritzs aeroplanes are ever so high above us, and shrapnel is bursting round them; shrapnel which never seems to fall anywhere. This is an old and stale game to us, would there were here in our place men who would be interested in such things.

The weather is still almost cloudless and may is on the hedges, foam on green bosomy waves.

The post today may bring a letter from you, which I will wait for before enquiring after your health.

The title "Severn and Somme" might sell the book a little better. It sounds like a John Bull poster, but otherwise there is nothing objectionable about it. Severn people may buy if Somme people dont: my French not being equal to translation of works so delicate of language. At present my desire is to get the thing off my chest, and my chest out of Khaki.

(Please excuse dirt.)

Your letter of April 2nd has arrived, there is nothing that requires an answer or a reference I think. Thank you for it all the same for its interest.

We are going out for an all night and next day stunt, Heaven pity us! Still we expected it — on Rest.

Mrs Harvey has not heard from FWH since late February, but his book has arrived. How we would have argued about that book — what discussions strolling about Hygrove by the pines and in the Orchards! Curse it, there's "nothing left remarkable beneath the visiting moon" for me, save a hot time to come. I could do him a lot of good now, since I have learnt by writing. (Have you received the

Yeats book yet? I did not send it myself, but left it with another.)
Next Day.

They say Fritz has retreated again, and if this is so, more marching, more road making, short rations again. May General Russky be right about victory coming by Autumn.

"The Cossacks" is a fine book, too small to be a great one — but accurate and life like. One cant help thinking that such a life is going on there, while in the Victorian books one is continually reminded of the fact that "this is not Life but only a description", And by such gentlemanly people too!

I will take a huge dose of Russian stuff apres le guerre. Some of the short stories of the lesser known writers are extremely interesting. How often, I wonder, did Thackeray really look at life? He shows at his best in the "book of Snobs" and "Travels and Sketches" (is it?) — things related more to books and form than actuality. In fact he was an artist at one remove from things; the opposite of W H Davies in "The Autobiography of a Supertramp", that most fascinating of records. Brahms music at its not-best shows the same thing also — the mind of a man as satisfied in his study as in the open air. There are not many things that make worthy art. They are, Nature, Homelife (with which is mixed up Firelight in Winter, joy of companionship etc.) The intangible Hope (which means all music only can hope to express). Thoughts on Death and Fate. And there are no more. It is right, as RLS wrote, for a young man consciously and of purpose to regard his attempts as Art only, but this is a half stage, and should soon end, if the young man has anything to say.

End of the Treatise: Your sincere friend   Ivor Gurney

To MARION SCOTT   41.99

12 June 1917 (P)

Sent a week after June 6

My Dear Friend: Your letter of the 25th has just reached me.

A letter to you has just been posted but still I write. You, of all my friends, write the most interesting letters; and a most unusual thing, there is always something in them to comment on or reply to. A thing of strange and enormous significance.

You seem to be getting better, which is a meet right and sensible thing to do. Please continue.

So I have a new service to thank you for — the preparation of the book for printing. I had clean forgotten there was anything more to do.

It interests me to hear about peoples preferences in (yes!) "Severn and Somme". The prophet must always be annoyed when a friend tells him how much better slippers and a churchwarden become him than the splendid mantle, and so your sisters liking for the "Estaminet" does not please me. I see Siegfried Sassoon has published now. Do try to see it, and if you can do so, spot a poem on the subject of a man unconscious from the time of his being wounded till he was in train in Blighty: then recognizing what part of the scheme of things he saw by the advertisements. It is very good; and came out in the Sat: Westminster. I see Osborne calls him a great poet.

My second premonition is not vivid — probably only a pious opinion, a hint of the price I am willing to pay.

Russia still seems to strengthen. Perhaps the first successes of her offensive are needed to complete the cure. And Italian news is great news.

I am glad you like the photograph; your liking it may embolden me to send it to others also. I had twelve; one you have, 5 have got spoilt in my pocket and have been dumped, the rest I still have myself, till such time as the spirit moves me or carelessness to send them off.

Your description of Frederick Bridges organ playing amused me very much. Would I were back under the old boy! He was my counterpoint master, and it is my chief excuse for my weakness therein.

O to be back cracking my head over Orchestration and Fugue and the Mass, the Mass! I foresee a quarrel even at this distance about that last, which must be got through. Shall I ever be able to outmanoeuvre Sir Charles? For argument does not long continue to be polite in the Army. Well, well, civilisation may yet touch me to gentle speech. The time of the scarcity of letters is near at hand, I think; which is also that where most information and material is found.

Will people continue to write letters when Peace comes? Or retire and take a well earned rest behind huge fortifications of PC^s after the Field Postcard fashion?

Peace

I'll write no letters in that happy season
When Peace illumes the world like the Sun's Lamp.
Laziness will be in part the reason.

But — shall *I* pay a penny for a stamp?

No, no, it cannot be! And if some female
Is soft enough of head to lose her heart
To Me, she'll have to settle as to the Mail
And pay for both. I'm damned if *I* shall start!
    Your sincere friend   Ivor Gurney

To MARION SCOTT   41.101

11 June 1917 (G)

My Dear Friend: Out of the line once more, but for once, not hungry, for the Lord and the ASC have been kind to us, and liberal gentlemen have bestowed cake upon me.

I have heard from Mrs Voynich who tells me you are not able to walk as yet. This is hard lines my esteemed correspondent, but you have courage enough to win through, I feel sure.

How are Mr Scott and Audrey?

HNH wrote me a long letter, and interesting. He says that the end of the Raleigh song is not so good as the beginning. This is true, but I do not agree that it needs rewriting. Though the details are hardly considered there — that being only a sketch I have sent you. If he decides to orchestrate it, he may do as he pleases, use a free hand. In my head is "On Wenlock Edge" waiting to be written and the details of that will be far more difficult.

Yes, the College Mag: and the TLS[s] have arrived. I am sorry I forgot to thank you. If there are any complementary copies please send them to Mrs Chapman and Mrs Hunt.

It is good news you are going to Sevenoaks, where there is a clean air untainted with petrol, and where an invalid has reason to get strong. (Your letter of June 7th has gone to the making of this, I should have said).

———————

Today there are orgies of cleaning, and men brush and polish frantically at brass and leather. The weather is beautiful, and there is plenty of water to wash with, so we are not unhappy. Also there is plenty to eat, and in estaminets plenty to drink, but ah — les pauvres Anglais; one charges here half a franc a small glass for vin rouge, 3d a glass for doubtful beer in small measure, and so on. Matches are scarce now, but I have been lucky, and the men who smoke cigarettes only are in a bad way. French biscuits are very inferior things; there cannot be much flour of wheat in them.

Rondels

1. *Letters*

"Mail's up"! the vast of night is over
And love of friends fills all one's mind
(His wife, his sister, or his lover.)
Mail's up, the vast of night is over,
The grey-faced heaven Joy does cover
With love, and God once more seems kind.
"Mail's up"! The vast of night is over
And love of friends fills all one's mind.

2. *Shortage*

God God! No Jam! No Bread!!
  No Butter!!!
Whatever are we coming to?
O desolation, anguish utter —
Good God! No jam, no bread, no butter.
I hear the brutal soldiers mutter,
And strong men weep as children do.
Good God! No jam, no bread,
  no butter!
Whatever are we coming to?

3. *Paean*

There's half a loaf per man today?
O Sergeant, is it really true?
Now biscuits can be given away,
There's half a loaf per man today;
And Peace is ever so near they say,
With tons of grub and nothing to do,
There's Half a Loaf Per Man today!
O Sergeant is it Really True?

4. *Strafe (1)*

I strafe my shirt most regularly,
And frighten all the population,
Wonderful is my strategy!
I strafe my shirt most regularly;
(It sounds like distant musketry.)
And still I itch like red damnation!
I strafe my shirt most regularly
And — frighten all the population. . . . . . ?

5. *Strafe (2)*

The "crumps" are falling twenty to the minute.
We crouch and wait the end of it, — or us
Just behind the trench, before, and in it,
The "crumps" are falling twenty to the minute;
(O Framilode! O Maisemore's laughing linnet!)
Here comes a monster like a motor bus.
The "crumps" are falling twenty to the minute;
We crouch and wait the end of it — or us.

I wonder if the proofs are with Sidgwick and Jackson yet. That
will interest me, and also (when the time comes) to know what
Gloucester people think. Last night I read some to a friend of mine,
and was surprised to find how little I cared for them, and how
remote they seemed. As for Spring 1917, it is as I thought long dull,
and unvaried.

Later

This letter had better go now, as it has waited long enough.
There is a chance of my getting a transfer to the MGC, which is
plus bon, and does not involve sticking people.
With best wishes: Yours sincerely   Ivor Gurney

To MARION SCOTT   41.111

Late June/early July 1917 (?)

My Dear Friend: Here am I, sheltered from the sun by the parados
of a trench behind a blockhouse; reading "The Bible in Spain."
That's finished now, and "Robinson Crusoe" need not be begun for
we are being relieved tonight, and O! the relief! "Robinson" may
follow; we shall have tomorrow off anyway. What a life! What a life!
My memories of this week will be, — Blockhouse; an archway there
through which a sniper used his skill on us as we emerged from the
rooms at the side; cold; stuffy heat; Brent Young; Smashed or stuck
Tanks; A gas and smoke barrage put up by us, a glorious but
terrifying sight; Fritzes shells; One sunset; two sunrises; "Bible in
Spain"; The tale of the cutting up of the KRRs in 1914; of Colonel
Elkington; of the first gas attacks also; of the Brigade Orderly; and
of the man who walked in his sleep to Fritz, slept well, woke,
realised, and bolted; Thirst; Gas; Shrapnel; *Very* H.E.; Our liquid
fire; A first sight of an aeroplane map . . . . . Does it sound

interesting? May God forgive me if I ever come to cheat myself into thinking that it was, and lie later to younger men of the Great Days. It was damnable; and what in relation to what might have happened? Nothing at all! We have been lucky, but it is not fit for men to be here — in this tormented dry-fevered marsh, where men die and are left to rot because of snipers and the callousness that War breeds. "It might be me tomorrow. Who cares? Yet still, hang on for a Blighty."

Why does this war of spirit take on such dread forms of ugliness. and why should a high triumph be signified by a body shattered, black, stinking; avoided by day, stumbled over by night, an offence to the hardest? No doubt there is consolation in the fact that men contemplate such things, such possible endings; and are yet undismayed, yet persistent; do not lose laughter nor the common kindliness that makes life sweet — And yet seem such boys — Yet what consolation can be given me as I look upon and endure it? Any? Sufficient? The "End of War"? Who knows, for the thing for which so great a price is paid is yet doubtful and obscure; and our reward most sweet would seem to depend on what we make of ourselves and give ourselves; for clearer eyes and more contented minds; more contented because of comparisons ironically to be made . . . and yet

etc (Not quite correct)

Forgive all this; and accept it as a sincere reflection; a piece of technique; only one side of the picture; trench-weariness; thoughts of a not too courageous, not too well-balanced mind. Like Malvolio, I think nobly of man's soul, and am distressed. God should have done better for us than this; Could He not have found some better milder way of changing the Prussian (whom he made) than by the breaking of such beautiful souls? Now *that* is what one should write poetry upon. Someday I will say it in Music, after a while . . . .

Now I must go into the Blockhouse, may get a Blighty doing so . . . and O if it were but a small hole in the leg! But I am lucky only in my friends, and existence has gone awry for me, not by any means wholly my fault. Maybe I am strong enough to prove the truth of "Character is Destiny" now. God, how I could work, how train myself in Blighty now, were it over! Dyspepsia or no dyspepsia, I'd "be a marvellous kid!" And yet (O the Shakespearian insight of me!) Had I used those earlier years, still I must have come out here for all my promise and accomplishments, and — there you are; here.

I have made a book about Beauty because I have paid the price which five years ago had not been paid. Someday perhaps the True, the real, the undeniable will be shown by me, and I forgive all this.

There is a great gap in my mind, very thirsty, which shall be filled with sunsets, trees, winds, stars, and children's faces; blossoming fairer after so long a drought my mind shall turn freely to that which once was effort to contemplate. I, even I, may experience Present Joy — but not yet. But were I home, with this new ability and Passion for my work, O then perhaps . . .

It is a hard thing to accustom oneself to the resigning of life at any moment, and to become aware and more aware of what that leaving means. Meanwhile, while I am thus thinking and writing, our guns pour almost incessantly a thin musical complaining watery trickle of shells; for what purpose one may rise up and see. "After all I might have gone to Liepsic, to Bonn, to Munich; and they might have been my friends and companions in Art." There goes a dud, and I am glad of it.

Who will dare talk of the glory of Waterloo or Trafalgar again?

There now, I have written myself out, and feel happier. (Theirs or ours? Theirs. Bash!)

I do not forget in my preoccupations to hope you are getting stronger, and that Mr Scott is now on holiday. Nor forget the funny side of things. A few yards away are three walking cases; perhaps "Blighty" men. To get to the Dressing Station is a slightly risky thing, but far less so than many ordinary things a soldier does. Will they risk it? In day light? Hardly! For they have that which is more precious than much fine gold.

Tea's up!

TEA!! O magic word.

Late reading with a pipe and a teapot. 5 oclock at Cranham. Willy Harvey and wonderful Mrs Harvey. Framilode. Twigworth.

O what not? All these memories have music in them. Bach and Schumann. Perhaps there are two men of that name over there:

Your sincere friend   Ivor Gurney

I wish I wasnt so lousy.

Dont trouble to sympathise. I take that for granted or would not have written comme ca.

To Marion Scott   41.104

7 July 1917 (P)

My Dear Friend: I am glad you are enjoying yourself among natural things, instead of hoping for health in smoky London, where the air that should be such a joy is petrol laden and dusty.

Really, I do not see why you or Mr Scott should be bound strictly by food regulations, having done your best and suffered by it — for conscience' sake. But that is the BEF view, which takes all it can get in view of a probable shortage some time or other. Anyway Devonports rules must have exceptions

I have told you about "Cap'n Stratton's Fancy".

Thank you for the T.L.Ss, the article on Tolstoi was very interesting.

It is hard to live a fine life in surroundings like these; not impossible, but nearly so for myself; who need intellectual work to steady me; good solid hard grind all the morning, and a long walk in the afternoon. And then — who can talk with me, as teacher? For I love better to learn than to teach. And since Music and books and my friends are not of this life, therefore Life itself lacks the vital impulse and natural joy. One has to ignore so much, that only one capable of magnifying and concentrating on such pleasures as there are is at all comfortable, I do not say happy. It is the same with you too, I suppose; longing to do so much and so cruelly tied, so thwarted.

Tonight I have reached the happy state of being broke — nothing can touch me farther. My desires are automatically lessened in all directions save only that of newspapers. One obtains freedom and a view from on high; chocolate becomes a vanity, unwholesome also and hard to digest. Smoking becomes a real pleasure and rare. Also one reaps the reward of past generosity and may be suprised by a treat at any moment.

Yes, we have Summertime all right, and, if we turned in at the official hour would lose half lights. But we dont.

Tis cold and rainy and July 1st today. I hope all of you will get really well, and soon, in not-so-distant Kent.

Today the guns have been muttering fairly loudly: you also may have heard.   Best wishes:

Your sincere friend

Ivor Gurney

To MARION SCOTT   41.108

8 July 1917 (P)

My Dear Friend: It is delightful that you are living so pleasantly,
and those surroundings should have a good effect on your
perversely behaving body.

This village is still delightful, and today the weather is perfect.

Two days ago, I had a dinner of salad and deux pain-beurres. It
was perfectly wonderful to have such a dainty meal after aeons of
shackles (Englished — skilly: stew.)

Your parcel has arrived, and thank you very much for it.
Especially the lemonade powder and the fruit, which are summery
things; but do not suppose that the cake, cheese, biscuits and OXO
go unappreciated.

I am sorry about Mr Scott, and only hope Lord Rhondda may be
able to do something for him, and that a proper holiday may be
found possible.

Gloster county is packed full of beautiful things, and pink
dogroses of the most delicate miraculousness find place therein.
Also wild strawberries by the million, and would I were on Coopers
Hill looking over to Malvern and Wales while easing my back at
times. O God, that goes too deep though!

We are having really a pretty easy time now, and this means Over
the Top, I think. Well, let come what come may, as the Victorians
said, I shall have had my day. (And a — poor one at times.)

Alan Seeger's poems must be interesting. I like "I have a
rendezvous with Death" very much.

O Sincerity, what had you to do with Elizabethan prattlings like
"My true love hath my heart", and "Tell me where is Fancy bred"!

I have no change now, but next letter shall contain a 5 fr note to be
applied to the purchase of Ralph Hodgsons "Poems", for you. So if
you like to order it, the money will arrive in time (Macmillan 3/6).

I remember "facing a difficult hill, with sparkling and delight".

Or would you prefer the Second Book of Georgian Verse which
(I suddenly remember) contains (I think) that "Song of Honour"?

A Frenchwoman told me she never heard French soldiers sing
half so much as English. This pleased me, and indeed 7 Platoon has
been songful of late, "Whitewash on the Wall", "Everybody's
Happy in the Old French Trench", and Ragtimes galore ("Charlie
Chaplins Walk" being favourite.) "Rolling Home ", "Old Man
Brown he had a little farm". I hope to play em to you soon.
Meanwhile

Vive les Russes!!!

Et les Ecosses. (Scotts.):   Your sincere friend   Ivor Gurney

To Marion Scott   41.106

15 July 1917 (P)

My Dear Friend: Your letter of July 7th has just arrived.

I am sorry you are sick again, but hope this will be the final lookback and a short one, on your journey toward health. And glad that your father was out of the mess in London. (Have any of our fine buildings been hit?).

Is Mr Scott's laryngitis pretty well yet? As to remembering numbers, who has a worse memory than my own? And yet, if one thinks of numbers in the Army way; 24-12-81; it is far easier.

As to Mr Dunhill — Tray bon. Very well.

I thought you might like to put some names and dates below my verses. (If the Censor doesn't object.)

All written up to the end of October; may be mixed up between Fauquissart, Laventie, La Gorgue, Merville.

November — Robecq, Neuvillette, Bouquemaison.

December, (my soft job), Crucifix Corner.

January, etc. Gapennes, L'Etoile.

("Song of Pain and Beauty" — Ablaincourt. February or March). I remember Harvey had trouble with S and Js, and had to tickle them up; this has just emerged from my queer memory. Macdonald, I think would have decided sooner.

Last night there was a pure colourless October Sunlight, and I could smell apples in the Minsterworth orchards and feel for a moment that soon we should go in and company with Bach, to talk of books and things of peace. How later I should go swiftly under the night towards Orion, home; there to smoke and read myself sleepy, and not to go upstairs till just this side unconsciousness.

The News. The News. Que pensez vous de tout cela?

Again the Miracle breaks all bounds, and Russia is strong; again the German dovecots flutter; more strongly than ever before.

Peace in the Balkans: Secession of Austria; Belgian coast and the North of France reconquered. All before Noël? Je le pense, m'selle.

Tomorrow "The Old Bold Mate" will come to you. It has been a grind to write it, please excuse the writing so scrappy and obviously hurried. The whole thing was more distasteful to me as it might have been the writing of something I loved, and even then I find it hard to settle all the details, which is the real meaning of setting stuff on paper.

Beaucoup journaux ici — a day late, to be sure, but reading 5 papers a day one gets a general idea . . . . . .

Did you mention leave? Well, it is nice to hear someone mention it . . . .

Good luck: Your sincere friend   Ivor Gurney

To MARION SCOTT   41.100

15 July 1917 (?)

My Dear Friend: They have attached me but 5 minutes agone to 184 MGC; that's my address for a bit, probably permanently, unless I turn out a dud.

This is a far, far better thing than I have ev — er done, and when one thinks of the Winter . . . .

True, it is a pity to lose so many good friends, but I console myself by thinking how many of those would have jumped at the chance.

Thank you for the papers, very much:

Your sincere friend   Ivor Gurney

To MARION SCOTT   41.112

22 July 1917 (P)

My Dear Friend: Well, I got your letters, your telegramme and the summons to the MGC, all in one crowded half-hour of glorious life. Never was I so flabbergasted to get anything Postal as that telegram. Who could it be from, and what about? Its being French in form put me off, the flimsy blue after our larger yellow.

Well, S and J have not made the Great Refusal. I take this as an omen.

I hope your courage and humourous tenacity will meet with its reward, and I cannot see why this should not come — after the War; perhaps; perhaps not now.

As you will concerning Mr Dunhill.

I have heard that they have heard from Harvey, who is still pegging on. That's all to know.

When the summons came to "proceed" to the MGC, it was rather a wrench. I have many good friends there, and (I am proud to say) those showed real regret at my leaving; though most thought I was lucky to get the chance: as they nor I do not like the thought of sticking Germans, forbye the chance of getting stuck. And it is a far more interesting game, — a better fed; one does not do fatigues;

one usually gets a dug out in Winter; does not go into the front posts, which in winter are feet deep with slime and water; and, as I have said or hinted, is a safer service on the whole. Since I have never really reconciled myself to the thought of sticking a man, it is a release also. As I am in No.1 Section of 184 MGC which goes in with the Glosters, I shall not be cut off at all, really, in the line. Isn't this good luck?

Well, to return to my book, I hope you will triumph and get joy therefrom, since you have done all the dirty work. I doubt whether it would have been written but for you. ("A most valuable document", say the biographers). If you would care to adopt any more of them please do. Dedications are yours for the taking.

Here is the beginning of "The Old City" (that is, Gloucester).

> "Who says "Gloucester" sees a tall
> Fairfashioned shape of stone arise,
> That changes with the changing skies
> From joy to gloom funereal
> Then quick again to joy; and sees
> Those four most ancient ways come in
> To mix their folk and dust and din
> With the keen scent of the sea-breeze.
> Here Rome held sway for centuries etc

This is dedicated "to all Sons and Lovers of Caer-glow, Glevum — Gloucester."

Dont send any books please, for a consignment of my own has just arrived.

Has you read any books of Belloc's Essays? Just try "First and Last", "On Everything", "On Something" or "Hills and the Sea"!

Do as you please about the Georgian (2nd) Book. I don't know it at all.

The boy who had "Friends", (in the TMB) was sent to Blighty — sick — so there goes what I did not lose when I was wounded. When a man is wounded or in hospital, all parcels are divided amongst his section — a thing I agree with, but greatly regret for some things. The Taylors also had sent me "The Mirror of the Seas."

"Wild Wales" was my most constant delight until I was wounded and lost everything worth having in my kit. It is a coloured book, full of friends, long to remember. There is no time for more, if you are to get this. I rather envy you the fun of correcting proofs. Again

Do as you please.

I believe that soon you may hear Our Guns. Germany seems pretty visibly upset already, dont you think? I hope Mr Scott may escape by miles any bomb-dropping. It must be horrid — it is — for though only two were dropped at Chelmsford, it was not nice.

Goodbye, good luck.

I suppose

(O this is so timid)

Sidgwick and Jackson

cannot be

made for fork out   ever so little?
No? well I thought not.

Your sincere friend
Ivor Gurney

To MARION SCOTT   41.109

27 July 1917 (P)

My Dear Friend: Your letter of terms etc has arrived. Thank you
for it. It seems to me you have done very well, but still — that is no
reason why you should not try to do better still, since publishers are
our lawful prey and natural enemies. Personally (again) when the
book was written there was not thought of making money behind it,
but chiefly an occupation and mind exercise. For all that I really do
not see why the book should not pay, though I do not expect any
very laudatory reviews in the "Times" etc. You have won the
preliminary skirmishes anyhow.

My own opinion of the book is, that it is very interesting, very
true, very coloured; but its melody is not sustained enough, its
workmanship rather slovenly, and its thought, though sincere, not
very original and hardly ever striking. For all that, the root of the
matter is there, and scraps of pure beauty often surprise one; there
is also a strong dramatic sense. Where it will fail to attract is that
there is none, or hardly any of the devotion of self sacrifice, the
splendid readiness for death that one finds in Grenfell, Brooke,
Nichols, etc. That is partly because I am still sick of mind and body;
partly for physical, partly for mental reasons; also because, though I
am ready if necessary to die for England, I do not see the necessity;
it being only a hard and fast system which has sent so much of the
flower of Englands artists to risk death, and a wrong materialistic
system; rightly or wrongly I consider myself able to do work which
will do honour to England. Such is my patriotism, and I believe it to
be the right kind. But how to write such poems as "If I should die" in
this mood? (Also, I am not convinced that poets believe what they
write always. Brooke was a sincere exception, but then, he was
lucky; he died early in the war. So often poets write of what they
wish to believe, wish to become, as one prays for strength and virtue
not yet obtained.) Golly, what a lecture! Serves you right.

Well, I have been thinking. To all appearances, the War looks like ending between July and September 1918. So my resolution goes, and there probably will be another book. So look out! But angels of ministers of grace defend us, another year!

I should like a talk with you, and yet would a talk be sufficient? For one forgets so easily things which one knows too well. Details wearisome to write but interesting to hear. Then I have met a boy of twenty who was an expert amateur conjurer, a great lover of Boswell's Johnson, a lover of machinery, who had read and admired (Cary's and Dore's) Dante, also "Paradise Lost", (though he knew that he did not understand them; a rare modesty;) the common soldier's attitude to classical music and literature; his cheerfulness, his loose talk, his petty thieving, his nobility; his songs, his literature; his absolute acceptance of any rumours of "Conferences" concerning Peace; his grumbling at his own country; his admiration of Fritze's, and especially Hindenburg; his (lessening) contempt for the French; his activity, his sanity; his praise of and scorn of wanglers; his cleanliness, his hate of being considered as Tommy, or of being thought a soldier, or patriotic. He is a queer and lovable character. Not in twenty talks could I tell you what I know.

We had a concert here last night. Really, some ragtimes are most exhilarating. "Mississippi", "Dixie", "Alabam", "Charlie Chaplin's Walk". The one about the amorous shopkeeper also. I hope to play you these some day. They are not "Georgia" nor "Sambre et Meuse", but I know worse music.

So you have decided to call the book "Strange Service", which is a very exact description of the feeling that made the book; it would sell better as "Severn and Somme" perhaps, but that is your business; you are my War Cabinet but far more stable than the real. (What a justification for the old cabinet principles all these changes are! The S. Westminster and the Nation have been fully justified.)

Do you think there will be much more fighting this year? Shall we not wait for USA, or the collapse of Germany?

Be happy and get well. You are hereby appointed G.L.A. (Grand Literary Agent) with double salary: With best wishes: Your sincere friend   Ivor Gurney

I hope Mr Scott's laryngitis is nearly gone by now.
P.S. How many complimentary copies?

To MARION SCOTT   41.110

31 July 1917 (P)

My Dear Friend: I think you have done very well, and hope you have enjoyed the wangling, (as is not improbable, I think.) They *are* good terms for a first book; from such a publisher, and you are to be congratulated on your strategy. Do as you think fit about a Colonial and a cheaper edition; I leaves it to you, pardner.

"The Old Bold Mate" has gone, after much procrastination. Sorry — waiting for favourable opportunities means long waiting in the Army; the thing was written 10 days ago.

I am glad you are flourishing, and hope Mr Scott will soon be on the same good way; but that will do for this letter.

We have moved — to a flat land of continual cultivation; whose cottages are cleaner than those of other parts; where one may see windmills with the old new delight and pride in man's cunning and masterful mind; where churches are a landmark, and houses loom large, a country of faint continual haunting charm almost entirely of man's fashioning. A Scarlatti, early Mozartish atmosphere, restful and full of home-sense, and heart-ache.

It is good news that you have Sassoon's book; which sounded interesting and sincere. Please tell me about it.

Nicholson, I should say, may become a big man someday. He is new and speaks of real things, and has the knack of saying much with few words — a vital test. The difficulty with myself is that, once in England and once with a healthy mind, I shall forever chuck the Muse of Verse, (if she was ever mine to chuck) and grind hard at Music.

And the signs of the Times are — that there will be very sufficient opportunity for another book; and you talk of playing Sonatas with you!

My halidome! Gadzooks!!

By the way, did I dedicate "To an Unknown Lady" to anyone? I do not remember, but, for its title's sake, it must not be dedicated at all.

Why not let S and Js have the 5 triolets and the "Song at Morning"? There is lots more to come. The next volume or tome will begin with "Gloucester", and — O let us live dangerously and give much for the money. Please dedicate something to my sister Dorothy; also Winifred, who deserves something; being a good sort, though I never remember her existence, save when she writes. Father and Mother are provided for I think.

The Immortal Hour

I have forgotten where the pleasure lay
In resting idle in the Summer weather,
Waiting for Beauty's power my spirit to sway;
Since Life has snatched me up and flung me hither,

Here where the days' routine goes dully on
So evenly, so greyly that the heart
Not notices nor cares that Time has gone
That might be jewelled bright and set apart.

And yet, for all this weight, there stirs in me
Such music of Joy when some perceivéd flower
Breaks irresistible this crust, this lethargy,
I burn and hunger for that immortal hour

When Peace shall bring me first to my own home,
To my own hills; I'll climb and vision afar
Great cloud-fleets, line on line, up Severn come;
When Joy's great flame shall cleanse the stain of War

————————
————————

Question and Answer

What shall I say, O soldiers unforgotten
And friends most dear, but fallen, when they shall ask
"How died our sons that were in pain begotten,
Whose boyhood's making was our daily task?

And what have you to comfort our most lonely
Our undivided anguish, what word to tell?"
Soldiers, what can be said, what told but only
"Your work was nobly ended: they died well."

This is for the next book, not this.

May you soon be fiddling away on better bread than ever, and
with better news to please you.:   Your sincere friend Ivor Gurney

To Herbert Howells   3.6

31 July 1917 (P)

My Dear Howler: Time deals astonishingly with you, and to my
sense has treated you very well; considering all circumstances, quite
wonderfully, and your friends rejoice at it, I among them. Dont be
raided, my man, or go down very deep when the row starts.
    Not since I was first out here have I had such a soft time as since
the April affair — only once in since then! However, that no doubt
will have to be paid for.

You know by now what I am, and what the address is; in case you do not, here goes — (Name) 2/5 Glosters attached No.1 Section 184 M G C B E F (all cheques cashed by sanitary man.)

What's happening I wonder (as did you) when these guns are hammering, or, what is going to happen? I should guess it would be an attempt to outflank Lille north and south.

How is your heart now? Let's hope the New Tribunals will deal more wisely and gently than the old. Dont do too much. Forge ahead slowly till Time settles your erratic innards.

Well, you must know now that Miss Scott and myself have passed the first most dangerous channel with my book, and soon I hope will be bearing strongly out to sea with Publication (and, after, soon or late, Oblivion.) on the port bow, and Reviews to starboard. By Heaven, though, what stuff there will be to set apres la guerre! What Names! Brooke, Sorley (I have not read him), Katharine Tynan, Nicholson, Sassoon, Gibson, John Freeman, Laurence Binyon, F W Harvey, Masefield, and . . . . . . (but not for me,) Gurney . . . . apres la guerre, toujours l'apres! O how much better than to seek through Palgrave and Bullen for something not wishy-washy yet settable!

So an Elegy of yours has greatly taken Dr Allen? So much the better. There is the Mass, the "Chosen" quartett, the Concerto, the Suite, and this well in the public eye. What of "Sir Patrick"? Dr Allen is a man of courage, I am glad you have got into touch with him.

Best wishes from your fellow pupil and envious writer of the list above: Ivor Gurney. M. G. Corper

To MARION SCOTT   41.113

3 August 1917 (P)   Tuesday

My Dear Friend: It is certain you must have heard the guns lately, for they have been labouring terribly, and you should hear them as well as we can hear.

But it is M. G. mechanism which has up till now engaged my attention, not the dodging of shells. However, we can hardly remain neutral, as this is probably the Big Push.

There are several Scots and men of the North in this section, and it is delightful to hear their soft voices against the harsher English. Our instructor is a Scot, frae nearby the Forth, and he is a remarkable man. Talk of concentration, of patience! His remarks on mechanism are endued seemingly with the authority of Fate. Nothing draws him from the point. I feel a poor creature beside him, for while my mind wanders from heaven to earth, from earth to heaven, he has one idea only, the present idea. Terrible to offend, he is pleasant enough to those who bow down to his judgements. A fine chap, but doubtfully useful as a household pet. But the Scots surely are finest race on earth; taking them all round. But they must find it hard to learn languages, since foreigners frequently say things one does not expect. (Curse them!).

We have just heard that all first objectives on a 50 mile front have been taken. I wonder what this means?

Russia seems about to settle down a little; the essential death penalty should make a great deal of difference to anarchy, and as to the retreat it seems to be in order, and to be engaging German troops fully enough to satisfy us on the Western Front.

"The Course of the English Novel" is a very good article I think. In the Novel as in the Play, English genius rebels against perfection and turns rather to Content rather than Form. And our critics of music must take note, must beware of requiring that from Englishmen which may not be the truest national expression. Our best works of Art are interesting because of the sense of open air in them and a surpassing human interest. As Belloc says somewhere, A man who reads "King Lear" feels as though he had been out all night on the empty uplands in a great storm. Such things must move us more for ever than perfection, a good aim, but a bad desire; and so, it seems to me, a work of Art never should be greatly praised for its perfection; for that should set off its beauty, and its beauty or truth should be the chief impression on the mind. To praise a thing for its faultlessness is to damn it with faint praise. (Please dont tell Sir CVS or R.B.). But all this has no connection whatever with my own work.

I suppose one of the bitter-sweet musings of your weakness is your book: (this lecture recalled it to me.) and I hope indeed soon you will be able to start on that and your fiddle; for when that stage comes you should not have to wait long.

There was no mail today, but perhaps tomorrow may bring straw for my bricks.

Meanwhile:

All best wishes from your sincere friend   Ivor Gurney

To MARION SCOTT   41.115

8 August 1917 (P)

My Dear Friend: Your letter of July 31 and August 1st has arrived, and thank you for it.

I am glad Will Harvey has written to you, and hope it is not the last of your acquaintance. That he "is too mouldy to write" is a sad thing to read, but a brave thing to write. He is naturally subject to melancholy, and himself only in sourroundings that suit him, and so must have a bad time anyway. Perhaps it may be the slow accumulation of a small dulnesses that have affected him. I hope it is no worse.

As to "Severn and Somme", I have another criticism to make, in spite of your vigourous defence, (which of course you *would* make, being GLA for the same; theres a nasty one!) that is, outside the one line "Fragile mirrors easily broken by moving airs", I do not recall any line of real beauty. Answer that now! Perhaps by now you have "Camps" or "Works of War", or whatever I called it, and "Rumour of War" will reach you soon. And after surely some autumn poems of Minsterworth, the spirit is stirred by a wind uncontrolled, and moved by disconnected memories queerly rising up from the past; usually those thought on most often but not always.

As to the attitudes taken by certain writers to the present time and to their land; dont forget that this usually represents what they wish to think, and on some rare occasions actually do. These are intense moments and live in memory afterwards when the exercise of writing is sometimes used to recreate an emotion. As for FWHs "Though unto me you be austere", it is obviously, (I will underline) *obviously* a poetic exercise, not a very good one. It is not a sincere expression anyhow. You are right about the state of my mind. So am I. It is a sickness caused by real surroundings now, not by imaginary. A great step as you say.

The weather is rotten; our usual luck of weather in offensives.

The "Times" article was not at all bad.

I have seen one famous battlefield since my return from hospital much of it was hardly scarred and thick with flowers. Surely there can hardly be a lovelier colour than cornflower blue? It is the colour of Mozart, of Schubert in lighter moods.

Your story of the chalk uncovered is really very stirring. I hope we shall read some more on this subject. Perhaps the guns heard so plainly in Surrey, may not be the coast guns, but those on chalk — Arras way perhaps. But where the particular strata lie will be an interesting tale to hear.

Russia appears to be getting better, n'est ce pas?

We shall see some exciting things when the Rhine Bridges are kept broken, and a 50 mile sector of the front dominated by aeroplanes. Also, a huge attack on Kiel and the German munition towns. It might start in January and last till — Spring or the collapse of Germany. It is the best way.

Best wishes: Your sincere friend   Ivor Gurney

To MARION SCOTT   41.118

13 August 1917 (G)

Dear Madam: You will kindly delete *all* dedications save three —
"To Certain Comrades"; and one each to yourself and F.W.H. This
is a final irrevocable decision. I have the wind up about — and —
and — ; and besides, it will look absurd. Out with them! Slay, have
no mercy!

   You will realise that this action implies no disrespect for you, and
the next book shall show that, I hope; of which four masterpieces
are already extant.

   But what a hell of a lot of letters I write you nowadays. Enough to
show you that this letter is no forgery; no cheat, but is from
                         Him-who-must-be-obeyed
                         Ivor Gurney

Author, Composer, Soldier-of-a-sort, and your humble sincere
servant, Miss Marion.

To MARION SCOTT   41.122

18 August 1917 (P)

My Dear Friend: Is "Field Daisy" yours? Then I may congratulate you very much, for beyond the repeated "star", the
internal rhyme in line 9, and the awkwardness of line 8 (to which I
can suggest no improvement) it is very good indeed. I took it for
Sassoon — and — do you remember that Elizabethan thing sent me
a long time ago? You have learnt a lot since. Lines 3 and 4 are
charming indeed. (Might not line 8 run — "Of such things symbol as
unchanging are"? The accent on "such" puts me off.)

   Line 9 (to escape star) might have the common word "wonder".
The sonnet might have been Masefield's, might have been
Sassoon's. Cheerio!

   I had not paid it the compliment of copying, but all the same had
kept it folded in my notebook. It is a far, far better thing than you
have ever shown me, for the words become alive and are abstract
representations no longer.

   And so Ledwidge is dead. If the new book is not too expensive
you shall have it from me. He was a true poet, and the story of his
life is (now) a sad but romantic tale, like that of so many others, so

wastefully spent. Yet the fire may not have been struck in them save for the war; anyway it was to be, and is.

I am glad you are pleased with my communication to S and J; a most unlegally direct document, I think. Yesterday I heard from them as to the date of publication; till then I shall live in a pleasing state of anticipation, as near happiness as is possible to me. I hope it will look as well, be as small and give as much pleasure as FWHs book.

The "Round Table" arrived and was welcome. Some good articles it had. That one on English Education was truthful enough and its recommendations perfect, I think. Many thanks to the giver.

I am glad you are taking on more tasks, more amusements, since, I know, impotence must be very hard for you.

Russia seems to be kicking pretty hard now. I think with you, that we must not expect with certainty but can look forward to great things, for that offensive, betrayed, but not by cowardice, was a great thing, and so is the present resistance.

"And after a while he came to himself" . . . .
After his unaccustomed liberty had been seen for what it was — a responsibility, a burden. On the whole, out of my ignorance, I believe more in Russia than do you. Perhaps the French papers are more optimistic.

This is a darling land, and its children the most beautiful most healthy I ever saw; as a whole. Goodness is in the faces of most men, a mellow merciful spirit founded on centuries of beautiful living. (I should like to read Cammaerts and the other man.) The cottages are perfectly charming, and there is no ugly house, in the country at any rate. The roof is thatched, or like those of Sussex, red tiled. Low and longish, one has painted them white with window frames and shutters and doors in pale green. In France, blue often, brown, yellow, dark red, but not often so here. The men that would have destroyed and mastered this country have a great guilt, for such peasants are the salt of the earth; the only true test of good foundation; the essential of health; the preservation of simplicity and gratitude, and common kindness of a happy state. That Prussia also may become as she one day! — yes and England also, that is cancered and defiled by ugly towns and commodious villas, born of vulgarity, sluggish liver, greed, and all uncharitableness. (Never mind, Tewkesbury stands up so across the plain and is noble and golden of colour in autumn. And Frampton on Severn, that wonder, villages of the hills also are precious and still clean.) My dear lady your eagle eye will detect Belloc here; and why not? I am unashamed, as of a debt to Shakespeare, for both are greatly healthy, both bombastic, and both nerve on nerve alive.

Damme, I envy you those proofs! Perhaps I may be in Blighty by

then though . . . Qui sait? Five francs not enclosed yet. Though —
there is some danger of its being wasted to me if I keep it . . . . —
just now. With best wishes: Yours very sincerely   Ivor Gurney

Dont send books just yet.

To MARION SCOTT   41.123

23 August 1917 (P)

My Dear Friend: I feel a talk would do me good, and so here goes.

My gun team is in the line, but I a relief, am modestly in the rear at
present, near the big guns. Fritz tries to bomb them at night, bless
him.

The poem on Gloucester has been returned, but with request for
more. My feelings are too seriously hurt for that, though, at
present. How dare he?

One of our men just returned from England says that the bread is
much better now. I hope this is true, for one does not like to think of
friends as badly fed.

Henderson seems to have played Hamlet with singularly poor
effect. And what does that consummate old maid the Pope think he
is driving at? And what will be the effect on Catholicism of all this
pother?

I hope you will send me some more Sassoon, for his touch of
romance and candour I like. He is one who tries to tell Truth,
though perhaps not a profound truth

This is dull and hard work writing, compared to the easy speed
and interest of the spoken word. O to wake up tomorrow to find it
all a dream, myself in London just before teatime, making ready to
visit you. For, I believe, unless the flood of matter stopped the gap
of speech by sheer pressure, there is stuff enough in me to talk for
ages, since no-one is really interested in the things [that] are vital to
me. I would fix you with my glittering eye, "to move thee to a
si-i-i-gh, and chearm thee to a tee-ee-eear. Yarns that I think would
strike you pink, and petrify your ear. Of most disastrous chances,
and moving accidents in flood and field. Not arms, but *Men* I would
sing.

Perhaps I shall be able to extemporise a little after the war since
my mind is steadier than it was. But why when there are the 48 and
Schumann and Chopin and Beethoven. Why pipe on scrannel
straws at all? And what have I to sing about? The only thing I have
seen in France which absolutely took me, is Rouen, with its great

golden rock under the sun. As for England she has made copy for me, and has to be absorbed afresh — How differently, you will know by my music.

So here's a scribble all about myself, but that is because I feel lonely tonight. But do not forget you, or to hope you are getting stronger and have not to "calculate" your pleasures so much now.

With best wish: Yours very sincerely   Ivor Gurney

To MARION SCOTT   41.123

[enclosed with preceding letter] 23 August 1917 (P)

My Dear Friend: Your letter with Conan Doyle's "Guns in Sussex" arrived yesterday, and Sassoon today. Thank you so much for the trouble and patience it must have cost you to copy them. The Conan Doyle is not very good; sincere but dull. The Sassoons not so good as a whole as they might be — but true. Hodgson's "Moor" very fine.

Now your letter.

I do not know what is the cause of the unfinished letter. It is possible that being in a hurry I sent it off all tout' suite.

Surely I have thanked Mr Scott by now for his present? But all the same my mind retains no memory of the other 5 francs making 20. My memory of such things is horribly uncertain however, but my first impression is of 15, and that never has been strongly corrected by any other.

If you would like all the books I sent, save "First and Last", please accept them, and give me pleasure. (O, except of course "The Shropshire Lad".)

Nicholson has not yet arrived. I shall be delighted to see him, suck his brains and return him to you, to keep for me. I could not wish for a better birthday present. Thank you so much. (Is it a good thing to mark with presents a day which only marks another year of wasted time?)

Rumours of War
Yes, "On Sussex hills".

Verse 2. stet.

Verse 4. "No one dare speak", if you think so. But the effect is not so creepy.

Verse 6. Yes, that last line cost me trouble, and I am not sure of it yet, but stet for the sterile present.

Send "Rumours of Wars" to some paper if you like; would it be better to wait till the first book is known a little?

The Guns in Sussex has one pretty good verse — the first.

Now then — Sassoon!

"*Tree and Sky*" Mps!

Wisdom's last line is good.

Whispered Tale. True and good.

Absolution beautiful. But — one finds in it the fault of minor poets who make beautiful lines of unmeaning or not of any particular significance.

Why is time a *wind*, a *golden* wind, why does it *shake the grass?* I'll tell you; because of "pass" and because it is a good line as a whole. He was proud of it, and may have written the poem round it.

"*Golgotha*" is strained, though true, but not poetry.

"*They*" needed to be said, but is journalism pure and simple. What does "Before Day" mean? Again, line 4 means — what? This is the key, the chief part of the puzzle, so to speak. He cannot fully manage his material as yet. Line 8 ditto. As a whole "empty".

[But

you must remember that a lot of this has been written to free himself from circumstance. They are charms to magic him out of the present. Cold feet, lice, sense of fear — all these are spurs to create Joy to such as he; since Beauty is the only comfort.

Stand-to : Good Friday Morning.

Not perfect; not what he meant, but good; and the end absolutely true, save *perhaps* "old". The triple ryhmes are wrong as in other places of his poems. 3 similar endings are almost always trivial in sound. But there are tears there. That was Southern Somme front by the sound of it.

"The Moor" perfect; save perhaps for the three repeated "miles".

Why not "at miles and $\begin{Bmatrix} \text{stretching} \\ \text{desert} \\ \text{lonely} \\ \text{dreary} \end{Bmatrix}$ miles

What does Line 4 verse 2 mean?

Thank you again. These thing stimulate me and give me hope. My Anthology enlargens. Theodore Maynard is naught.

I am sick of being away from all my friends.

And last night on fatigue I had the roughest chanciest hour I ever had. My shrapnel helmet has an interesting dent in it.

However today is lovely, lovely. And yesterday we had a thrill. A German aviator was shot down from thousands and thousands of feet up (Guynemeyer did it they say.) He fell not 30 yards from me. The only exciting, really thrilling thing I have seen in France!

Best wishes for all good things:

Your sincere friend   Ivor Gurney.

190

24 August 1917 (G)

My Dear Friend: Beaucoup ourages maintenant. The bivvy sways
and wrenches at its pegs, and so do I — for I am sick of all this, all,
that is, save the shining spirit of comradeship so modestly, so
naturally, beautifully shown by certain men.

As for what has been happening, please keep the accounts of
fighting on the 22nd. There is no news at all as yet of my old
Company, but, I am sure, like the rest they did well. Luckily for me,
I am new as an M.G. and had to go up on fatigue only to return
where Fritz was lobbing shells every now and then. We got caught in
a barrage for an hour on the fatigue, and shrapnel caught me twice
— once on the blessed old tin hat, (dint and scar) and once on the
belt (no mark.) Pretty hot just there.

Thank you for copying the poems, once again. There are twenty
altogether in my book.

Curse the weather! Is it going to change again? Ah, but were it
Autumn and I in England! Such golden-pathed days I remember,
on Cranham; wading knee deep in rustling leaves, or exulting in
some miraculous sombre-passionate sunset over Wales, and in such
peace as nothing but the very presence of God may give.

I hope you are still Excelsiorising, toddling upward toward
strength. Soon the violin, soon the book, and then — what?

Well this is all for the present scribble. Best Wishes:

Your sincere friend   Ivor Gurney

                                   [enclosed with preceding letter]

24 August 1917 (G)

My Dear Friend: August 24th 10pm

The books have just arrived . . . My Goodness! Thank you
beaucoup ! Have you looked at them? Some of Brett Young is
perfect. As for Freeman, listen to the end of No. 1

  "And England lovelier looked than when
  Her dead roused not her living men."

What more do you want?

Why the Ruddy Hades did I write "Spring 1917"?

Why, O why did I, did I write . . . .

My book is far better than FWHs as a whole, but the artistry, the assurance, the matter and manner of these two absolutely puncture me.

Well, mine is interesting too: Yours   I.B.G.

All I have is 2.20!

For the present, my most grateful thanks.

To MARION SCOTT   41.125

30 August 1917 (P)

My Dear Friend: We are off up again, and this is the last letter written in the quiet. (We can write up there however, and do you write). I go up with Brent Young, Harvey, 6 Tragedies of Shakespeare and "The Bible in Spain", with nothing to fear on that account therefore.

You will find a fresh pome below, though there is no question of volunteering . . . .

And here I break off because they say no letters will be censored up there. "May all the infections that the sun sucks up — fall upon Fritz and make him by inchmeal a disease."

(Today is August 29)

To M.M.S.
      O, if my wishes were my power,
   You should be praised as were most fit,
   Whose kindness cannot help but flower.

   But since the fates have ordered
   So otherwise, then ere the hour
   Of darkness deaden all my wit.

   I'll write: how all my art was poor,
   My mind too thought-packed to acquit
   My debt . . . And only, "thanks once more".
                                    August 27, near P——

For the beggars haven't paid us yet! 30 francs in 8 weeks!

The Volunteer

I would test God's purposes;
I will go up and see
What fate is mine, what destiny
God holds for me.

For He is very secret,
He smiles, but does not say
A word that will foreshadow
Shape of the coming day.

Curious am I, curious . . . .
And since he will not tell
I'll prove him, go up against
The flary mouth of Hell.

And what hereafter — Heaven?
Or Blighty? O if it were . . . .
Mere agony, mere pain the price
Of the returning there.

Or — nothing! Days in mud
And slush, then other days . . . .
Aie me ! "Are they not all
The seas of God?" God's Ways?

That's not so bad, I think. Are colours turning yet in Kent? Perhaps.
In Kensington Gardens I have no doubt leaves are turning colour,
are drifting to please children as in other years, but the country is
different and holds its ways longer, especially in the West Country,
that greener and fairer land than poor old smoky Middlesex.

Herein you will find also a dissertation on Nicholson's book,
which would be sent off today, had I the money, but that lacking,
the book must stay behind, safe in a sandbag. You shall have my
second note book when that parcel comes.

Things look pretty hopeful now, dont they? The Italians seem to
have remembered Caesar and his far wars and glory. What the
Austrians remember I cannot say (Austerlitz?) And the French
dont seem exhausted, and as for the English . . . . Our guns would
frighten imps in the lowest concrete dugout of Hell, so they shake
me up pretty considerably.

Now write to me, prattle sweetly in your accustomed fashion, for
how long we shall be in we do not know save from that fickle jade

Rumour, whose information is rarely much good. And by all means send the proofs if you can get a double set. Goodbye With best wishes:

Your sincere friend

Ivor Gurney

To MARION SCOTT   41.132

31 August 1917 (G)

August 31st 6 pm

My Dear Friend: Still moving along life's weary road, not very pleased with the scenery of this section of it, and wishing the guns would give over; for these literally are never still.

When the parcel comes with the books returned to you, you will find a small packet wrapped in newspaper (if it is allowed to be sent, as I suppose it will). In this there will be a local German newspaper of August 10, and a fragment of filthy notebook which you might like to have — it being as I think a piece of a section commanders book.

This morning I was exploring some ruined Tanks but not with any striking success.

And tomorrow is September 1st !

Summer almost gone . . . . . .

Seven years behind accomplishment !

Today I have been reading "The Bible in Spain", that brilliant curious book. Indeed, but Borrow is indispensable — "Lavengro", "Wild Wales", Rommany Rye and "The Bible in Spain"! A queer chap though, and often purposely queer. Also FWHs book has been in my hands, but I desire before all things to learn, and he has not much knowledge. But it is queer to look from the real sight of this tortured ground on to that picture of my old School House taken from the playing ground !

I.B.G.

When windy, "write letters," and so — here you are.

For Fritz has been shelling and it has rattled me.

Thank you for your two letters — August 26, 27th. It delighted me to get them this morning.

As for the "Fifth Gloucester Gazette" I am indifferent. The only public I could get to that will not be accessible in the ordinary way, is that class of people who would not care for what I write.

As to the "Field Daisy", it seems to me that the first version is better than this last, of line 8; with which there is nothing seriously wrong anyhow. But here is a bit that pleases me.

"Even before this pain was set upon the Earth, this scourge of War"

For I do not altogether agree with you that it is all Man's fault.

It is very good news to hear that Fritz gets a hotter time of it on his present raids on England than he did. The Foul fiend. I hope you will escape ever being bombed at all, wherever you pitch your tent and make your stay.

Cyril Scott writes as one expects.

The lights you saw on that Wednesday were Aurora Borealis, so I read; not lightning. Mein Gootness! Now I remember seeing something of the kind most wonderful about that time perhaps, but took it for a coast bombardment, yet heard no sound, which was strange. These illuminations are connected in some mysterious way with sun-spots.

You are right about Sassoon; you are right about Hodgson. Sassoon is the half-poet, the borrower of magic. But as for the talk about poetry . . . . . well, I think about that sometimes in this little concrete and steel emplacement holding 25 men, but O the crush! Slum conditions if you please.

As for your book, I doubt whether you will get much help from me, whose convictions are firm but nebulous.

As for the Imagists — I hate all attempts at exact definition of beauty, which is a half-caught thing, a glimpse. What the devil *is* a "cosmic poet"? Surely a better name would be cosmetic ?

Hodgson is really the true thing, and so I would rather put off comment till later when I am better able to think of such things, and have read the "Song of Honour" in full. If it is much longer, O please dont copy any but the very best parts, for to tell the truth, I do not like being obliged to people for kindnesses I would not return, and to copy out the "Song of Honour" would about kill me. Thank you very much for your beastly decency, as boys say.

"When I'm among a blaze of stars" is very clear-cut, well and truly seen, but not poetry. Good verse.

"The Bells of Heaven" is splendid. "Reason has moons". I will refer to again.

Ruined Tanks in front of me against a flaring west of tomorrows wind and rain. A country like the last Hell of desolation. And to write verse, and abstract perfection ! And so I quiet my nerves and set my mind on another train of thought. I am most grateful for your friendship for you are the only one of my real friends save my while-lost FWH that can talk about these things, and can stimulate me. I am convinced that without you "Severn and Somme" would have been either not written, (as most probable) or written on pieces of letters etc and drifted piecemeal away as fast as written:

Your sincere friend   Ivor Gurney

To MARION SCOTT

9 September 1917 (P)

My Dear Friend: Your letters of August 30 and 31st reached grateful me in the line. Je vous en remercie !

You have had a great patience in copying out the "Song of Honour". I would not have asked had I known its length. Do not copy any more Sassoon please; I have absorbed him. He is a neat picturesque interesting writer who occasionally reaches poetry. The "Song of Honour" has great passages but is not the poem all we have been waiting for. (But for that, afterwards). No, I dont like "Ave (Autumne", I should think; if a second declension.)

"The leaves are preparing to die" is prosy.

"The amethyst asters (are) gemmed in imperial hue" is a good line, but could be used better

The amethyst asters gemmed in imperial hue
Most royal, emerald herbage flaunting its riches.

Line 2 of v. 3 is weak, and line 3 annoys me with "like". Say boldly things *are*. (Also 4 "The's" at the beginnings of lines.)

The golden-rod lifts processional torches of splendour,
From sapphire heaven gentian catches a gleam.
Topaz the phlox, and luminous, pink other worldly,
And daisies silver-of-dreams.

The last verse is good, especially the last line, but not coherent, yet easily made so. As it stands it does not make sense, to me.

The "One legged man" is good. "The Bells of Heaven" glorious.

I will talk of the "Song of Honour" when I can see it whole. Meanwhile many thanks. When they pay us, perhaps tomorrow, I will return the books mentioned before.

(Second letter)

I am glad you have managed to get some concession in the way of flour, and very glad you have managed 2 miles, say rather over 3 kilos! You will do it with a pack someday for fun !

I do hope you will manage to stay at Sevenoaks, and in a nice house. Indeed you deserve luck, since it is luck to have you as a friend.

(O "Reason has moons" is perfectly delightful, and O delighting me).

Well, we are out now, but for how long is doubtful. It may be the out-of-the-line feeling, but I do not think I shall get killed. That is the only premonition, save a slight one that there is no Blighty just yet.

Leave is quite possible when this fighting season closes.

I have no more to say, save that on such a September day as this I should have been picking apples and shooting rabbits with Willy Harvey. Crack not my heartstrings! Best wishes: Your sincere friend   Ivor Gurney

September 7

My Dear Friend: As this letter has not yet been taken, I may as well add a P.S. to say what a devil of a temper I am in — what with flies, lice, and being on guard.

They have paid me — 10 francs! So today if possible Nicholson and Co shall set out youward. I wish that I could write some more now, but dont feel up to it. What's up with the weather? What's up with everything? Everything's up what, and that's the truth of it. Meanwhile go you on and prosper.

To MARION SCOTT   41.134

9 September 1917 (G)

My Dear Friend: Thank you very much for your letter of September 3, which reposes peacefully before me on a pack. Conditions : beautiful morning, which we must spend in a concrete affair, once a peaceful farm; now called after that farm, but O how unlike ! ("How unlike the state from which they fell !")

I am sorry you get well so slowly. The War is probably the cause, and War diet. May it not be so for long!

Russia does seem in a hole now; but the declaration of a Russian minister that the cause of the retreat was concentration of technical force and not cowardice sounds better. (Tanks?) The enormous majority against Stockholm at the English Trades Union Conference is very good and encouraging. So also is Gerard's statement that he thinks Germany can hold out not more than another year, economically. Gerard must be a man worth meeting !

I am glad you like my last two things, especially that for you.

Yesterday I sent off to the postman a parcel containing, "Five Degrees South", "Presage of Victory"; and Nicholson's book; which (as you suppose) has taught me something; my second notebook and anthology; a German paper; and, lastly, a noisome fragment of a German NCOs note-book, as I should judge, at least.

The best way to learn to write is to read classics like Milton, Keats and Shakespeare, and the Georgian poets. (Do you remember V. Williams said the same about Music?). One learns form and the true use of language from those, and flexibility and the modern touch from these. Remoteness and Modernity mixed, is the best diet for youth — or age. In my notebook you will find some things you have not seen. Do as you will with them. By the way you have never acknowledged a poem called ————— (because the name may not be written) and a Shakespearian sonnet that came with it, of which I am rather proud. These are written in the note-book though rather illegibly. Some things there may help to pad out a book if I happen to return to Music sooner than — 40 poems shall we say? Though, if the first book is successful we ought to do with less, and then not be considered mean.

I do not ask you how you are for Form's sake, (since nearly always I forget Form,) but because I wish to know. Thank you for telling me, and please keep on. Do you feel ill or merely weak and helpless or what? I mean, can you Live a little now? Your letters are alert enough anyhow.

"The Song of Honour" was good enough when it was written, but it is better still now. Could one, dare one write a hymn to the honour of Man now: It would be too high a thing. Only a Bishop could not see that. Only the professional Churchman is blind, who "goes lack-lustre" all his days.

The Five Francs have not been sent. Please excuse this, but — well it was only 10 francs after 3 weeks, and the Line to follow. In a certain case I must refer you to my executors, thats all.

My books up here are few — Tolstoi's "Master and Man etc", "A Gloucestershire Lad" and verse taken from your letters. (By the way I spotted Corbie the other day, near Peronne.)

Do you care for "The Late Last Rook"? I cant say it attracts me much.

Tolstoi's short tales are perfect. No one but a Master could write so well and simply: anyone must love them.

By the way, I *did* write to thank Mr Scott for his long letter and present, surely ? My memory. My memory!

Such an afternoon! Golden September sunshine which should be seen flecked in the grass of Redlands paddock with FWH and I strolling round — talking, talking.   With best wishes:

Your sincere friend   Ivor Gurney

To MARION SCOTT   41.135

12 September 1917 (G)

Letters of Sep 3 -7
Sep 12

My dear Friend: Thank you, in spite of what I wrote about not thanking.

I am very glad you like my two last things, two more toward your book. Today I have been writing, but will polish up a little before sending it on.

—— (you are right about the title!) was a mere exercise, a fill up of time, written because I had not written for some time. Your praise of it shows that I have some technique now! Of the last line of verse 2 — there is an influence further back than FWH. "And they shall die like men; and fall like one of the princes."

I am very sorry to hear of your sisters illness, and hope she is getting well in a proper manner. It does not sound dangerous anyway. May old Dr Burnett prove right that you yourself will have a free time from illness for the rest of your days. After all, it may be true that a radical defect is now removed, and though the trouble caused thereby is great a good time follows after. It is reasonable to think so, surely?

You need not be disappointed at your birthday present being a failure. It was not; since my own book appears to be better than Nicholson's! I only wish things were quiet so that the book could be studied by me, but that will come after — when there is no need. Now you add the three other books, your present appears royal. You will enjoy Brent Young, a poet — though not a big one, and a master of his craft, through studying Robert Bridges chiefly. There are some lovely things in that book, and it was good to come across Bredon mentioned. This is the Gloster-Worcestershire Bredon, not Housman's.

I hope you will manage to stay at Sevenoaks, since it suits you and pleases you, and since the soil seems favourable to letter writing.

By the way I am still in the line, but not having at all a bad time of it. My throat is sore from gas; it is just (or was) as if I had had catarrh, but only an occasional explosion of coughing is left now. No luck! One cannot smell the new gas. One starts sneezing. The old gas had a heavy hothouse Swinburnian filthy sort of odour — voluptuous and full of danger.

Yes, "Eternal Treasure" is good. The use of "safes" is purely Shakespearian, not mine; though I have forgotten a passage to quote. "Macbeth" perhaps has it. O yes, and "Antony"

I am glad Harold Darke likes my things so, and of course he may use my song.

As to Sassoons book, you will find the pretty but thin "Before the Battle" in my note book. The other isn't bad. Violent of course = weak. Please do not trouble to copy out things of this standard; they not giving me pleasure enough to compensate for your trouble.

We go out tonight, it is likely, thank Goodness !

Outside the guns are hammering, but they will have to hammer well at this remnant of a German blockhouse before they hurt us, and anyway it is mostly our guns. 10 shells to one is a usual procedure.

Goodbye, and dont worry, and get well as quickly as you may, for the War must end someday, and it will be a joyful thing to find my friends fit. Best wishes:

Your sincere friend   Ivor Gurney

To MARION SCOTT   41.131

September 1917 (G)   September — Monday

My Dear Friend: Thanks be to goodness I am out of it for a day or two, gassed in the throat 5 days ago — but not thinking to get anything out of it. How long will it last? Couldnt say, but not so long as I would wish. Being gassed (mildly) with the new gas is no worse than catarrh or a bad cold.

Well, everything in the way of letters will go astray for a bit, and it is probably of no use to send an address now, as anytime we may be shifted.

So — to correct Proofs !

Luckily they arrived the day before I went sick. Please cut out the dedications as I have said. So many are they that one arrives in the end at giving them to those who expect it rather than those to whom one would wish.

Yes, I agree, considering the poor paper, the book looks very nice, but O (yes, "O" !) the "I"s! Confronted with the thing in cold print, I am struck with the thinness and futility and egoism of the thing — but wont say more. I have arrived at more pages than FWH, but he has oftener long things like Ballades. From that last word I turned aside to look "Severn and Somme" through once more, and finished the corrections, as I think. Dont you think from what you have that Book 2 will be a better one than this? I hope you have the notebook by now, as perhaps you may think one or two things worth using.

Yesterday I met my pet RAMC man, who knew Tolstoi. He gave me a surprise. Told me his girl was Brett Young's sister! He has often spoken of her, but until I read that book, Five Degrees South, it could mean nothing to me who she was; while we are in France anyhow.

I am very glad you are able to find something to suit you at Sevenoaks; in all ways it is better to stay there, and for your sister to come too soon.

Well, there will be no letters for me now; probably not till I settle down somewhere, and that will be the MGC again I think, for there is not much hope of staying in hospital for me. By the way your letter of Sep:12 arrived just as I left. With best wishes:

Your sincere friend   Ivor Gurney

To MARION SCOTT   41.136

21 September 1919 (P)

My Dear Friend: Still at the C.C.S. but expecting to move today, through the blowiest white flecked weather of September, every gust of which brings a memory to me; of scent, of sight, or of sound of the hollow echoes of woodfelling or some such thing at Highnam. I dont wonder you wish to stay at Sevenoaks, Chelsea and the Gardens have their charm and Yoshio Markino has told us about the Colour of London. (By the way have you read that most fascinating book?) O that I were worse! It would not have been too difficult to get to Blighty with a real serious case now. Just my luck !

Strong protests and representations have been forwarded to the Lord Almighty, but I expect no yielding in that quarter, and on account of so common a complaint.

Again a term beginning draws near. O what a wasted time! Can it be possible to acquire a balance of experience of life, of clear sight and strength of character to make up for all this? Twenty-seven, and not yet trained! I feel a boy still; a boy who has not yet had his chance, with the ability and determination to make one if necessary. That is in the abstract. In the concrete, the continual question recurs, "Will you ever be able to build, to construct? Could you write one good Sonata movement?" No, I couldnt; but let me get back to soak myself properly in music, and to feel alive again and secure, and then — En avant ! Full steam ahead! And then (to alter the image) I hope to have sufficiently hard work to hold the tiller. O comforting dreams !

Today should send you out walking, and far, if the wind is not too much. For the air, here in this tent, is as clear and pure as any of Kent, I suppose. It is a 25 mile day, though you will hardly manage that yet awhile. It is a day to see Cranham above you and Portway in front, to stalk knee deep through drifts of early fallen leaves; to climb higher for the sight of Severn, Wales, Malvern, Bredon and Clee Hills — I chuck in the Severn plain as buckshee. A sunset and the road over Coopers likewise. But Arcturus over May Hill I reserve for myself.

I hope your sister is getting better still (It is some time before I may hear anyhow) and will be able to get to you soon. She might as well convalesce at Sevenoaks as near Hyde Park. The puddles of Kent are better than the rivers of Middlesex.

I am very sorry the proofs will reach you in so dirty an envelope. Your own, but it had travelled, and such things must be shoved any old where in the Army. Curse the Army!

This is an annoying wind; it gathers or seems to gather the sweetest things one has ever known to drift about and taunt a poor private of no renown at all, at all. Curse the wind!

By the way, I moi meme have got the name for being extremely cool under shell-fire. It may be so to the view, but could they read my mind sometimes! So you see, neurasthenia leads one to a strange praise. By conquering fear-of-Life one may learn at once to love Life and to scorn death together; but neither has come yet in reality.   With best wishes: Your sincere friend   Ivor Gurney

III

BLIGHTY

To MARION SCOTT   41.137

26 September 1917 (P)

My Dear Friend: To write to you on common notepaper, white
and smooth, to be in between sheets white as snow — yesterday, but
I smoke in bed! — and to hear noises domestic and well known
flurries and scurries about one — how sweet are all these!

And to be within 17 miles of Enbro, that old city of Scott and
R.L.S.; such is my nature that this last idea in fact is sweetest of all.
Ward 24, Edinburgh War Hospital, Bangour, Scotland is my present
address. Only slowly and uncertainly is the conviction leaking in
through the strong covering of frost and use that I am *really* in
Blighty. You remember FWHs parable of the man who was in
Heaven and did not know it? Even so is it with me!

Last night started the change moving a little quicker for I played
for two hours, mostly in accompaniment, and I found to my joy that
what I had hoped is true — the effort to concentrate is a pleasure to
me; which means that in so much neurasthenia is a thing of the past,
and that what I have would go if I lived in my old life once again,
with an added incalculable Joy added thereto. Rejoice with me my
friend, for that which was lost is found; or shall I say rather — its
hiding place is known.

I hope Autumn with its crisp air and beauty is bringing you some
treasure of health also, you who are Captain of your soul though the
body play all manner of fantastic tricks. And you sister too, whose
sword of spirit is also too keen for the scabbard, as one has said.

Now look at that! O Sherlock Holmes, could you not deduce
somewhat from the arrangement of these two pages? [*The single
sheet is divided into two very uneven columns.*]

I shall be delighted to hear from you again. Please send the old
letters on. Are you in your new house I wonder? What about the
book ?

(I wont say anything about the state of me — medically speaking,
being profoundly disappointed, and not hoping to escape the
Winter as I had thought).

How lovely to hear the voices of Scottish women, and see the
faces of women pitiful, proud, humorous, strong, lovely of spirit.

Not that the Frenchwomen are not fine. They most undoubtedly
are. But the strength of our Islanders is very fine. And which is
likely to be the finer strength I would ask — that of men who have
controlled themselves in danger and long cold nights of mud and
frost, and under a hateful discipline; or that of women doing day
long duty of pity in routine? I would say that of women who are
always active in service, will be finer and stronger, only there are

comparatively few of them. But there — I am lost in admiration of all Europe, driven by forces beyond their control. The contrast between the magnificent behaviour of Man to that of the apparent callousness of God is most striking, and were it for no other reason than that of having companied with good men one could face God with (almost) a slightly cynical but interested expectation. His debt to Europe, to the world, is very great.

Two or three things I have read that are good. Walpole's "Maradick at Forty", and G A Birmingham's "The Bad Times". Also an article by Belloc, which has been forcibly abstracted from "The Western Australia". I know you will be interested to see it. What "Nights at the Mermaid" must have gone to the making of this essay! Also, "Snaith's "Fortune" a splendid bit of braggadocio. Swank at its best.

I wonder if you have seen "Gloucestershire Friends" yet?

Of course I will come and see you if every Fate will not contravene me. My ten days leave will come anywhere from 1 — 2 months time. The farther off, the luckier, for I do not wish to go Back There just yet. On the other hand, there's nothing the matter with me.

I am not well of course, but the thing that struck me on the boat coming over was that no one looked well. There was not any more jollity among all that crowd going to Blighty than if it were merely Another Move. The iron had entered into their souls, and they were still fast bound; unable to realise what tremendous changes of life had come to them for a while. Dear Marion, this was sad to see, and a tribute to the power of the Old Sweats and Prussians generally, But the river — that magnificent river, the Seine ! From Rouen to Le Havre it is just one splendid Symphony, the greatest I have ever seen. I could only try to forget I was so weak of soul to remember a feeling of sickness in my body, and wish they would give me three days rations and a small sailing boat. By the Lord, I would have sailed her clean across if there had been sight of any star. Airships were patrolling the harbour mouth.

Now I must go down to shave — in front of a real mirror! Clean sheets, clean clothes and skin; no lice; today's papers; ordinary notepaper . . . What next?

Good bye, and all good wishes for all good things:

Your sincere friend   Ivor Gurney

To MARION SCOTT   41.137

26 September 1917 (G)

My Dear Friend: I have just finished Vachell's "Quinneys", and would like to talk about it. Surely the book will last? (You see I assume you have read it.) For the characterisation is so good, the play of events so inevitable that — since Cranford can last — I can see it in the hands of people of 2005. Perhaps it is Qs love of his craft that pleases me most, but Susan, Posy, Tomlin the stranger of Brittany, Lord Mel — all please and delight me infinitely, especially after slogging at Classics so long. Soon, I suppose, the curious observer may be able to see me strolling round Enbro, browsing at bookstalls, for one glad hour forgetting myself. If I see any very extra especial bargains here you shall hear of them, be sure. I love buying books, but when that is not possible, luring my friends on has an equal pleasure for me!

Since I must live in the past, why not live in the company of great men, by stalls laden with tattered books of their making? If they can know, it must please them to see a soldier weary of arms and routine forgetting himself in a delicious agony of uncertainty, caused partly by his divided love and (bond of sympathy to them) a loose purse ? Did I buy all I wished, should I read all I bought? That is very doubtful, but the touch smell and appearance of books is very lovely to me.

I wonder if you are in your new house by now, and whether you find it in some way home. You have a great house in London, but I doubt whether it can be to you what a tiny house may be, even if it is hung only with framed pages of the "Studio" or "Jugend", and the piano leaves little room for free movement, and three pipes going would soon asphyxiate the careful landlady. How are the creepers round your house? The winds are chill here today; soon frost will enforce the colours of Autumn on your walls, to delight yourself and as I hope your sister too. (I am not sure she is not right about liking "Estaminet" best.)

Life will begin to widen itself for you soon, with the violin and your book; let but the winter be but kind, and you should be finely set up by May, and see what Spring can do for fragile things of Earth ! Why, even playing "The Rosary", "Friend of Mine", "Drake's gone West" etc has bucked me up no end. What power shall not Bach have on you, that is full of all sanity and sweetness and a great restoring power of health? When Peace comes, all the air now full of uneasiness and hate will sweeten; when Europe is sick it is not strange that a spirit like yours should be affected; but it is hard lines you should have to suffer more or less passively. But will you remember that soldiers also suffer passively but under direct orders that lead them to act — as machines of boats that go among hidden mines, risking destruction.

War brings greater self-control — or breakdown. You also must have mastery of yourself, or perish. And whether the pain be or complaining nerves or of waiting on age long nights of cold and wet to pass, it is all the same, and the use of patience brings the same reward. There is even the same uncertainty with us two, for instance — the same aching thought; whether we shall get the chance to use the rewards of patience. Indeed there is no difference in our conditions, save that I have the right to wear two "wounded" stripes, and you can only want to do something — anything, to justify yourself to yourself. There again we are equal; for War is simply a necessary but horrid nuisance, and my aim is work in art, not a medal or a ribbon. Another consideration. Supposing I did get a DCM, I know well that braver men than myself have died without, and how to wear a distinction without shame, that is so uncertain in the earning?

Please do not accuse yourself of uselessness. At any rate not to me, who have so much to thank you for.

Our positions are reversed, and I am trying to cheer *you* up for once, instead of writing interminable complaints to get wise consoling words.

Today there may be a letter from you, perhaps many letters from France sent on, but it is not wise to hope for all that to happen after 4 days of hospital.

Today I will write to Howells, and Shimmin. There is Sir CHHP to come, and one or two others of lower degree.

For the length of this letter you must accuse the lack of magazines and books here. For the lack of matter a dull life, but what you have endured so often you may well last out again. If there were no M.M.S. it would be necessary to invent one. With best wishes:

Your sincere friend   Ivor Gurney

To MARION SCOTT   41.138

29 September 1917 (P)   Ward 24, Edinburgh Military Hospital, Bangour.

My Dear Friend: I have just turned over a page, just finished writing a most unsatisfactory piece of verse with which I shall not trouble you. And would you really be polite enough to ask how I am getting on? Then you shall learn that the will of the doctor still keeps me in bed and on Light Diet; as that does not include bully-beef and biscuits I am not unsatisfied altogether, but it does mean *Lightness*, and that is not good. And the little baccy I have is of the most distressing; cigarettes are no companions like a pipe, and one tires of them. They do not care for classical music much here; my head is thick; my fingers stiff; the weather dull; there is nothing worth reading.

So there you are out of my grumbles. For to lie between clean linen in a light room is no small thing; nor to be able to buy todays papers a small blessing. It is good to wander surreptitiously from ones own room to another and listen to Scots tales of battle and winter hardship — if one does not look forward. Rest is good, and for the present that is all my business. Would to God I had a cough — a cough! What can a gassed man do without something hoarse or rattly? My chances are small, for my chest betrays me, of staying peacefully "in silk and scented down".
I have a rendezvous with Fritz
By some disputed barricade"
and that before long.

Perhaps you would like to hear something of our movements lately. When I left Rouen, the first place we got to was Nesles, which had been ours not more than two months or so; and well preserved, not destroyed at all; pretty and soberly charming. However, our division had left that front the day before, so after that one night, off we went to Amiens to catch them 10 kilos the other side. (There was no time to see the Cathedral.) I have forgotten the name of the place. A few days after a 23 kilometre march with a sick foot about settled me — but there! one gets used to dying out yonder; so there we were in Neuvillette, near Bouquemaison. More Marching. Wavans, I think. Then in the line for 8 days at Arras, to the right of Mouchy, watching which hill-village at dawn, I thought of the "Song at Morning"; Out again, somewhere. Then by train to Buire-au-Bois, near Auxi-le-Chateau. Beautiful country and very nice people. There we had training for some time, and trampled down crops and crops enough to make you sick. But what cared Brass-hats for all-daylight labour gone to ruin? I left the Glosters at Buire au Bois for the MGC at Vaux. All this country is marked with old encampments, and full of memories. A beautiful land — but not my own. From Vaux to Saint Omer by train. From Saint Omer to Buysscheure, 10 kilos. Training awhile. Then up through Arike by train to the Ypres front, near Poperinghe, that neat clean dignified worthy home of dignity and civic life, now being shelled every day, bombed every night. And then up by short marches to the right of St Julien. Where sheer, hideousness is the prettiest thing. Where peace often reigns because men are tired of shooting each other. Where I searched the Tanks with two other men, but — too late. Where I was an hour getting tea and sugar from dead mens kits and salvaging a mess-tin, which was sniped. Where I stopped a panic; the best thing to me so far; and found that filthy fragment of notebook, and that paper you have, (I hope.) for it was sent off some weeks ago,

smelling pretty foully. I was half afraid to send it, but knew you had
liberty to drop it in the fire if you so wished, and had curiosity to
know what it was exactly.

O the souvenirs I might have had! But only officers have any real
good chance of souvenirs, since only they can get them off. The men
find things, and people who live in dugouts will hang them up and
brag of great deeds in that old time. But the men, who could not
carry very well, *and had no place to store things* and hardly a leave,
will be empty-handed. You see, if one finds something interesting,
it may be in a hot corner, and how is one to carry it, for the
haversack is full. Suppose one gets it out the line, then one must
wait for leave, or a friend's leave. And if a wound comes all your
stuff is lost. A man found a quartermasters stores at Omiecourt,
near Chartres, with hundreds of brand new helmets, but all that
could be done was a little traffic with officers. I had two books and
some papers for you, all lost at Vermand. Men hang on to revolvers
and badges, watches and compasses etc, all that can be easily
carried. There is too much sniping for the fighters to get souvenirs,
the salvage and burial parties get them. (Will this letter interest
you? And if so, why?) People unfitted for the line, lunatics, funks,
bosseyed idiots and such like, from whom an officer with 50 francs
may make himself rich with booty — and reputation, the ASC do
well, for they have room to store. R.T. officers, with Real Homes.
Brass Hats can get what they would. Only the poor fool who goes
over the top — and under the bottom — seems to be without
anything at all. It is only fair to say that he is easily contented — with
bare life, warmth, and food he must be counted rich; so by all means
load weights of discipline on to him till he cares not whether he is in
Rest or in the Line. And doesnt care a ha'peny obscenity about
souvenirs save in his leg or arm; marketable, magic-carpet-like,
transmuting talismans as they are. What an ode Burns would write
to a Piece of Shrapnel! I hope for a letter from you very soon:

    Your sincere friend   Ivor Gurney

To MARION SCOTT   41.139

1 October 1917 (P)   *Ward 24, Edinburgh War Hospital,*
Bangour.

My Dear Friend: I have just discovered a letter which should have
gone days ago, which might have been answered by now had it not
been overlooked. But — have you had my address at all yet? If not,
my carelessness brings its own punishment, for letters from you are
a pleasure to me — even in Blighty, where one may be in bed and

read that strange fiery record of "Villette". What a queer magical sort of tale it is, and what an uncanny tortured other worldly yet supremely real atmosphere she can bring one into! Was she one of the people who can find no peace on earth? Or, rather one who would have done very well in Canada, Australia, South Africa? It is a dreadful thing to realise that moving but a few yards into the company of next door people might bring one out of Heaven into Hell or vice versa.

And what a style! In a few words she can give you an Autumn evening in a way not equalled by any writers of that time — if even they ever seriously attempted such description. We are used to such moments of beauty in our books in this later day.

In Chapter 12, there is an exquisite description of the night sky with its crescent moon, and then this —
                    the thunderstorm.
"Within the dormitory they gathered round the nightlamp in consternation, praying loud. I could not go in. Too resistless was the delight of staying with the wild hour, black and full of thunder, pealing out such an ode as language never delivered to man — too terribly glorious, the spectacle of clouds, split and pierced by white and blinding bolts.'

Where is R.L.S. and the tribe, one and all of conscientious makers of style?

How lucky I am not to have read her, to come fresh to a great classic! Bon! I lick my chops and will continue.

Did you see the review of F W Hs book in the TLS? Golly, but there is nothing to give my poor friend a swelled head in that notice. It *is* true that in a "Gloucestershire Lad" there is not much good stuff, but what of that when "In Flanders" is there — a pure beauty, actual colour and wistful distance of blue hills on the page? As for my own, they will not say much to affect me, for the sight of the whole thing in proof convinced me that humility should be my proper mood, and gratitude for a hobby found when one was needed. Neither he nor I have lived in the proper atmosphere to write much yet — the company of men who are trying for the same end and prize of a modern techique. That matters little to me, who have another larger and finer string to my bow, but for him — he must be thirty now and has a living to earn —at law, which he hates.
                    (Another dirty sheet.)
Ah! a light bursts on me suddenly, I believe, know, that I have sent you a letter: Belloc's article which has gone proves it; so that soon I shall be hearing from you, perhaps in an hour or so. Who knows?

Margaret Hunt has written to me of your new address, and so it shall go there direct this time. I hope you like the house well, and can feel at home there, and that with you it is sunnier than with us near Enbro, where the sky was grey and austere on the day that papers told us was Londons most beautiful day of Autumn.

Allons, I am nothing but grumbles because staying in bed makes me unfit in no time — a bundle of oppressed nerves; and those ruddy drawing room ballads set me afire. It is true that they want an accompanist, and he *might* stay on some time beyond ordinary, even till Christmas, but, though a refusal will mean France before then perhaps, rather than play accompaniments to songs I hate, and the little good music that stays with me still to a more or less unwilling audience; I will become a leader of forlorn hopes, a pot-hunter, a scalp-seeker of high renown. Four blessed hours I played yesterday: four ages of exquisite torture.

Two extracts from Scripture. "Lord help me". "For I am not as other men are".

The TLS praises Drinkwaters Plays a great deal. He has a fine technique, and only now have I acquired concentration adequately to appreciate such work, so it will be well for me to make such haste as I may to know these.

If we were playing Bach together now . . . . Or Brahms, if he were not too difficult for me! Or if FWH and I were walking the Minsterworth roads, talking hard of books, and I encouraging and stimulating him, O what joy! Now and here, in this light clean room, there is nothing for me but the old feeling of inefficiency, sadly wasted time, still buried talents, and a sense of shame at my continual grumbles where others are content. Just to see the face of a Scot not 12 yards away, what a humiliation of weakness must I feel before such strength! I swear that if happiness and utility do not come to me after the war, I will first earn some money at picture-palaces and then go to sea with such men, whom I do admire so, and who take me along with them to some extent; in a rough life to live in free air, to word oneself clean out with the joy that comes from sticking it well to follow.

Sorry, but you get always the full flow of my grievances!
Your sincere friend   Ivor Gurney

To MARION SCOTT   41.140

1 October 1917 (P)

My Dear Friend: Your letter of the 28th has arrived, and the enclosure, which is hereby returned, properly dealt with.

Indeed I am distant — Here follows a confession I have made to noone else. There were 6 districts to which one might be sent. The Gloucester district ranged from Bristol, Cardiff, Birmingham to somewhere East. If one asked to be sent there, it might be that Fate would manage it. That is, it was both doubtful whether you would be allowed to stick to your district, and how far away from home you would be *if* you got there. But — so I was told, Scotland was sure; took even the overflow of other districts.

Now I knew that my getting to England was practically a fluke, and my stay in hospital certain to be short — I wished to see Scotland, Edinburgh in particular, so why not? And here I am. But the chief fact was that railway fares were fearfully high, and visits fearfully short. So why bother about being near friends, when the bother was not likely to land one within 75 miles at least of the place desired? I did not bother, and so have saved my friends' money and time, and from worrying as to whether they *ought* to come and see me.

There is nothing the matter with me as far as I know save fatheadedness and unfitness and indigestion from doing nothing and eating too much. (I am in a horrible temper, so dont interrupt; Weltmuth and indigestion together. Of course it *might* be gas. I only hope they keep me here till I am cured under that impression!)

I am as Ratty as can be, but nobody knows it, save you. So much France has done for me.

For Business —

Here you are and Damn the Censor!!

(Down, down my heart — {King Lear}).

You may have both "Pain and Beauty" and "Purple and Black". It is my wish to please you. As for the cover, do just as you please.

And so the parcel has not come!

Brett Young and all! Souvenirs as well.

My voice breaks. I can no more.

Tears. General snuffles

This must go now if you are to have it soon.

I am glad your sister is better, and with you. Floreat soror tua: Your sincere friend   Ivor Gurney

To HERBERT HOWELLS   3.12

2 October 1917 (P)

My Dear Howells: One thing in your letter interested me hugely. Have "they" been writing you "anonymous insults"? If this is connected with your music, Cheerio; you are getting on. You dont tell me much about yourself. As for your work, is it suspended in the summer holidays? Anyway, dont give me silly or unpleasing answers, for I am in the devil of a temper. I am not *quite* sure whether the gas has not slightly aggravated my ordinary thick-headedness and indigestion. If this is so, then there's hope for the Wangler: if not, then no hope; I should be merely a Lucky Blighter soon to be cast out into outer darkness again. Anyway, I am that spoilt pet of Society, an accompanist that can read at sight. But O! what that same Pet has to endure! The rapturous soulfulness that disdains tempo. The durchganging baritone that will not be stayed long by interludes of piano, whose eager spirit is bars too early for the fray. The violinist that will play *songs* — not only the voice part but any choice twiddly bits that a careless writer has left to the piano. The universal clamourous desire for ragtime. Topsiturviness of diseased vanity of all sorts, kinds, conditions. Enbro is indeed a magic name. Its glamour is increased (as usual) by distance and denial. 16 miles and regulations of the most strict. I wonder which was Henley's hospital? There are many memories round this city, but the dearest to me are those of R L S, that friend of Everyman. Henley and the Great Sir Walter, Dr John Brown and Holyrood come after him in my mind. There is no blooming (well done!) music in my head. I am frosted up. Last night, I felt the beginning of the thaw, the first hint of what joy music might give. I was playing Beethoven, and for one golden minute my wandering mind was fixed and could see the stars; I forgot the restraint that so long has been partly self-imposed on myself and flew free. Why I had no indigestion to speak of! A glimpse up the shaft of Hell.

Perhaps some songs may come from me before I return, but there is a lot to do before my mind will freely conceive anything. You simply dont know what France means, not in horror, but in everyday trial. If this letter is to go, it must finish now. "Hoping that you are in the pink": Yours ever I B G

To MARION SCOTT 41.141

4 October 1917 (G)

My Dear Friend: Your letter of September 30 has arrived. With it, the first really presentable weather North Britain (I will be rude) has seen fit to give us. This morning has shadows and there is a velvet look to the distances, the sky seems new again, the strength of the hills is not grim.

It is to be feared that yet another parcel is lost. The poem I was writing is also lost; they dropped my vanity bag carrying me from train to hospital — the fraud that I felt !

Perhaps it wasnt bad, but my brain was really getting stuck over there. How much, last night showed me. The Presbyterian Chaplain gave a lecture on Adam Smith. He was a capable man, what do I say! He was touched with greatness, supremely alive, warm-blooded, interested, interesting, fine looking with eyes of humourous power. A man from Fifeshire. For two solid hours I was what *I* know as yet for happy. I could have sat all night. He had a slip of paper with subjects for the next ten weeks, and O but I wished him to use them all — to start at Adam Smith and go on to Nelson !

Next to me was the most astonishing man I have ever met. A coalminer of Fife, he had the Celtic temperament, which shamed my half-vitality where I sat. He could hold an audience in his hand, and never feel the weight. He was over 50 years of age, had been out to the front and still was affected by some sickness contracted out there, but spoke with no bitterness of that fact. He could see as well as any the greatness of the times and spoke like Lloyd George to the men. He was pretty well read, and through mere interest in the thing had worked through all Prouts Harmony exercises and the R.C.O. papers for thirty years. Bach made him drunk with glory. "Man, but it's fine". (The spelling of that last word is inadequate to *his* speaking.) He should be one of the leaders of British Music and is but a coal-heaver beating his dusty wings, but without complaint. But fancy having to go back to the front after meeting these two! Wumman, but it's awfu'!

I am likely to be here another fortnight, for on the colonel's inspection I was one of the very few not marked Con: Camp. "Why?" "Accompaniments, my dear". For once, I saw the Army winking its eye at me, and wunk back.

I hope that what comes from an Italian source as to America's Peace offer is correct. These are none so bad. And, barring an absolutely complete military victory, as good as we can get. Of course, the terms are too generous for Germany, but without generosity I cannot see how she is ever to assert herself against the Junkers. So much priceless blood has been spilt, the organisation has been so perfected, that, right or wrong, a commercial blockade for 25 years would mean an eating cancer in the heart of Europe. We have to encourage democracy, in this case by discrediting a ruling caste. I dont believe a commercial blockade would do more than pull Germany together under the old rule and keep Europe safe — granted! But there is a better way. To crush Germany more than is needed of effort. France cannot ever be hopeless again. So much we have gained. To sum up — It is a great pity that Europe cannot gain the same unconditional surrender of Germany as a parent may exact of a child, but if things are properly managed, *in the event of German accepting the proposals of U S A of course*, then the price is too great to pay any longer. It is time we left off, with a Faith in God, and an International agreement which would make aggression hopeless for any country.

Lastly, a complete military victory will not guarantee South Eastern Europe for long, if Russia will not see reason. This arrangement is far more likely to keep peace and to make reason a moving force in International communication. A military victory will not guarantee peace, neither will this; but it has more promise as a birth or potential force of peace, because further conflict will leave Germany weaker than ever. It is more unwise to weaken her, than to trust that her people have learnt a lesson; because in the essential things of self-government we cannot interfere.

Excuse this long, long dissertation.

As for getting into Enbro, it has not proved possible so far, but if human effort can manage it . . . .

I am so glad you like your new house, and very sorry the Germans will not leave you alone. It must be a strain. (This letter must be off!) I will write to Mr Dunhill and Erbert Owls. Concentration! I thought I had none, till last night. Only Joy can make me fit of mind, all this half-sickness is due to half-vitality, half-use of capabilities. About FWH, I will write again.

I can see (in my masculine vanity) a romance springing up between Audrey and 241281. Even though there is a great longing in me to see my Chapman again, and the rude and turbulent Mick. With all best wishes to you and your sister:

Your sincere friend   Ivor Gurney

To MARION SCOTT   41.141

4 October 1917 (P)   [*enclosed with preceding letter.*]

My Dear Friend: Hearing a few casual catchwords flying around, it struck me that you might like to know some of them — such as I can remember. Poor bare jests, almost too familiar to remember at will.

There is one (just heard for the thousandth time which brings a picture of a tragic roll call. A man may be shouted for who is not present, and the room answers, "On the wire, at Loos". A lighter answer, a mock of this last, is "Gassed at Mons".

A coming strafe means carrying parties, and they are greeted with "More iron rations for Fritz". Germans are known, affectionately, as Fritzes, Allemans or "Johnny". The Scots use the last name chiefly.

An intimation of a charge for crime is made by the phrase "You're *for* it".

Intimation of death is made as "H—— has got it. "Poor old Bills snuffed it". Or "Shant see old George again". To see Germans kill the wounded, is to see "the boys done in".

One "goes up the line with the Boys". Or "over the top with the Boys".

Practically *all* swearing ceases when one reaches Blighty, though the language out there is frequently foul. A commentary on the life! A bad officer, that is, a bully, is a ————! A good officer, that is, a considerate, is "a toff". "I'd follow him anywhere". "The men's friend;" or simply, but in significant tones, a "*gent*leman"! A funk is "windy", a bad funk, "as windy as Hell".

An officer always takes whisky into the line, and his being drunk on any critical occasion is always condoned. I have never known any of our officers really funk an order. Exact orders are always obeyed, or practically always. A bombardment is of course "a strafe", a bad one "some strafe". Men are "glad to be out of that". A premonition of Death is given as "My numbers up." A ditto of Blighty — "I'm for Blighty" "Blighty this journey". A box respirator is a "Gaspirator". A helmet a "tin hat". A rifle a "bundoob" (Hindustani?) A revolver "a peashooter".

The Germans, in anger, are referred to as "them ———— bastards". The English soldier has an enormous reverence for Hindenburg and his strategy. An almost complete belief that man for man he is far better than Fritz. A doubt of our air-service. A conviction that the Germans are as he is — a sufferer under discipline, no better nor worse than he; only unluckier. A belief that our discipline is stricter than his. A longing for home, and English girls. A contempt for everything French, although he has learnt to think better of the soldiers. French girls, towns (as a rule), houses, farm implements, are all objects of scorn. He admires the .75 gun very greatly. As for French beer, cigarettes, baccy . . . . . the comparison simply must not be hinted even by dashes. For all his amorous intentions once he reaches home, he thinks the French girls highly immoral. For all his stealing, the French unspeakable thieves. He likes Church Parade. Loathes most of all disciplinary parades, kit inspections and the like. Marches till he drops. Loves to frowst, and has a marvellous ability for the making of fires, "bivvies" etc. Fritzes splendid dugouts always move his praise.

His Guide, Philosopher, and Friend is "John Bull", Horatio

Bottomley is recognised as a scoundrel, but, for all that, the finest man in England, the only one to sympathise with a common soldiers woes and oppressions. Lloyd George is also admired, and, slightly, the King. Asquith is simply "Wait and See". Their faith in newspapers has been sorely shaken for ever by the comparison of accounts with realities. But chiefly by the contrast between the phrase "Mastery of the Air" and the reality. Parliament is a haunt of people who talk and dont care what happens to him and his like. Still he preserves his faith, how and in what, is obscure, but I believe it to be his feeling that Englishmen would not condemn him to suffer longer than was needful. But he never says so.

I may remember more, if so and it interests you, you shall have it.

To MARION SCOTT   41.142

8 October 1917 (P)

My Dear Friend: For the first time since when-God-knows I dip pen in ink and indite friendly unimportances. And it is very nice too, as the slang says. To write in pencil, is to be casual, careless, informal, unworthy of the true inner seriousness of letter writing; is to show ones lack of appreciation of the texture of paper, of the lovely gliding of the pen — but not this one, — of the beautiful look of clear script black against white paper, — why is this blue? Of the use of ceremony in life; to show oneself altogether unappreciative of those finer points that divide Man from the Beast, and make a penny worth the spending.

The man who would attempt to write verse with a pencil when a pen is handy and convenient to him would rob a church without more thought than he would give to the flicking of cigarette ash — which indeed is frequently the trick of the melodramatic villain. For the writing of music there can be none so foul of spirit as to contemplate aught but the pen as instrument. The pencil here is beastly and detestable beyond chaste thought; let us pass by with averted face, or even shuffle sideways like a crab; avoid the thought as base indeed with shame not to be told.

The soldier is exempt from all these considerations; For he is unwillingly vile. Ink, pen, and blotting paper haunt the dreams where only he may be himself.

Let the Gods judge in this — the worst of his crimes, the deepest of his woes, wherein he is more sinned against than sinning, the blind constrained tool of Destiny.

I hear you say, "but this is all Nonsense", in a withering tone, without effect on me, who reply with a complete answer, a snub, a saying of great beauty and intense meaning; to wit — "It is far better, Madam", (with courtliness also, you see!) "to write nonsense reverently with a pen than to have graved the Ten Commandments with a diamond pointed instrument of Gold of Ophir, on loveliest marble of Carrara, such as Browning wrote of (with a pen, you may be sure!) in "The Bishop orders his Tomb at St Praxed's". The Artist respects his materials, loves their peculiarities of texture and management, and deals with them gently as with his own flesh and blood, or the priest his sacrament of Bread and Wine; red and white; Passion and Serenity."

Let us use ink whenever Fate and Supply allow us, for so we shall show ourselves cognisant of and grateful for the civilisation of Europe, that once again has survived onslaught of the barbarian; who showed himself nakedly to all when he would destroy a "scrap of paper", and the work of pen and ink without a pang.

After Music

Why, I am on fire now, and tremulous
With sense of Beauty long denied; the first
Opening of floodgate to the glorious burst
Of Freedom from the Fate that limits us
To work in darkness pining for the light,
Thirsting for sweet untainted draughts of air,
Clouds sunset coloured, Music . . . O Music's bare
White heat of silver passion fiercely bright.
While sweating at the foul task, we can taste
No Joy that's clean, no Love but something lets
It from its power, the wisest soul forgets
What's beautiful, or delicate, or chaste.
Orpheus drew me, as once his bride, from Hell
If wisely, she or I, the Gods can tell.

Halfway through this effusion the mail arrived with the RCM magazines and a letter from you (In order of size.)

Alack. It seems only too likely that another parcel has (or has not?) Gone West. Nicholson was there also, wasnt he? Have you had him back? Regrets are useless. As for the verses, I can remember nothing at all of them; as they were quite ordinary. "Quinney's" is better than the "Hill". Have you read Wister's "The Virginian"?.

A certain Sister borrowed "Gloucestershire Friends" and has not yet returned it. My first impression is disappointment. He is farther away — FWH — from the reader than in "A Gloucestershire Lad."

"My father bred great horses", if it were a little better would be first-rate. "The Ballad of Army Pay" is good. "Seth bemoans the oldest inhabitant". And a poem which includes a line "with one high morning note a drowsing man". The poem written at Douai (O questions!) has very good stuff in it. That, also, which would "work Thy Will with Passion". That also (though I do not like "big" glory) which has a refrain, "and in the little valleys thatch and dreams". The best thing, I believe is — "We have taken a trench".

My poor friend was tired: do not judge him by this. It is the ineffectual beating of wings, a sick mind's desire. So fine a footballer, cricketer, man, cannot wait many years after the war for his fulfilment. *This* is not it, anyway. It will do as a source of quotation for Bishop Frodsham, who will also obtain a pleasurable glow of satisfaction at his great work of uplifting the People by Literature. Obelise him !

Will Harvey is an untidy careless dreamer, who has known much sorrow, chiefly because his mind was not occupied as fully as it needed to be. He is chivalry itself, and the detection of Fear within his heart is merely the spur to action. He sings well, and is indeed born a lover of all Beauty. He is capable of great Wisdom, of glorious foolishness. Loves Life which loves not him.

Some men have to form themselves, to control their every tiniest movement of spirit, and indeed to create their own world. And such is he; who has now learnt all bitter things, and has only to gather the sweet with experienced hand. A mind of sweetness allied to strength which has never known itself and cannot live as most men by habit. But dont look at "Gloucestershire Friends" to find all this.

Another letter will ask you how you are getting on yourself meanwhile all best wishes from:

your sincere friend   Ivor Gurney

To HERBERT HOWELLS   61.173

October 1917 (?)

My Dear Erbert Owls: This is a sad shock for you, bear up my man. There is nothing dedicated to you in "Severn and Somme".

Why? Because there were too many friends to whom I wished to dedicate, and all took away from the prime dedication. Miss Scott in consideration of her faithful service has two; Will Harvey has two more which directly refer to him. No other living people are there.

I hope you won't mind and will understand. However I propose to write a symphony in Canon. Its length is directly dependent on the patience of the audience. The first, leading part goes over the top, say, at 8.Pip. Emma, and reaches its first objective (Common time till now) at 8.27 PM. Starts again (3/4 Largo) at 8.29, and is again found digging in at 8.51, going over immediately for its 3rd objective, and finally turning up at its fourth objective at 9.48, when the working parties (that is, the last-entering voice) have just started. It has two alternatives — go to straight backward, bar by bar, or to start at the beginning again, *but it must not stop.* An artillery of 200 Italian combined-instrumentalists (16 to each man, you know them?) provide the barrage. And Ha! you blench! It is to be dedicated to You!!   Yours   IBG

To MARION SCOTT   41.145

Early October 1917 (?)

My Dear Friend: Sixteen miles from Enbro, and cant get there; not a sight of it. My parson is going away for a week, and afterwards is going to try to manage it. He is a great friend of Lord Guthrie who owns R L S house, and promises me a complete tour of everything that can be packed into a short stay. The same Ratcliffe Barnett is the man who is keeping myself and a singer here. The man who told us after service yesterday. "I hate parsons!" That rare thing, especially among his kind, of being a Truth-teller, Lecturer on English Literature, Mountaineer, Lover of Men, Music, and Books. One does meet men of this kind occasionally, not often, God, I do feel wise and old and grey with waiting! He has eyes that can look you through, and a fine head with a Roman nose defiant at the fore. A character that can hold a crowd as easily as one man. A master of Life, consequently of Death also. A great reader. A great admirer. A great man to finish with whose aim at present is to set men at ease when they talk to him.

After all this, let me thank you for the baccy which was most companionable to receive.

Nielson (O that you might see him) tells me tales of Norroway over the faem with it, tales of She(e)tlands, Iceland. Tells me what men do at sea, and what sad carelessness landed him the Army. What eyes he has, and fine wrinkled long humorous face, wise with seafaring and long contact with men of the sea. Obviously he is as brave as a lion, obviously as tenderhearted as a child. To lead up to the purpose of all this — Damn the War!

Your gift is not unappreciated by him, and I spend hours in his room. Tomorrow he goes on furlough, but has saved up an ache and a pain that will yet be useful, after three weeks or so.

Last night I played Bach and Beethoven for two hours, and got a little into swing towards the end. That was good. I am too lazy to write, and besides nothing will come to me when I try to pump — the bilge pumps, I think, by the results.

> *Memory, let all slip*
> Memory, let all slip save what is sweet
> Of Ypres plains.
> Keep only autumn sunlight and the fleet
> Cloud after rains,
>
> Blue skies and mellow distance softly blue;
> These only hold
> Lest I shall share my panged grave with you,
> Else dead, Else cold.

To Marion Scott   41.146

16 October 1917 (P)

My Dear Friend: This is a most lovely morning, and I ought to be out on the hills somewhere instead of writing letters, even to you. For letter writing is work of a sort, though I like it not badly here, and in France it is often a pleasure.

There is not much to tell you, there is no masterpiece of chiselled and exquisite verse. To be sure there is "A hundred papers and a' " running in my head but you know *that*, surely?

Your tales of the Down country interested me. If you had ever told my ear that Richborough was the last port held by the Romans it went out of the other ear, for I remember nowt about it.

As for "After Music", the last line is meant to be quizzical, and is true of myself. *Is* it wise of me to play music? Well, I do, but know only too well that the effort to forget will be an extra difficulty against the little serenity I shall have in France. Unless I grow stronger of soul of course, and so much stronger is unlikely.

The things I should most like to write are things of beauty with a vinegary ending, something after "The Fire Kindled". Heine I believe is famous for that sort of thing. It is best to be Shakespeare but good to be Heine — though not Thersites.

So the same was meant for "Memory let all slip". The beginning of which seems to me to be just ordinary — excused by the end,

which is (as you suggest) not all it might be. And it was meant to be
"pangéd"(two syllables). But if you prefer —
"Lest I my panged grave must share with you.
Else dead. Else cold.
(and even there, why not "pangéd"?)
I think there should be a semi-colon after "It from its power" in
"After Music".
As for the cover, Red so be it. L A bon! and while I think of it, it is
not enough to shame me to read over the name Edward Shanks,
this, in the S.W.

The Fields are full

The fields are full of summer still
And breathe again upon the air
From brown dry side of hedge and hill
More sweetness than the sense can bear.

So some old couple, who in youth
With love were filled and overfull,
And loved with strength and loved with truth,
In heavy age are beautiful.

Which knocks most Lyrics in "Palgrave" senseless, it is so packed
with thought, so musical and significant.

Yesterday I was wiping cutlery and plates and things after
breakfast and dinner, and it tired me out. I hate that sort of thing so.
Nurses are really wonderful people to do so many things distasteful
and still to smile. There is a very nice set of nurses here (have I told
you?) that could hardly be better. They call this the "Ragtime
Ward", a name of envy given by men oppressed in places of female
dragons and discipline. The courage of women is certainly not less
than that of men. To my mind, that is, The serene performance of
hateful duties, and the refusal to be depressed by them *is* the finest
form of courage. The more sensational are the wilder forms — no
higher. There are a few soldiers who go on till they are knocked out,
not heeding wounds, most of these comparative few have supported
their nerves only too freely beforehand. The rest may be the flower
of earth, but the man who can be brotherly and crack a joke on a
winter night in a shell hole has undoubted undeniable unsupported
courage, which is not always certain of the spectacular gentlemen,
who may be Berserk or drunk. But there! it is only my preference
perhaps for serene and quiet strength rather than for the violent
kind. Violence is waste of energy.

Here endeth the umptieth lesson.

As for fearing the Front — well, that is only because Life is too pleasant here. They'll soon alter that out yonder. (Theres a dramatic Lyric someday!)

The lucky people are the Scots, who can concentrate. The unlucky men are those who may be surprised into a single thought in the heat of (rather excited) conversation, but at no other time, if there are such men, and not only one! For this one wanders anywhere while he is playing Bach; yet they are not such black thoughts as they were.

Wise people are the Scots, anyway the nurses among them — for they had giving up trying to make me so uncannily tidy as other men are. So I turn my locker to the wall, when the (U S A) doctor comes.

The attitude of a fairly ordinary type of man to Classical Music is — that he does not like it, ought (yes, I think so) to like it and would like it if he had had a proper education. That's not so bad. But perhaps my courteous attitude to Ragtime makes a little difference here. And I never swank. The British respect sincerity, and they can *see* I like Bach, and believe there is something in it just as there is in what astronomers say of stars beyond ordinary view. They are willing to believe that something lies behind that inextricable tangle of notes, a reality beyond the mystery. I hope both you and your sister are getting on well, and that Audrey has not had her beauty-sleep broken lately.   With best wishes:

Your sincere friend   Ivor Gurney

To MARION SCOTT   41.148

23 October 1917 (G)

My Dear Friend: Thank you for the letter and postcard just arrived, one of them gave pleasure anyhow.

Mr Barnett has been informed of my literary dealings, and it excited him. We are to exchange scalps, for today he will bring me a little book of his own. Casual anecdote yesterday. He was playing at a Hall, an ordinary parish concert I believe, and had some success. When he was leaving, and old "habitual" and street player came up to him and said "Man, it was Fine!!! In the old days of Homer men exchanged swords. Me and you'll exchange fiddles". Which is the cause of the appearance in Bangour of a suspiciously raw looking instrument apparently made of packing case and — yellow yellow yellow varnish.

(By the way did you ever read the Yeats book that came out with Yeats "Responsibilities"? I believe that had anecdotes of the same kind.)

No light coloured fiddle will ever please me like a dark one.

Mrs Voynich has just sent me a short story of hers "And so be patient, be wise and patient, friend", for I know pretty well the attitude from which it will be written. That it will see life unsteadily and as an awful Hole. Allow me to recommend you a book. Why I read it is because the authoress is a poet we have both heard of — Rose Macaulay; and because the Y M C A is chiefly "remainders". "The Making of a Bigot" is the title, and the book has some fine sketches of people, a beautiful tolerant satire, and some proper stodges.

The Sonata in D I mentioned is the one you suppose, and I have one or two striking improvements to offer. First movement

Yes, the word in "Annie Laurie" is "flame".

Sorry, it is Hugh Sidgwick that has been killed. You say no word about your own health so I suppose you are still just slowly forging ahead. Peace should bring a double rate at least I think.

I have "Gloucestershire Friends" in front of me.
No1. Not bad. No 2. H'm No 3. chill breeze-birches? But not bad. "Prisoners" has a good last verse. But to complete the picture, the last line should have rhymed in "-ed". Why does he so often upset his form? First verse of "Christmas Wish" is good. "Christmas Prison" foreshadows the full Harvey. Ballade No.2. is good. The second part especially. "Solitary Confinement" is good — is touched with the Shakespearian influence that will grow on him, and has a charming thought about the white arm of the Lady Moon. A "Rondel of Gloucestershire" is slightly boshy, but not bad. "The Little Road" shows increase of technical power in some of the lines? (*Why* doesnt he keep his form?) Sestett of "Sonnet" is good. The "Sleepers" not bad. "Army Pay" has excellent sentiment at least. "Afternoon Tea" — perfect. "To the Unknown Nurse" has a good second line. "The Horses" is also "future" Harvey. Not perfect, but good. "The Drums of Death" "The Oldest Inhabitant" "Marriage" "The Wind in Town-Trees" (Future Harvey) — all good. The Villanelle has pure poetry. The last part but one very good.

"Kossovo day" has two good last lines. But why (save for metre) "tortured"?

Last night — O lucky me! — a Scottish Rifle sat up besides the stove with me, which glowed and made believe it was a fire. And he had travelled and could talk, and we had the same politics and the same tastes. His eyes were steady, his laugh open and easily provoked, and a smile that could not be long checked being chiefly an affair of the eyes. O well, it must have been 12.30 when we illicitly walked under the stars, watching Orion and hearing his huge sustained chord

through the night

Of Courtesy it is not less
Than Courage of Heart, or Holiness
And in my walks it seems to me
The Grace of God is in courtesy.

That's true and memorable enough. And then what of

"But heart, there is no comfort, not a grain
Time can but make her beauty over again.
The fire that burns about her when she stirs
Burns but more clearly. O she had not these ways
When all the wild summer was in her gaze.
O heart, O heart, should she but turn her head,
You'd see the folly of being comforted".

The great test of Art — the Arts of Music, Writing, Painting anyway is to be able to see the eyes kindly and full of calm wisdom that would say these things behind the page. I will not try to write verse in England. Once out there, it will leak from me in vulgar streams. With best wishes:

Your sincere friend   Ivor Gurney

To MARION SCOTT   41.149

26 October 1917 (P)

Details of the Life and Crimes of the private named Gurney.

Gloucester Cathedral 1900
  Head boy sometime
Dr Brewer Jan 1906

I have forgotten when I got the Scholarship (I have asked Mrs Hunt to tell you.)
Stanford — Composition
Mr Waddington (whom I like very much) for Counterpoint
    Also the Westminster Board.
Mr Sharpe (a good man)
    for Piano
Dr Davies. Dr Allen,
    Centre-forward for Kings School
Owner of the "Dorothy" (defunct)
    2nd best batting average
    3rd best bowling — last term of school
crack platoon shot July 1917
    Author of "Severn and Somme"
    and a further unborn imbecility.
Army Feb. 9th (?) 1915
Proficiency pay. C.B. every now and then. Sang Widdecombe Fair
blushingly at Albert Nov: 1916
    Wounded Good Friday night — or rather on the Sat:
    Gassed (?) at Ypres.

To Marion Scott   41.151

31st October 1917 (P)

My Dear Friend: Thank you very much for the history, which I enjoyed very much, and which has set me eager to read the "Old Road" as soon as possible: I know the Gloucester library has it — the big edition, with good illustrations.

I have 3 Poems, and O — a new song for mezzo soprano. One of my best, madam; that being a setting of those wistful magical words of Yeats — "The Folly of being comforted".
   There is one passage
       "O she had not these ways
       When all the wild summer was in her gaze."
which will raise your hair. And the full completion of meaning in the words at the cry
       "But heart, there is no comfort, not a grain" —
of course it cannot be as fine as "By a Bierside" but it is more difficult and hard to form than "In Flanders", and quite as successful. Perhaps "In Flanders" is slightly more beautiful as a whole, but there is a sorrow for wasting beauty and such tragic

passion here that puts it above any but "By a Bierside". Yet what hard luck! (It was written in one sitting the night after I had been up all night helping in the wards. Some stunt!) Well, I finished a fairly completely written sketch, and then found I had left out

"The fire that burns about her when she stirs
Burns but more clearly."

O Blasphemy! My balance upset! Well, there is not enough M.S. to copy this out, it shall come next time.

As to being cleared out I know no more, nothing. Last night Mr Barnett took me down to play to the officers who listened beautifully. The piano had once a touch and a tone — an ancient but not yet hopeless "grand". Yet some notes stuck, for a vase had upset on the keyboard that afternoon. Well, well.

Programme

Beethoven — Sonata in D
Bach Prelude and Fugue in E♭ (*2nd*)
    Preludes F♯mi(The folly of being comforted)
             Dmi
Chopin Ballade in A♭
    3 Preludes
    1st half of Fantasie in F mi
Beethoven — Final movement of Funeral March Sonata.

Mr Barnett sat by, and listened in a pure ecstasy. What a fine thing it must be to have a mind so single, joyful, childlike. Then, as I had copied out "By a Bierside" for him, he would have me sing it; and afterwards "The Folly of Being Comforted".

Your down-talk makes me desire very much to go into certain things more. Geology, for instance, to find out how deductions are made; and other sources of early history. It delights me to hear that the roads run south of the churches, because of that reason. Is that not a more satisfying reason than that the Christian Churches give for the position of their temples? The sun is glorious to all, and not perplexing. And it is also delightful to hear of the artistic renaissance of the 7th century. And strange; so queer a thing is Time, so difficult is it to realise that these men we read of were men like ourselves.

What a book G K Cs "History of England" must be! And what a prose he can write, and does! I always love G K C the man when reading his books; for he is so great-hearted. Never will his review of Masefield's "Gallipoli" fade from my mind, nor an appeal to the American People. There is no style in music quite like that . . . or is there? Yes! by the Lord and it is in Chopin — the Fantasia in F minor! The A major and A♭ Polonaises. Some of the studies! Who would have dreamed of connecting the two men? Eureka — a discovery!

What a frightful hit poor Italy has sustained! What a blow! And we, for if Russia does not recover we shall have a hot time of it on the West. Indeed Britain is the rock of hope now. The news will pull Germany through another winter I suppose, when the signs were that there would be bad trouble at least.

With the selfish fear I have, mingles still sorrow for all humanity suffering under this strain. Some day men will read history books, and say with Brett Young, "Poor savages that wrought in stone,
                              Poor savages that fought in France."
How shall formal religion console one? It is only Music that will comfort the heart — mine does already, and when more dross is burnt out of me, perhaps then I shall see Beauty clearly in everything. Yet O, that this purification should come by war! Obscene and purely dreadful!

I am glad my songs were a success at Reading.

If they liked "By a Bierside" as much as Mr Barnett, then my place as a prophet is secure. Well, I will do all I can to get "The folly of being comforted" ready for the next letter, but may let it wait till I see you in person. But here's one set of verses — the others are not quite ready.

Hospital Pictures. No.(1)
Ulysses

A soldier looked at me with blue hawk-eyes,
With kindly glances sorrow had made wise
And talked till all I'd ever read in books
Melted to ashes in his burning looks.
And poets I'd despise and craft of pen,
If, while he told his coloured wander-tales
Of Glasgow, Ypres, sea mist, spouting whales,
(Alive past words of power of writing men)
My heart had not exulted in his brave
Air of the wild woodland and sea-wave.
Or if, with each new sentence from his tongue
My high-triumphing spirit had not sung
As in some April when the world was young.

Bangour Hospital.
Oct 1917.

If hope you will like this Nielson-Kelly mixture. And sincerely hope you are feeling pretty well, and will be when we meet again. How is Miss Stella now? with best wishes:
Your sincere friend   Ivor Gurney

To MARION SCOTT   41.152

3 November 1917 (P)

My Dear Friend: Well, to business, (probable.) Chuck out —
Tuesday. London 7.30. High Wycombe, Friday Morning.
Gloucester Sat:night (as late as can be.)

There's a bit of luck; owing to slight indigestion (presumably due
to gas; wink, wink!) I am to go to Command Depot for two months
— a sort of Con: Camp in Khaki. I hope they *will* keep me for two
months, and then of course, if the indigestion isn't cured . . . . .

No, the song is not done, when I'm with you perhaps. Two
months Con Camp! O Composition.

Tomorrow I will write out
       Hebridean
       Ulysses

   for you, with best wishes: Your sincere friend   Ivor Gurney

To HERBERT HOWELLS   3.25

17 November 1917 (P)

My Dear Howells: The time we had together pleased me very
much, and I am glad we are such good friends.

What I want to say is, O dont worry yourself to write now; write if
you must; perspire it; let it leak, but dont O dont get impatient with
the slow days, and overwork yourself. If you were well, you would
be wasting time in the Army, "and so be patient, be wise and
patient, friend", for it is best to be wasting time as you are doing
than for you to be lost.

Well; here am I, back in harness, and not to be sent to Command
Depot. (Dear old Army!) The notices of my book were out
yesterday, and you will probably receive one soon. Could you collar
the Morning Post reviews anywhere? The New Statesman? New
Age? Nation? Possibly you might see one lying about and collar the
bit. It is a crime, but here excusable, I think.

I hope Miss Dorothy is properly gracious to you. Not yet has any
letter come from the Princess to me, but still I feel that all is well,
and feel that our hearts are conscious one of the other; which brings
a kind of serenity after the heat.

My address is a pretty good one

Pte Gurney I.B. 241281
 B Co
  4th Reserve Battallion T.F.
  Gloucester Regiment
  Seaton Delaval
  Northumberland
   (Hear, hear!)
   So write sometime.

A horrid rumour has reached me that we shall get our embarkation leave next Thursday and be off on the next draft. If so, I shall apply for a commission, just after the 6 days. (Shudders of surprise *after*) Farvel! Au Revoir. Auf Wiedesehn. Goodbye:
Yours ever   I.B.G.

To MARION SCOTT   41.154

21 November 1917 (P) Pte Gurney 241281, B Co 4th Reserve Batt:, Gloucester Regt, Seaton Delaval, Northumberland.

My Dear Friend: Alas, for the two months! Today I am on ordinary training, and that means but a short stay if nothing happens.

I hope you are getting on all right. There have been no air-raids, at all events; which is lucky. I wonder how London is looking now, that was so charming for the days I saw her — well, some of the days.

Two of the local reviews have reached me. They are just what I expected — and didnt want. But I got a delightful letter from Haines — the man who knows Gibson and Abercrombie — which said how pleased he was at his first glance, and how it seemed to be a not unworthy companion for Sassoon's Book, and Sorley-Turner; whom I have not read.

By the way, some time ago Sassoon walked up to his colonel, and said he would fight no more. Flashes, of course: and blue fire. There were questions in the House, and a general dust-up; but at last they solved it in a becoming official fashion, and declared him mad, and put him in a lunatic-asylum; from which there will soon come a second book, and that it will be interesting to see.

Will you let me know what poems you have received lately? I have been rummaging in my Bangour notes, and have written a little since I saw you. There must be 7 or 8 things to come, not all quite polished up and hairparted but nearly so.

Thank you so much for "Friends", for I love that book. Of

course, Rupert Brooke is exquisite enough, but one can always read "Friends". Mrs Gibson, probably affected by W Gs being called up (a C3 man!), has fallen downstairs, and spoilt one eye for ever. When Rupert Brooke went abroad, he left his copyrights equally between Gibson, Abercrombie, and De La Mare. They have had £2000 each! That's why Gibson has not died, and his family. Poetry pays — it took a War to make it; but still, there you are. Best wishes: Your sincere friend   Ivor Gurney

To MARION SCOTT   41.155

24 November 1917 (P)

Recompense

I'd not have missed one single scrap of pain
That brought me to such friends, and they to me;
And precious is the smallest agony;
The greatest, willingly to bear again —
Cruel frost, night vigils, death so often ta'en
By Golgothas untold from Somme to Sea.
Duty's a gray thing; Friendship valorously
Rides high above all Fortune without stain.

Their eyes were stars within the blackest night
Of Evil's trial. Never mariner
Did trust so in the ever-fixéd star
As I in those, And so their laughter sounded —
Trumpets of Victory glittering in sunlight;
Though Hell's power ringed them in, and night surrounded.

Bangour
October 1917

The Plain

The plain's a waste of evil mire;
And dead of colour, sodden-gray.
The trees are ruined, crumbled the spire
That once made glad the innocent day.

The flowers, the flowers are buried deep
With friends of mine who held them dear;
Who lie with innocence, asleep,
Dreaming of April's covering there.

O if the Bringer of Spring does care
For Duty valorously done,
Then what sweet breath shall scent the air!
What colour-blaze outbrave the sun!

Ypres-Bangour
September
1917

Hospital Pictures (no 3) *The Miner*

Indomitable energy controlled
By Fate to wayward ends and to half-use.
He should have given his service to the Muse;
To most men shy; to him, her humble soldier,
Frank-hearted, gracious, bold.

———————

Yet though his fate be cross, he shall not tire,
Nor seek another courage than his own;
For selfless valour and the primal fire
Shine out from him, as once from great Ulysses —
That king without a throne.

Bangour
Oct 1917

To MARION SCOTT   41.156

29 November 1917 (P)

My Dear Friend: Your delightful letter was good to get in this
wilderness. What weather it has here you can hardly imagine —
however damp and cold are always present, though today for once
we incredulously saw the sun. It is very nice to hear you are going on
well in health and with (O Lord!) "Youth and Music". ("Babbling
limpidity" is a good phrase!) Yes, there *were* good things in that bad
time a year ago; good things. One feels far more fed up here than in
France, as a general thing. It is good to go to one's limit, and good to
see men facing hardships well and coolly facing vile Deaths.

If we get a clear formula of demand from Germany, and give a
clear one back, I shall ask no more, but remain satisfied. Do you
know, dear Friend, the thing that shocks a soldier is that not many
civilians guess at. The fact that men at last do things not from
courage or for their Country, but because of discipline (as I was told

in 1914 and more still in 1915, but refused to believe.) It is that which revolts one, and makes one long for the finish. And O, if men died in a mood of glory occasionally instead of in a mere state of being fed-up!

I am so pleased about the photograph. It is natural, is it not? I got Pitcher to put up one of his studies which struck me and it was that, not horror, produced that look. Night operations! Dont talk about 'em! Monday, Tuesday, Wednesday! so far. And you talk about sending me a book present! I will accept the Third Georgian with a pure pleasure, but not yet, not yet. It is mere fact that I never read. You shall hear at once when the reading mood returns, which it must, in spite of everything.

There are rumours of a shift to somewhere South; O if it might be.

I cannot say what the Cathedral Sidney has sent may be. Beauvais?

Again I have to apologise for carelessness; for the Glasgow editors letter is nowhere to be found. This is a bad fault, and I am very sorry; if it does turn up you shall have it at once.

How in the name of goodness did high-explosive shell stick in your house? From a big bomb was it?

I am glad you have joined the Poetry people. That is a good circle.

But as for getting any from me, O help! Well I lie fallow; and am about to send you Thomas' poems. Very curious they are, very interesting; nebulously intangibly beautiful. But he had the same sickness of mind I have — the impossibility of serenity for any but the shortest space. Such a mind produces little. The news about Herbert is sad. O Lord, what if *he* leaves his work half-begun only? One cannot help fearing that, poor boy.

Is Beauty to be made only for breaking?

Mr Dunhill has written, wants to set "Firelight". Of course he may.

A friend of the Hunts tried in London — at the Times Book Club — for Severn and Somme. Out of print it is! Harveys two books, a "Shropshire Lad" and mine are selling like hot cakes, they told her! So all your efforts have not been in vain; and the Music Reviews have not yet started!

You have stirred things up well, with a long arousing stick.

Will you please alter that dedication "To Puck, if she will write" to — simply — "To Puck". And a horrid thought strikes me. Did I leave out Mrs Chapman ("La Comtesse Tilda" as I call her)? If so, she must have this; Puck can do for Book two in this case. But only *if*. O black-avised year, what dost thou bear to us? The Times says each successive year has been bloodier than the last. And here's another on us. "Dear houses, the very God does seem asleep." with best wishes: Your sincere friend   Ivor Gurney

To MARION SCOTT   41.160

December 1917 (?)

My Dear Friend: It is kind of you to write such letters and take
such trouble while you have neither much time nor health, and I am
grateful to you. And for your criticisms, which are justified, but at
present I simply cannot alter. The words are to me undoubtedly
the right ones, and "innblinds" and "valourously" must be dodged
by separating the poems. "Innblinds" does so much express what I
want to say, and so well.

Which is the right spelling of Laventie or Levantie, I do not know
— the first I believe. Personally the repeating of a phrase such as
"And yet, and yet" does not annoy me. But it becomes a mannerism
when found 3 times in a batch of poems. Thank you, there's one
altered.

As for "Innocent" and "innocence" — well, I must think of
something else, but can't yet. This is barracks, not ten days leave,
alas! Your account of your visit to the T.L.S. man is most
interesting. You find a way to tame lions; anyway they dont sound
terrible.

It is good of you to take so much trouble; certainly I cannot work
up enough interest in them to worry so much . . . Well, not now; if
they gave me a months leave however, there might be stirs.

(This letter is written at Mrs MacMahon's. The mother of an old
2/5th friend who was lately here on leave. My poor old Batt: got
caught in the Cambrai do, and O well Lloyd George is delightfully
confident.)

Bruce Richmond was very nice, I think. I am glad to know that
De La Mare had not quarrelled with the "Times". Haines said he
was in the sugar department, but also that his ideas were not
Northcliffe's, and so they parted. But he may not have told you of
that.

There is a review in the "Sunday Times" today of "Severn and
Somme". I will get it and put it in with this, and the Bristol paper's
review.

"Blackwoods" is high indeed, but if it could be managed — Bien!

And that would be a nice start, indeed. It is good news about
"Severn and Somme" getting a second review.

Ah, mam'selle, an Ode, a "Hymn to the Honour of Man"?
Perhaps, but not here, where my mind is sodden. But O to write that
Hymn!

Part (1) Courage of Joining up
     (2) Courage to bear up when what-Army-Life-is was really
         seen.

(3) Courage under fire

(4) Courage in the wet and cold

(5) Decency to each other, comradeliness in all states of lousiness and other evils.

(6) Courage of dying.

I should like to write that, dear Friend. May be in France, not here. And on a quiet front, if there are to be any.

The Situation?

Well, one forgave the Paris speech, because it might have reasons. (Or half-forgive). But O not this latest. What is "Victory"? Breaking the German line, and compelling them to status quo, loss of Alsace Lorraine, an Independent Poland, and restitution to Belgium and Serbia. That's victory, nothing else + indemnities and all our War costs.

Because, as Lord Rhondha says, "When the Lusitania sank, I made a vow to get even with the Kaiser." To get even with the Kaiser! There you are! The real Prussian attitude! Besides, Germany has a case against Europe. The case of a Power that became great between 1850 and 1900, yet got no seaports comparable with their power. Of course it was not right to take Belgian seaports, but still, they had a case.

And, as to atrocities — Well, the Germans have been on the *unfortunate* side as regards morality. We should have disregarded precedents had we been in their position, with Time on the other side, and comparative plenty. One *cannot* allow the Lusitania to sail the seas with valuable goods for enemies. One cannot refrain because of passengers that have been warned. This is the horror of War, not of Prussia.

Have you heard anything of Sidney Shimmin? I don't think he will have a bad time altogether.

Do you know anything of the sale of "Severn and Somme"? I am afraid you do, since you threw out a hint about a first edition being plenty, and have said nothing more.

Directly I get a large enough envelope, the other verses shall be returned. (I have noted any corrections.)

There are signalling operations three nights a week now! Three evenings gone! O Lord! So you will see that time for writing or forgetting the army will be scanty. with best wishes:

Your sincere friend   Ivor Gurney

To MARION SCOTT   41.163

January 1918 (E)

My Dear Friend: Thank you for your long and most welcome

letter; and here are two poems to thank you for it. But O you dont know how difficult it is to write anything — the shortest note — in this freezing, ugly, uncomfortable Hell of a Hole. (You see I am still fed up.) The other men get round the fire and take the bench, one cannot write in the billet on the table therefore. Only warm weather, or France, will alter things. Yes, you did tell me of your visit to S and Js. I am almost sure of having written about it, and their asking for my second book. Yes, the first edition is gone, but the blighters have not sent my copies yet, which is rather mean, even for verse publishers. Thank you again, about the Third Georgian. If you think it would spur me to write please send it. But I warn you that noone else on full duty reads verse at all here. Small blame to them!

As for Herbert, you know as much as I do, save that Sir James Mackenzie says he will fight the case if Herbert is called up. Have you seen his new photo, taken at the same time as mine? A very good one it is, but the eyes look so ill. Hadow has written to him, sympathetically and saying that he considers H N H to be the chief hope of English Music. I wonder if God is fool enough to end him first?

Thank you about "La Comtesse Tilda". Yes, that will be her title; not Mrs Chapman. I am so sorry about Mr Dunhill; he looked fagged and thin when I saw him in November.

As for the "Music-Student" think no more on't, friend; although fools are annoying enough when they try to hide foolishness so.

Thank you for all the trouble you have taken about the "Elizas". You are a good friend indeed. There are two songs coming to you from Herbert — The Folly of being Comforted, and Severn Meadows. All I have done.

Sir Hubert is a great man, and my admiration of him has been great from the first. He speaks with authority, not as one of the scribes. What has been his illness? Indeed, the human race often seems to shame God, for even the most wise Deity and most pitiful could hardly refrain from triumph and shame to see how nobly men endure in schemes far beyond their comprehension — doubting indeed whether there is any plan to comprehend.

As to the War — I feel much happier. Our terms are definite (though of course to be receded from) and Germany is still ruled by bullies and liars. Well, we soldiers wanted to know that, so the knowledge has rather overshadowed Lloyd George's other disgraceful speeches.

We cannot accept the German terms, which are fatal to Freedom, so we must go on being harried by our Old Sweats still a while longer; though I do not forget the faces of men hobbling down with trench-feet, while our War-makers take no danger.

To spur me on, I bought More Soldier Songs at Blyth. O dear! perhaps I am a poet after all.

How are you now, physically and mentally? Are the articles for the brats finished? And can you practice? Please tell me, not for politeness sake do I ask.

And thank you for the T.L.Sˢ The Rob Roy article and the review of Georgian Poetry were very good. The papers go a round — I do not keep them. Letters and papers are not what they are in France; but they keep alive in me the resolution not to be broken by the Army, as some men are broken; keep alive hope, and memory of the pleasure that filled me in your music room — a sense that there is a port, and I shall arrive there.   Many thanks and best wishes from your sincere friend   Ivor Gurney

To Marion Scott   41.163[sic]

11 January 1918 (P)

My Dear Friend: Your gift came today, received with pure pleasure and sincere thanks. It looks most fascinating, and will be read as soon as possible. The song is ready written out but must be tested on some piano.

And now I'm going through your long and most interesting letter.

You say you have a sick household. I hope Mr Scott is much better — or at least, able to amuse himself; but he must be really ill not to be able to do that, with his clear interested mind.

Your review of my book has given my people great pleasure, and they are very proud of me, you may be pleased to hear. Mr Bellows sent the R C M Mag: to them. Sidgwick and Jackson have sent no books.

Yes, Edward Thomas is a very poetic soul indeed, and English at the core. Please write about them. Haines knew him intimately, and talks of him a lot.

I do hope you are still getting well now, Mr Scott, the "Aunt who lives with us", your Mother, and Audrey, and hope that the Air-raids have made no difference to getting well. Goodness, what a dose at once! Is the weather bad in London now? It has improved here, and they may all be flourishing.

Yes "Wenlock Edge" is written out, but I will not send it till tested. Also a new song — Gibson's "For G", which certainly wants tinkering with.

You may show my songs as and when you please, of course.

Why should not "Orpheus" come first in the Elizas? If not why not, and something rowdy must begin, put "Spring" first and "Orpheus" last.

As for the first two bars of "Sleep", — certainly. 2 first bars as written, then in octaves — the notes written, and an octave above. Yes, play it *almost* slurred.

comme ca!

Thank you so much about Bruce Richmond. You are a more than superhuman Literary Agent, because you do these things for kindness' sake.

"And which has brought such honour to the College" is a reference which greatly pleases me.

Please talk about yourself when you feel inclined, for I like listening. My inquiries about your health are quite genuine. For a person with your pluck and with your health deserves solicitude. So — "How are you Miss Marion, this evening, Ma'am?"

That you can walk with enjoyment is very good news. If it werent for the War, you would probably be quite well in no time at all, with your determination. Hang on, my Jolly Literary Agent, and smile even if only for cussedness. About your work I am going to be simply honest. I don't know what to say, and that's true. Should you go on writing? Well, I care only for Music of strong individuality: Bach, Beethoven, and Herbert Howells and Vaughan Williams. It is the same with verse — I care only to hear what I could not do myself; I like what is beyond me.

But as to the use of making a body of *English* music there is no doubt, whether it has genius or not; but I, who am paralysed by doubt, before writing, as to whether it is worth while or no, cannot be expected to give advice. Literature? Now could I — *could* I give any opinion? Can't you ask Mr Dunhill, who must have read some things of the kind you mean? I am simply in the dark — dont know.

Consider what I am — the semi-invalid who tried to write and the fairly fit man totally out of touch with everything!!!

Your influence may be strong for good anyway, but you have a perfect right to please yourself, not ask hopeless, fed-up, people like myself. (They paid me 5/- last week.)

You write as clear English as your handwriting — judging by your letters. As for your music — further darkness — I know only your tiny songs. So there you are — as if you had not asked me!

Is Germany waking up? It rather seems as if any unsuccessful offensive on this front would lead to trouble. Anyway we know now that the present German terms are quite unacceptable, and can go on fighting with a clear heart.

The quotation from Newbolt is very beautiful. And thank you so much for the trip to Chamonix and up. You can write you know, and in this your personality was clearly felt.

Yes, I think you must be better, could not have written that evening out of you before now. Cheerio!

I feel ashamed to close now, but even this must be paid for by writing illicitly tonight after Lights Out at Signalling notes for an hour.

It's worth it.

You are a good friend indeed. Letters are not here what they are in France, but gratitude (I like G K Cs definition) has not become so dead in me that I am not glad to get your warm hearted vivid letters.

And your Symbol and mine look very well in the Georgian Book, placed just right, and, of course, well done. Perhaps you'll set me writing with your much-desired gift, although Time is so scant. With best wishes: Your sincere friend   Ivor Gurney

To HERBERT HOWELLS   3.32

January 1918 (?)   [*Mouse-eaten and incomplete*]

My Dear Howells: That was a lovely note of yours. (I sent it on to her!) And gave me great pleasure. Save the news about yourself. Poor old chap! I am the luckier of us two at present, I think, for you have a distressed mind.

If I do well here, there may be a chance of my staying for a considerable time, so I'm going to try to do well. Anyway there is a probable five months still to go.

Here is a new, more orthodox, song. Please send it on to Miss Scott when digested. It is beautiful, isnt it. You know why . . . .
[   ] she could hear it.
[   ] Nelson Drummond is older than I thought — born sooner I mean. She is 30 years old and most perfectly enchanting. She has a pretty figure, pretty hair, fine eyes, pretty hands and arms *and* walk. A charming voice, pretty ears, a resolute little mouth. With a great love in her she is glad to give when the time comes. In Hospital, the first thing that would strike you is 'her guarded flame". There was a mask on her face more impenetrable than on any other woman I have ever seen. (But that has gone for me.) In fact (at a guess) I think it will disappear now she has found someone whom she thinks worthy.

A not unimportant fact was revealed by one of the patients at hospital — a fine chap — I believe she has money. Just think of it! Pure good luck, if it is true (as I believe it is). But she is more charming and tender and deep than you will believe till you see her.

O Erbert, O Erbert . . . . .

I forgot my body walking with her; a thing that has not happened
since . . . . when? I really dont know.

To Herbert Howells   3.20

[*enclosed with next letter*]

Going North to Edinburgh

My Dear Howells: I have just written you a letter telling you of my
coming up here. Please dont say anything about it to anyone but the
Taylors. It will need explanation I am not ready to give yet, and of
course my people will want to know why I did not go home — but a
week-end leave is so short.
　　Compree mong bong Amy?   Yours   I B G

To Herbert Howells   3.20
16 January 1918 (E)   Wednesday 16

My Dear Howells: Enclosed with this you will find a letter
enclosed written just before I was hastening North to Edinburgh.
　　What I think of your photograph is — that it reveals you in a fine
way, but O poor Boy you look ill.
　　Hadows letter delights me. He is an honest critic, and right in this
instance besides; a letter of this sort must buck you up. Just be as
serene as possible. Let not the eager fire of your mind eat your body
any more than it must, for you are great and shall do great things.
　　Your criticisms are true. As to similarity — well, perhaps I wont
admit anything but similarity in method. As to linking them up
more tightly, that may come; but as to setting the things I do in an
orthodox fashion — well it could be done; but I live attempting
difficult things, and this is my way.
　　Wait till I am out of this though.
　　Yes, I mean you to send those songs to Miss Scott (I told Mrs
Voynich so) and so please send them.
　　Make any copies you wish of course — but should I not do that
myself, Sick Genius? These songs are a success. They have pleased
you, and I want no more. As to "Severn and Somme", I have not yet
had my copies!! Damn S and J, they take a long time about things.
Sir Charles has a photograph of me though.

Well I have just been up to Edinburgh, about that magnificent place, and in and out to Bangour.

Herbert Howells, it is just perfectly and radiantly All Right. I have reach Port, and am safe.

I only wish and wish you could see her and know her at once. You and Harvey.

My Goodness, but it was a hot pain leaving her. We had a glorious Saturday afternoon and evening together. A glorious but bitterly cold Sunday evening. A snowy but intimate Monday evening. For the first time for ages I felt Joy in me; a clear fountain of music and light. By God, I forgot I had a body — and you know what height of living *that* meant to me. Well Ill say no more.

Being in the Army is worse and better for me filled with memories and anticipations and being where I am — in surroundings that mock all beautiful dreams.

But to get her and settle down would make a solid rock foundation for me to build on — a home and tower of light.

Like you I see in her first of all a beautiful simplicity — her very first characteristic, — As you see in Dorothy. The kind of fundamental sweet first-thing one gets in Bach; not to be described, only treasured.

Well, well; why bore you? You know what I think and how it is with me.

May good luck be with you in this thing and all things:
Yours ever   I.B.G.

To F.W. Harvey   61.390

February 1918 (?)   *19 Barton St, Gloucester.*

My Dear Old Willy: It's a dull day. I will comfort and renew myself by writing to you, friend of orchard and river; drawing life from memories of blue and silver seen together and great sights of sunset from the little hill.

There's not much to tell you of course. Things are going on steadily, and little by little I gain happiness and health and power over my mind and external things; and gain this not only by desire but because One Other is giving me such gifts as I may deserve.

You would hardly know me now, or recognise my piano playing (had I a month's practice,) and indeed there is a startling difference between the white-faced thin thing from hospital and what Pte Gurney is now. I think you would be pleased with your friend, Willy, a weed no longer: though hardly a smart soldier and never enthusiastic about cleaning up and such like spiritual exercises.

How are you now, being out of solitary confinement and able to mix with men again. You must be happier surely. Are your parcels coming? Your mother said you had not been getting them regularly when she last heard.

Dear chap, there's so much to talk about. I'll put my hand on your shoulder, and we'll wander about the fields and roads to talk of the Georgian Book, No 3 — which has several new names. (Willy, I hope you'll be in No 4.) Turner, Sassoon, Munro, J C Squire, Stephens, Graves. And old names. Drinkwater (a good selection) Gibson (a poor one) Walter De La Mare, Davies (poor) Hodgson. These young writers are very interesting, very much in earnest, and very gifted; out of them a great poet should come. Make haste Willy and start it!

O we'll do such things together yet!

You must be stale with imprisonment; but still, unless weak with hunger or sickness — force yourself: write.

You will be glad to hear of me, that though I am still neurasthenic and naturally gloomy yet the knack of kicking myself into doing things has developed a lot, and hardly ever am I idle. My evenings are quite full up, one way or another. O you just wait! Once you are back I'll fill you to the neck with music and wonderfully subtle criticisms of your own and other poetry. We'll frighten cows with gesticulations and hot outcries behind Hygrove. I think I shall be able to help you quite a lot, old boy, and strongly hope so. Especially as I am going on growing in insight in my own craft, and this must help me to see into yours. "Severn and Somme" has sold out one edition but my Authors copies have *not* arrived.

Its February — the years going round, and I have escaped the Winter out there Thank Goodness. It is likely my course of signalling will last till May anyway. Perhaps Luck will keep me in England till June, which will suit me better than wallowing in the mire of Flanders. I have been playing the piano — not a bad one — in the Recreation Room here. And there is no doubt Willy that I play better than ever in my life. I longed for you to hear some of the stuff I went through — a most appreciative audience you were always, and when you come back (if circumstances permit) I'll set you writing in no time.

Bell is Signalling Officer here — a decent chap. He says he knew you well in the   , and it is through his power it may come that I keep out of things for a time.

There is a new song and some new verses. Here is a song written in November.

> My heart makes songs on lonely roads
> To comfort me while you're away,

And strives with lovely sounding words
It's crowded tenderness to say.

––––––––––

Glimmering against the forward dark,
Your face I see with pride, with pain
So that one time I did desire
Never to see that face again.

––––––––––

But I am glad that Love has come
To bind me fast and try my worth;
For Love's a powerful Lord and gives
His friends dominion over the earth.

You know whom that's meant for.

The weather here is almost unrelievedly ugly — the colours and mellow grace of Gloucester seem a false phantom of a lovers mind, but are not.

Do you remember how, in Spring evenings, the gold of late sunlight used to be heavy on the floor of the orchard, that lies to the right of the road, nearing your house on a journey from Gloucester. And great sunsets? And Autumn afterglows, most tender, most "thronged" (You know what I mean.) You'll make words to catch that charm, and I'll make music, combine the result. Cheerio, Willy, things will come right in the end. Look at me — the sick creature of 4 years ago, and what I am now. If *I* can do it, what can you do?

Though you have to live on the last ultimate scrap of grit in your being — some day you'll live easily in Joy, because you like living for its sweet and varied interests, and think of any evil of the past as a necessary light price for so much content. Dear old Willy, if friendship is anything at all, you should be happy, for there cannot be one friend of all your many forgets or has forgotten you, who have the power of holding from a distance as only Great Lovers can — of increasing it, indeed. I'll write again soon to let you know anything worth letting you know, and prattle in my old egoistical style. Good bye with love: Yours ever   Ivor

To MARION SCOTT   41.165

25 February 1918 (P)   Pte G: I B 241281 Glosters, A 17 No 1 General Hospital, Newcastle.

My Dear Friend: My inside having been a little extra troublesome lately, I went sick and now am here! So long as the gas has no influence on my tummy after the War I dont mind. Well, I am trying to write, but my mind is appallingly rusty, as you may well believe. By sheer will power (no musical impulse aiding) I turned out a song today. But alas! I have only two books with me, "The Shropshire Lad" and your gift "Friends". So if you have done with E.T. please return him, will you.

I am so sorry Mr Scott is so ill, and do hope Time will bring rapid and permanent improval. It is overwork I suppose has done it — another War result. And Audrey — Lady Audrey — may she soon be rosy and jolly. May you all be, as you deserve, poor things. Thank you so much for all your presents. The Poetry Review has not much in it, do you think? It is too elementary; but some of the childrens stuff is interesting and "Ambition" (in vers-libre) is fine, it seems to me. One is ashamed of it — but Mrs Meynell is altogether too annoyingly "chaste" to live in this world. An enormous amount of good must be done by this Review however; and more still will be done when the young men return if there are any. (Monday morning)

Let us be tactful and not refer to the news.

My Father is surprisingly stronger, they tell me. Still, it needs another operation to make things shipshape; after which one may be allowed to talk of getting well. I think you would like my Father very much: he looked very fine and serene in bed, and himself was serene and fine — both.

You dont seem to mind Air Raids, Miss Marion! It is a great compliment to tell me that you were absorbed in reading my songs while aeroplanes and bombs and shrapnel were in the air. Thank you very much for that and for having the Englishwoman's Review copied.

Yes, I had read (and copied) Hodgson's "Time", but not at all closely, I think. It was certainly not a steal. Where I found it was in "Poems of Today" which I had not seen for a long time. Walter de la Mare's original I do not know.

There is nobody I can think of who would like to hear the "Elizas", save Evans, and the Taylors.

Now will you please send me some M.S. paper when you next write? The reason is, of course, that we get no money in Hospital. It will be my complete endeavour to return the sheet covered with master-work, but I doubt it. When you get "To G" from Herbert, I believe you will like that better than some of my things.

I feel an awful washout you know, but there is a certain pride in me when I think that some of my best things have been written in the Army. Have the others written at all? Save Benjamin?

I am so glad you are having success as an Author. Judging from the review of my Book, you are adapted to that sort of work as well as anybody. *And its important that these articles should be done well.* One ought to be interested in such things as you have written of.

Did you do well at the Photographers? Were the day and the hour and the facial control and the necessary brazen impudence and devil-may-careness all right? I wish it were Pitcher you had for photographer. He is now engaged on a perfect lovely study of Gloucestershire, which he means to be his chief work, I believe; it looks something like an East painting, judging from my casual memory.

Don't things look luverly in the East? Well, it removes all doubt. We have to fight until Germany will behave well on this front at least. On the other, nothing save an over-powering defeat can make any difference — and that is hardly likely, is it?

Our hopes lies in the fact, that German soldiers, though they may be willing to go on to the end, know perfectly well that the cost has been too great, and that the working classes can not allow themselves so to be cheated, bullied, misused, ever again.

I am out of it for a while, and hoped to be able to write and forget everything; but my brain is too rusty, and all stimulation is absent. One must be fired before emotion is released.

This dumbness would not matter, only that it makes distrust in oneself.

The day I came in to Newcastle, not expecting any more than a report, there were two books only in my pocket, but having heard the verdict desperation took me out 10 minutes walk or more into the town where I bought Boswell Vol 1 — lucky for me. But somehow in my mind there is a great desire to read the lives of great workers, Bach, Carlyle, Beethoven, Goethe, Michel Angelo, Da Vinci; and yet, what could all that do in Wartime?

Vain dreams, though not discreditable, and having hope for the future. It is unfortunate that there is no one in the Ward to whom I can talk — not unexpected, however.

With best wishes to you and the Invalids for all good luck:

Your sincere friend   Ivor Gurney

Will you *please* forward this to Evans? For I have neither envelope, stamp, nor address!

To HERBERT HOWELLS   3.11

25 [?] February 1918 (P)

My Dear Howells: How are you, old chap? Has Yorkshire done you good? Can you sleep? Are you stronger for walking? Can you write?

It was nice to come up with you, and talk about the things I shall always love to talk about, though now — through the lethargy of circumstance and disuse — my brain is unfit for such things. But you can't guess where I am! It is in Ward A17 No 1 General Hospital Newcastle; through stomach trouble caused by gas, though I needed a rest as well; and so lie on my back reading Boswell's account of the mighty Johnson and wondering when O when I can be back working towards my goal, where A N D lives.

I am horribly fed up, just as the Doctor himself was, when not really using his mind, but I wont trouble you with that, since you are so brave in far worse circumstances, bless you!

You know you thought something dropped from my pocket book in York Station? Well, something did. It was — O my grief! — a 10/-note; nearly all my worldly wealth, that was to take me to Edinburgh. So not being able to go to E: I came here to save money! Dont laugh, they might hear you!

I wonder if you could lend me your "Lady Audrey Suite"? No, dont send it! For my tenure here is absolutely uncertain, and it might get lost following me. But I *would* like something hard to chew! I shall buy M S paper and try to write, although my last attempt was disastrous. Who can write in the Army with a sick stomach? Not I, at any rate; still, the attempt shall be made.

What is the place you are staying at? Is it pleasant? Are your housecompanions nice? How nice it would be to see you, and talk, and wander as much as pleased us and you could stand!

Well, if Howells is impossible, I must content myself with Boswell, trying to drown the voice of my conscience . . . . . . Are you easier in your mind now that the exemption has come to you, permanent and final? O that is good news, boy, and rejoiced me, for selfish and selfabsorbed Moi is glad at your good-fortune, which is that of British Music. So much was clear with the Concerto, and it has become clearer still since, so they say.

Goodbye, old chap, and wish me well too. But I do wish that sense of guilt was lesser than it is. Mere weakness, I know!

May you find some Beauty to inspire you wherever you be, and your courage get its right reward: Yours ever   I.B.G.

To HERBERT HOWELLS   3.23

12 March 1918 (P)   *Gallery Ward, Brancepeth Castle, Co Durham.*

My Dear Howells: I am happy today with a letter from AND soon after another both charming, so shake hands; and her presence is strong on me as I write. O Erbertowls when will it come right? This morning I feel certain-sure for both of us, my jolly Genius, but hope that the meanwhile is not too dreary for you, Poor old Chap!

Can you sleep well, Ducky? Do you feel pretty well, can you write? Say "yes" and gladden the heart of a Dyspeptic Wangler.

There will probably be 5 songs or so out of this easy but dull time; one a love-song especially for Annie, whose eyes and lips are so bright in me this dull grey typically-Northern imitation of a morning. How are Dorothy's with you? She has been whispering most comforting things these last few days, and I have walked in my loveliest most beloved paths with her, drawing free glad breath from that sweet South Western Air.

I am so glad you like the place and people, and got on well with Bairstow. Perhaps it is because not all geniuses are ratty and porcupine-skinned that H N H gets on so well. I wish him all good luck, but O that I and he were just going north to Edinburgh! And then we'd All come South to see Dorothy.

Wow, wow! I feel skittish!! Best wishes:

Yours ever   Ivor Beegy

To MARION SCOTT   41.166

Received 26 March 1918 (E)

My Dear Friend: Here's some news for you.

You know how a neurasthenic has to drive himself, though he feels nervy and his heart bumps in a disturbing but purely nervous fashion? Well, Ivor Gurney determined to drive himself. His heart certainly did not feel right, but that was imagination and he must go on — through Salisbury Plain, Laventie, Somme, Caulaincourt, Vermand, St Julien. He was tested once or twice, but doctors said nothing. They marked him A 3 at Depot when he got there. It is true he never felt well, and had continual digestive and general nervous trouble, but that was presumably to be driven out. Which lands him at Depot getting weaker and fuzzier in the head without knowing why. On Friday he went to Durham 9 miles there and back, after which his pulse was waltzing irregularly like this as it is now

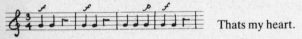 Thats my heart.

Surely a prostitute's job is cleanly compared to doctors who allow this and mark "Debility" on a case sheet so that a man shall not know? Shall leave the hospital a little recovered and go on till he

drops again? That's what they have done for me. By God, I'll do nothing more strenuous than clerical work for months, whatever they try to do with me, and *never* march again. Meanwhile the crisis of the Tragedy has been reached in France, and (whatever else may be) the British Soldier feels a glory in killing before he dies — such a contrast to last year! Our men will stick it however hard the task, but — they tell me Amiens has been fortified with barbwire and trenches.

Good old 51st! They are a glorious lot of men — Seaforths, Gordons, Black Watch, Argyll and Sutherlands. And how many left of you, poor boys? Yes, but this is so much better than Paschaendael! Now I'll walk a little, two miles an hour and tired at that.

Supposing after a month here, they gave me a Board and then a chance of discharge. What then? What will the College do? I would like to know that, It may be useful. However I am too tired to think of Composition with any pleasure. With best wishes for yourself and Mr Scott: Your sincere friend   Ivor Gurney

To MARION SCOTT

28 March 1918 (E)
[*I have not been successful in unearthing this letter from the Gurney archive but it seems important enough to reproduce portions printed in* The Ordeal of Ivor Gurney, *pp.122–3.*]

Yesterday I felt and talked to (I am serious) the spirit of Beethoven.

No, there is no exclamation mark behind that, because such a statement is past ordinary ways of expressing surprise. But you know how sceptical I was of any such thing before.

It means that I have reached higher than ever before — in spite of the dirt and coarseness and selfishness of so much of me. Something happened the day before which considerably lessened and lightened my gloom. What it was I shall not tell you, but it was the strangest and most terrible spiritual adventure. The next day while I was playing the slow movement of the D major [sonata] I felt the presence of a wise and friendly spirit; it was old Ludwig van all right. When I had finished he said "Yes, but there's a better thing than that" and turned me to the 1st movement of the latest E flat Sonata — a beauty (I did not know it before). There was a lot more; Bach was there but does not care for me. Schumann also, but my love for him is not so great. Beethoven said among other things that he was fond of me and that in nature I was like himself as a young man.

That I should probably not write anything really big and good; for I had started much too late and had much to do with myself spiritually and much to learn. Still he said that he himself was not much more developed at my age, and at the end — when I had shown my willingness to be resigned to God's will and try first of all to do my best, he allowed me (somehow) to hope more, much more. It depends on the degree of spiritual height I can attain — so I was led somehow to gather.

There! What would the doctors say to *that*? A Ticket certainly, for insanity. No, it is the beginning of a new life, a new vision.

. . .

I could not get much about Howells off L van B: (the memory is faint) he was reluctant to speak; whether Howells is to die or not to develop I could not gather.

. . .

How I would like to see your face! No, you'll take it seriously, and decide I am not unbalanced or overstrung. This letter is quite sane, n'est ce pas?

To Marion Scott   41.169

23 May 1918 (P)   No 2 Up West, Lord Derbys War Hospital,
Warrington, Lancs.

My Dear Friend: Your kind letter and all its interesting news about people and things gave me great pleasure, chiefly on account of the kindness shining through it. Thank you very much for it, for I believe that is an especial sort of kindness now that you are so busy.

It pleased me to hear about Dr Hull's enquiry about Herbert's music; and do hope that his notice of Herbert's work will make a difference — and that your account of H N H will produce its full effect. Thank you very much for your offer to send along the typewritten letter, and I should like to realize once more through your mind what his music is.

My Goodness! What an absolutely terrific amount of work you get through in your time; it is astonishing to think how you manage to stand the strain — what with visits to the dentist as a kind of sugar-icing to the whole. Please accept my best wishes as to the result of the hat adventure; it must be a triumph above the ordinary to manage to turn out something of one's own; and an adventure in thrift too; which is not an easy thing to accomplish.

Thank you so much for your trouble about my verses.

Perhaps some more may come from me while I am at the Front; hardly before I think.

Audreys letter does indeed sound Elizabethan, and "eskeyped" is very good indeed; someday she ought to do some individual work for she has eyes and forehead enough and character, which under your careful training ought to produce something worth having someday.

I was glad to receive (but surprised at this late hour) the review of "Severn and Somme" — but sorry that the reviewers think Graves cannot write; for he is a poet and I'm not.

Your "Muse in Arms" is in my kit-bag in the stores, and I shall make a real attempt this morning to get the corporal to let me send it off. I am afraid it is mere laziness that has kept it from being returned before.

Willoughby's things are occasionally very striking, dont you think.

Thank you so much for your most kind and interesting letter, and please excuse the dullness and flatness of this scrawl — which is so inferior to your own letter, bright and full of interest.

Yours gratefully with best wishes   Ivor Gurney

To MARION SCOTT   41.170

10 June 1918 (P)   *No 7 West, Lord Derbys War Hospital,*
Warrington, Lancs.

My Dear Friend: (Since that is how you start your letter)

There are many things to thank you for, including a most sympathetic and interesting letter, some Times L S , a paper with a thing of mine in, and today some flowers, for all of which thank you very much. It puzzles me why you are so kind — since your kindness is so little valued; still it is nice to think oneself remembered kindly — so thank you very much. I sent the poem to Miss M Hunt. The flowers which were small given away to different men — and the tall ones put in a jug since there were no vases to be had in the large room. But tomorrow I will try to get them placed on our table. Two I wore myself. I hope you are feeling stronger and are still able to work for other people, as you love to do — myself — well you know I was always selfish.

Tonight a letter has come from Evans to say he is well, but very fed-up. This is not surprising as he has a restless spirit.

This last month or two has been trying enough, but someday I hope to do better because of them. More than this you will not hear in this letter. Perhaps next may be better.

My Father is down at Weston, after a week or so at Framilode, from which place he returned very brown so they say.

Sidney Shimmin has received your type written appreciation of H N Hs work I hope. It was sent some days ago. If only something of the same kind could be written of me — now in shame and despair — with so little done, yet reassured by friendliness from you and others (H N H Sir Hubert and Sidney Pitcher) sufficiently to write letters: Yours   Ivor Gurney

To MARION SCOTT   41.172

19 June 1918 (P)
[*This letter is sent, unlike others from England and Scotland, without a stamp but with the words "Wounded Soldiers Letter" on the envelope where the letters from France had borne the words "On Active Service" instead of a stamp.*]
The Soldiers' Home, Bold Street, Warrington.

My Dear Friend: This is a good-bye letter, and written because I am afraid of slipping down and becoming a mere wreck — and I know you would rather know me dead than mad, and my only regret is that my Father will lose my allotment.

Thank you most gratefully for all your kindness, dear Miss Scott. Your book is in my kit bag which will be sent home, and thank you so much for it — at Brancepeth I read it a lot.

Goodbye with best wishes from one who owes you a lot.

May God reward you and forgive me.   Ivor Gurney

To MARION SCOTT   41.179

20 June 1918 (?)   6A West Ward, Lord Derbys War Hospital, Warrington, Lancs.

Dear Miss Scott   Please forgive my letter of yesterday. I meant to do that I spoke of, but lost courage. Will you please let Sir Hubert know?   IB Gurney

To MARION SCOTT   41.173

22 July 1918 (P)   *No 5D West, Lord Derbys War Hospital,*
Warrington, Lancs.

My Dear Friend: It delights me that you have at last come to the
West Country and seen what Howells and Harvey and myself have
seen — Malverns across the plain against Sunset. Today your p.c.
arrived, for which and for your jolly letter many thanks.

A letter from M H tells me you took the "Penny Whistle" down
with you. Thank you so much for all you say about it — the
suggested alteration does not seem to me to be very necessary; but
revision was always difficult, and light may come later.

I am sorry you are returning so soon to London; for Malvern must
surely suit you well enough; still I suppose it may be necessary —
work must be done. Please remember me to Mrs and Mr Scott and
say I hope they will be pleased with their West Country visit, and
improved in health, and also (to put it selfishly) as pleased with
Gloucestershire as you yourself are.

The Hunts were delighted with your visit, and say it was like a
visitor from another world "in our quiet backwater", but say you
looked rather tired. I hope that you will be like a giant refreshed
with the wine of Malvern air. (By the way, Malverns, so I have
heard, were the first part of Britain to stick out of the water). Mr
Haines has not written, but I shall expect a letter soon full of
book-talk he has had with you, for any contact with a booklover
such as you, would necessarily set him going; talking at his top speed
doubtless, and as well as usual; for he is a really good talker.
Dorothy fell in love with you at first sight, and wrote such a jolly
letter about your visit; she *is* a first rate sister, and I am proud of her.

Thank you once again for your attempt to wangle a fee out of the
Cambridge Press. Such things are of course safely left to you, who
manage these things to perfection I have no doubt. My father is a
fine chap, and has always been (I have no doubt) since the early days
of scaring birds off the corn; which is his earliest reminiscence. He
has a real appreciation of music, and has been more kind than
almost any father about all the time I have wasted in the past. May
the future be brighter! I feel that only France or the sea will do me
much good for a bit; there are no pictures in my mind — so repaying
him must wait longer than I had hoped.

It really does please me very much that you got in such an amount
of seeing people at Gloucester, and like the Cathedral so much, but
wish — O so much — you had seen the country round; Newnham,
Stroud, Tewkesbury, and the rest. The West Country is incom-
parable, though I daresay Devon may be finer as a county than

either Gloucester or Worcester, but dont care much — Anywhere between Newnham, Newent, Tewkesbury, Stow on the Wold, Bourton on the Water, Birdlip, Stroud will do for me; and doubtless for you too, poor town-dweller!

There's a lovely evening sky behind me as I finish this letter! I wonder what it looks like at Malvern; and what gorse is like, and whether you have been able to climb up much, and view the seven counties they say are to been seen high on (I think) the Worcestershire Beacon.

A long time it is since Father and my elder sister, my brother and I rode to Malvern and saw all these things — it must be 13 years ago! Fern I remember and Malvern beneath us — Ledbury on Severn, when Tom Jones stayed, and Tewkesbury — but nothing really of Malvern itself. I hope everything will please you there, and that without cracking yourself you have managed to see all you desired, and enjoyed yourself as you deserved. Fresh friends you have made anyhow. Not least M H and E H. With thanks and best wishes:

    Your sincere friend   Ivor Gurney

To MARION SCOTT   41.175

27 August 1918 (P)   *No 8 Ward, Middlesex War Hospital, Napsbury.*

My Dear Friend: I am sitting up in bed, after an afternoon at St Albans where I lay on the grass outside the Abbey and made various shots at my Scherzo, sent you a postcard, bought some tobacco, and did other various useful things; and now here's a perfectly delightful letter to begin to answer; full of appreciation and kindness which is most encouraging.

I am glad the verses delight you so — there are more to come. "Crickley Hill" I will see to when revision starts. The irregular rhyme was a mistake. "You" and "dew' are not perfect rhymes, but will pass without any notice among critics. There are some more to come later. It is good of you to say such pretty things, but I am no Edward Thomas. All I want is — guerre fini, soldat fini; and to go home without burden of any thought save music, and hard swot for a time.

               Migrants.
       No colour yet appears
       On trees still summer fine
       The hill has brown sheaves yet,
       Bare earth is hard and set,

But Autumn sends a sign
In this as in other years.

For birds that flew alone
And scattered sought their food
Gather in whirring bands; —
Starlings, about the lands
Spring cherished, Summer made good
Dark bird-clouds soon to be gone.

But above that windy sound
A deeper note of fear
All daylight without cease
Troubles the country peace;
War birds, high in the air,
Airplanes shadow the ground.

———————

Seawinds to Africa
Starlings with joy shall turn;
War birds to skies of strife,
Where Death is ever at Life;
High in mid-air may burn
Great things that trouble day.

———————

Their time is perilous
Governed by Fate obscure,
But when our April comes
About the thatch-eaved homes, —
Cleaving sweet air, the sure
Starlings shall come to us.

Which is one of my best things — to the authors mind, at any rate,
You shall have the book that was lent me so long ago — "The Muse
in Arms", that thing full packed with good stuff and thanks so much
for it.

No, Ma'am, there is no sign as yet that I shall be allowed to use
the piano while the others are out. The doctor did say something
about a Church Organ — which was only a mention, and not very
satisfactory at that — but nothing has moved since you came, and
went to your romantic dwelling house among flowers. It was a kind
thought of yours to send flowers to Warrington and sure it is they
will be appreciated by the poor folk tied up there. Some very nice
people were among that motley crowd and several I shall be sorry
not to meet again. There was an old coster (with his "attempt-
mark" still on his neck) a most sweet and plucky nature; who had
continual longing for his folk and donkey cart. He has full

expectation of my joining him in business after the War — with evenings spent fruitfully at the Picture Palace.

Twigworth Vicarage

Wakened by birds and sun, laughter of the wind,
A man might see all hearts desire by raising
His pillowed sleepy head (still apt for lazing
And drowsy thought) — but there a green most kind
Waved welcome, and the rifted sky behind
Showed blue, whereon cloud ships full sailed went racing
Man to delight and set his heart on praising
The Maker of all things, bountiful-hearted, kind.

May Hill that half reveaĺéd tree clad thing,
Maisemore's delightful ridge, where Severn flowing
Nourished a wealth of lovely wild things blowing
Sweet as the air — Wainlodes and Ashleworth
To northward showed. A land where a great king
Might sit to receive homage from the whole earth.

St Albans
August 1918

Interval

To straight the back, look up, and see the slow
Dispersed cloud-flocks of Heaven wandering blind
Without a shepherd, feel caress the kind
Sweet August air, soft drifting to and fro.
Meadow and Arable — Leaning on my hoe,
I searched for any beauty eyes might find.
The tossing wood showed silver in the wind;
Green Hills drowsed wakeful in the golden glow.

Yet all the air was loud with mutterings,
Rumours of trouble strange in that rich peace;
Where Wars dread birds must practice without cease
All that the stoutest pilot-heart might dare.
Death over dreaming life managed his wings;
Droning dull song in the sun satiate air.

St Albans
August 1918

There is one thing — perhaps two more — but those must wait till afterwards.

Mr Haines wrote me the jolliest of letters lately — Surely he has the real touch of talent or genius? A born letter writer surely?

Mr Pitcher sent me also a view of Gloucester Cathedral seen from the river, with one great cloud hanging over it ("overbowed with benediction" as, I think, Browning has it) and such a cloud came to delight me over St Albans red block of power yesterday. It was quite like old times and Tewkesbury to see that sight again — clouds and tower. God be praised that made Gloucestershire, and put it in the hearts of men to builds towers to perpetuate His praise, for what service is there like the making of a great thing in stone?

There's our call for out — and a lovely blowy blue sky to watch, during the intervals of Scherzo-hammering and welding. I *think* it will be a success, though there is too much of the old-fashioned Beethovenish smack about it to please me. But I want hours and hours of hammering anyhow at a piano to tune me up — such as I had at your house in London, how many eternities ago!

What do you think of the news? Peace seems impossible before Autumn 1919 at any rate; but it is best to hope that Fritz will see reason.

An officer-friend turned up here and took me to London where we had a little music and chocolate together and lemonade at St Albans — spirit and matter mixed. But it was delightful to see him; with talk of the Old Batt: and the changes in the Staff; gossip of the Front etc. He says his Brigadier has a great admiration for the French Staff and a contempt for ours — All daily orders are issued from Foch, and he believes that a vast improvement in all ways has come since that General took command. It was good to hear intelligent shop-talk again, and words like Merville, Lestrem etc floating on the air.

Mr Dunhill very kindly sent me his own "Wind Among the Reeds" as a present, and lent "Wenlock Edge", with some more of Martin Shaw. His own songs are weak, I think; but Vaughan Williams has always strength and colour, though to me the set lacks real musical instinct; to hear they must be very fine. Poor chap, I fancy he takes some time to heat up, and that his character has made him a musician rather than his gift.

Goodbye, and may you be wandering round that garden for some time yet, with books and music to read and not altogether uninteresting articles to hammer at. Anything I can help you in please send. With all best wishes:

from your sincere friend   Ivor Gurney
"Epic" is far too stiff for me to tackle I fear. The Muse in Arms shall accompany it soon back to you.

To Marion Scott   41.174

September 1918 (?)   No 8 Ward, Middlesex War Hospital,
Napsbury, St Albans.

My Dear Friend: I am delighted that you are delighted, and —
yes, aeroplanes is yet a stunt in poetry; and a memory of Willoughby
Weaving and a sight of starlings in flocks did it. ("Starlings rise in
roars, from the misty fields"). How are you getting in this new-
September weather. The wind has been jolly lately — jolly it has
been to feel the wind in one's hair. Your garden I daresay has been
full of it, and all your flowers tossing their head in joy to feel the rush
and thrill of Autumn coming once again — April — May —
September — October — these are the four months of life.
    Will you please excuse my having sent a parcel to Mr Dunhill to
you, for forwarding? By mistake, I destroyed his letter the day
before.
    And now for some new verses.

                            "Girls Song"
    In curtain of the hazel wood,
    From sunset to the clear-of-star,
    An hour or more I feared, but stood —
    My lover's road was far.

    Until within the ferny brake
    Stirred patter-feet and silver talk
    That set all horror wide awake —
    I fear the fairy folk . . . .
                _____

    And whether late he came or soon,
    I know not, through a rush of air
    Over the white road under the moon
    I sped till the square
                _____

    Of golden lamplit blind came, then
    Hand on my heart, I slackened, stood . . .
    Though Robin be the Man of men,
    No more I'll tryst that wood.

                        Solace of Men
    Sweet smelling, sweet to handle, fair of hue
    Tobacco is. The soldier everywhere
    Takes it as friend, its friendliness to share
    Whether in fragrant wreaths it mount faint blue
    In dug low, or surreptitiously to

Parapet in rimy night, from hidden lair
Of Sentry; staying hunger, stilling fear —
The old dreams of comfort bringing anew.
For from that incense grows the stuff of dreams
And in those clouds a drowsing man may find
All that was ever sweet to his starved mind,
Heart long bereft — Dear Friends, hills, horses, trees
Slopes of brown ploughland, Sunsets fading gleams,
The bane of care, the spur to memories
(As poppy and mandragora it is?) (which do you prefer?)

To F.W.H

Ink black and lustreless may hold
A passion full of living fire;
Spring's green the Autumn does enfold —
Things precious hide their bright in the mire

And a whole county's lovely pride
In one small book I found that made
More real the pictured Severn side
Than crash and shock of cannonade.

Beneath, more strong than that dread noise
I heard the talk of trees, and men,
The still low-murmuring Earth-voice . . . .
God send us dreams in peace again.

Girls Song

The tossing poplar in the wind
Shows underleaf of silver white,
The roughness of the wind unkind
Torments her out of all delight.
But O that he were here
Whose blows and whose caresses alike were dear!

The great oak to the tearing blast
Stands steady with his great arms wide,
So over him my anger passed,
When his rough usage hurt my pride
But O that once again
I might arouse that passion endure that pain.

September, St Albans

That's all for the present, Mamselle. Herbert has just sent me a packet of two-part songs to imitate — which is a new and interesting side of music to me. It will be good to read them in bed tonight.

There'll be a song in a day or two for you to see — a setting of "Had I the Heaven's embroidered cloths" which I think you will like; and an old resurrected Brancepeth Song — "The Fiddler of Dooney".

It's raining horrid outside and the paths are running; so no farm work will there be probably; swot today at Music which one grows to hate — having no piano; but I believe from today the Doctor is to let me have that hour in the evening. Last night he promised that but one cannot tell whether these folk mean what they say.

With best wishes: from your sincere friend   Ivor Gurney

To MARION SCOTT   41.182

September 1918 (?)   No 8 Ward, Middlesex War Hospital, Napsbury, St Albans.

My Dear Friend: Your charming and appreciative letter arrived here tonight when I was in the dumps rather and cheered me no end — cheered me up so that I was able to think once more of swotting at music. And O great news, the doctor asked me last night whether my people were willing to take me home! So my board and discharge are near I suppose and freedom, perhaps strength to work. O to slog on under Herbert's direction and develop all that is deep in me so undeveloped — and give you one really good V.Sonata. Well, with God's help that may come, but I need that.

My goodness you are a generous lady about praise though! Never was anyone so lavish and kind. It delights me you are delighted,

To MARION SCOTT   61.3

2 October 1918 (E)   No 8 Ward, Napsbury.

My Dear Friend: Thanks for the lovely day we had yesterday, and all the talk and cheerful chatter of my esteemed correspondent. This is to say merely that my discharge does not come off till Friday, so that means we draw kit tomorrow and do not come to our various destinations till next day.

Will this upset your plans? I hope not, indeed. Will Friday night suit you as well for my staying?

Let's hope all will fit in and I be landed safe in the arms of my people on Saturday.

    with best wishes I remain: your sincere friend   Ivor Gurney

To MARION SCOTT   41.177

7 October 1918 (P)   *19 Barton St, Gloucester.*

My Dear Friend: Thank you so much for your only too kind letter, and your mention of Mr Napier Miles. I have just written a letter to him to ask whether I might go there at once — not being sure of my impulses, and being anxious not only to save myself, but also my father, who must be more worried by my being here, than there under care. Also, if there is music, I could do as well there as here, until my time is past.

Perhaps Herbert has told you something of what I told him.

O there is one gorgeous bit of news — F.W.H. has reached Holland — Schevingen!!

This is written at no 54 Wellington St, and in front of creepers and trees of October; so beautiful. Alas, that I must leave freedom so soon, but I believe it to be best. Thank you so much for your kindness, Mamselle the Fairy Princess, and I am not without hope that this will turn out well by March, perhaps before.

With thanks and best wishes   Your sincere friend: Ivor Gurney

To MARION SCOTT   41.178

2 November 1918 (P)   *19 Barton Street, Gloucester.*

My Dear Friend: I am so sorry to hear that you too have come under the influence of this dreadful new thing, which strikes where it pleases, but why on you, who have had so much to endure during these last years? Surely that scourge might have spared you?

Well, since that is not so, may you soon recover; and find something in your sickness to interest you.

I am glad to tell you that I am better myself, after a fortnights hauling of heavy things about the Munition Works, but that is a job that wont last long — fortunately — by the look of things in the papers. Isn't the news glorious? What a week the last has been!

Poor Herbert is down with the "flu" also, complicated by

pneumonia, and not feeling any too cheerful I daresay, in spite of his being at the house of his lady-love, at Churchdown under that little hill of Chosen he has loved so well.

Coming back in the train today there was a great sight of Malverns to cheer me sticking up across the miles of plain — enormous enough, and reminding all whom it might concern of

May it not be long before you too may say "Look, See!" at them. Robinswood Hill looks fine too; our works are spread just along in under him, and every morning one gets view of that humpy crest. Well, there is no more I can tell you save that I may be "going to sea" again, and this time less ignominiously I hope!

Meantime, may you prosper, and recover your old self, and soon, under the influence of Peace Bread, and may that soon be dished out!!

with best wishes: Your sincere friend   Ivor Gurney

INDEX